WYOMING
Land of Echoing Canyons

by Beverley Elaine Brink

Old West Region Series

Edited by Francie M. Berg
Published by
Flying Diamond Books

dedicated to Lucille White

First Printing

Printed by North Plains Press

Library of Congress Cataloging-in-Publication Data

Brink, Beverley Elaine.
Wyoming, land of echoing canyons.

(Old West region series)
Bibliography: p. 173
Includes index.
1. Wyoming—History. 2. Wyoming—Description and
travel. 3. Wyoming—Social life and customs.
4. Indians of North America—Wyoming. I. Title.
II. Series.
F761.B74 1986   978.7   85-80478
ISBN 0-918532-15-9
ISBN 0-918532-09-4 (series)

FLYING DIAMOND BOOKS
Box 612, Hettinger, ND 58639
Printed in the United States of America

TABLE OF CONTENTS

Some things change . . .

Wyoming: a young state, but old in world politics

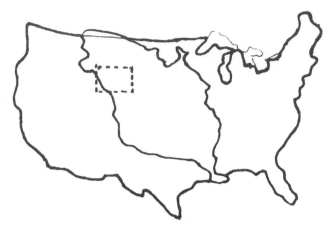

Acquired by U.S. in Louisiana Purchase, 1803
Wyoming has belonged to Spain, France and Mexico

SIZE: 97,914 square miles, 9th largest state; length 375 miles, width 276 miles.
CAPITAL: Cheyenne.   **COUNTIES:** 23.   **STATEHOOD:** July 10, 1890, 44th state.
LOCATION: Bounded by Montana, South Dakota, Nebraska, Colorado, Utah and Idaho.
HIGHEST POINT: Gannett Peak, 13,804 feet; lowest, Belle Fourche River, 3,100 feet; mean elevation 6,100 feet, second highest in nation.
POPULATION: 469,557 (1980 census), increase of 41.1% over 1970; per capita income, $11,780; unemployment half national average (5.8% in 1982 when national rate was 9.8%).
SCHOOL ENROLLMENT: Public, 100,000; private 3,528; University, 10,210; in seven community colleges, 9,544; second in nation in educational rank with average grade level 12.4.
INDIAN RESERVATION: Wind River, home of 2,381 Shoshone and 3,570 Arapaho.
ECONOMY: Mineral production, $5,852,764,024 (1981); recreation, $738,396,000; agriculture, $616,000,000; 9,100 farms and ranches average 3,870 acres, second largest in nation.
RANKING IN MINERALS: First in nation in bentonite, first in production of trona (soda ash), second in uranium, third in coal, fifth in crude oil, fifth in natural gas; other minerals mined, gypsum, feldspar, iron ore, vermiculite, jade, limestone, stone and gravel.

Others do not . . .

State Legislature meets annually, holding budget and general sessions in alternating years

'You are welcome in Wyoming. You'll see it in our smile, feel it in our handshake, hear it in our "howdy" and savor it in our unspoiled landscape.'

Gov. Ed Herschler

Flag—state seal on buffalo

Bird—Meadowlark

Flower—Indian Paintbrush

Tree—Cottonwood

Young bald eagle views canyon majesty with far vision

Water thunders 308 feet in Lower Falls, Yellowstone Park

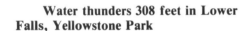

PART 1

Land of Echoing Canyons

Wyoming's natural wonders placed the state in the vanguard in developing recreation and resource management policies. Her people value and enjoy the state's treasures, acting to protect them even as they share them. Many of the guidelines were set in Wyoming for national standards in game, forest and park regulation.

•Yellowstone Park, the world's most extensive geyser area, was set aside by Congress in 1872 as the first national park.

•The first national forest, Shoshone, was designated in Wyoming in 1891, four years before the U.S. Forest Service was created to develop policies there.

•Wildlife management policies were tested here, where the continent's largest pronghorn antelope herds graze beside oil wells. The largest elk herd is here, as are moose, bear, bighorn sheep, mule and white-tail deer, and fur-bearing animals.

•Within the state are two national parks, Yellowstone and Grand Teton.

Geologic eons echo in the deep branches of Big Horn Canyon

1. LAND CALLS YOU OUTSIDE

Craigy malformations line the Big Horn River floor, rising 2,000 feet to where the canyon cuts a scar in the prairie. A raucous stream created this gorge which is still spectacular, though half-filled with water backed up behind Yellowtail Dam.

Fishing boats troll between sheer rock walls where once bull boats carried fur harvest out of the Big Horn and Pryor Mountains.

The 475-foot-high dam that created this boaters' and fishermen's paradise is in Montana but backs up Wyoming water. The dam and east shoreline are within the Crow Indian Reservation. It drains an area all the way to the Wind River Mountains, the river's name changing from Wind to Big Horn as it rushes out of the Wind River Canyon.

The story the Crows tell: Chief Big Middle of old was saved from destruction on one of the awesome crumbling cliffs by a big horn sheep. The sheep told him that if the name of the canyon is ever changed, the Crows will lose their land.

The Crow Tribe has developed Ok-A-Beh Marina, a half-million-dollar tourist facility near the dam. The U.S. Park Service has begun to develop non-water-oriented recreation, such as dude ranching, camping, biking and hiking. Two-million visitors a year are anticipated at this dam, midway between the Black Hills and Yellowstone Park.

Main entrance to the vast chasm—once stamping grounds for rustlers, trappers and pre-historic people—is from the south through Wyoming and by boat. The old Bozeman Trail runs through Fort Smith just north of the dam.

IN SUMMER,

OR IN WINTER, ACTION IS FUN

Competition skiers find sanctioned NASTAR events at major resorts, like the one pictured at Jackson Hole, left

White water rafters find exhilaration—and solitude—on Wyoming rivers

In winter, drivers harness up the huskies and mush —or visitors can bathe surrounded by snowbanks, center left, in one of many hot springs

Warmth of a campfire is time for dreaming, left, while yuccas burst with creamy blossoms, far left

Castle Geyser, one of oldest of 200 in Yellowstone Park

Frozen falls, sculpture in ice

Parks: From snow to sand

From sand dunes to eternal snowbanks, echoing canyons to rolling prairie . . . contrasts are seen in Wyoming's state and national parks. The action they offer, too, is just as various—fishing, hunting, snow sports, pageants, rodeos; tournaments in golf, fishing, and skiing; sightseeing, camping, history and art displays.

Two national parks within the state's boundaries, Yellowstone and Grand Teton, were designated for diverse reasons as well. Yellowstone, once jokingly called Colter's Hell, has over 10,000 thermal features—geysers, hot pools, mud volcanoes and steaming fumerols; unique in all the world, it is little wonder its discoverer, mountain man John Colter, was ridiculed for his fantastic tales. Grand Teton Park is built around the majestic Teton Mountain range, a tourist attraction since the days when visitors arrived by stagecoach from an Idaho rail point.

The deeply scored canyon of Flaming Gorge near Green River and Rock Springs was carved by the Green River as it passed through kaleidoscopic desert country to form a 91-mile-long lake. Fishing and water activities are superb in this national recreation area, as in the Big Horn Canyon which is a geologist's delight for 49 miles through sheer walls to a vast lake backed up by Yellowtail Dam.

Natural wonders in state parks range from huge white sand dunes and the world's largest mineral hot-springs, to a river which vanishes into a cave in a mountain canyon southwest of Lander. Eight parks focus on large lakes—Guernsey, Glendo, Boysen, Keyhole, Buffalo Bill, Seminoe, Curt Gowdy and Alcova. The ten state parks are located all over Wyoming, in mountains, prairie, desert and badlands.

BOYSEN STATE PARK in the mouth of deeply-cut Wind River Canyon is surrounded by the Wind River Indian Reservation, home of Shoshone and Northern Arapaho tribes.

BUFFALO BILL STATE PARK is an hour's drive from the east gate of Yellowstone National Park on the north shore of Buffalo Bill Reservoir. Trout fishing is ex-

GIANT BEAR CLAWED TOWER GROOVES, IN LEGEND

This awesome fluted tower rises 1,280 feet above the Belle Fourche River valley, visible for 50 miles and more. Devils Tower is such a spectacular landmark that it was designated the first national monument in 1906.

Once a mass of molten volcanic rock, it cooled and crystalized, then eroded until its 600-foot-high polygonal columns were left standing alone to tower over northeast Wyoming's Black Hills country. Mountain climbers often scale it.

A giant bear clawed grooves in the rock as it rose from the earth, in one of several Indian tribal legends. At the top, a lovely girl coveted by the bear, rose safely until she joined her seven brothers in the night sky, as stars.

Fort Laramie guarded trail in westward migration

cellent during most of the season, both in lake and the Shoshoni River north and south forks which feed it.

CURT GOWDY STATE PARK in the foothills of a mountain range dividing Cheyenne and Laramie, centers on two small reservoirs, Granite for water sports and Crystal Lake for shoreline fishing.

EDNESS KIMBALL WILKINS STATE PARK east of Casper is contoured on the north by the historic North Platte River, and in view of Casper Mountain.

GLENDO STATE PARK midway between Cheyenne and Casper, receives heavy regional use, so prized is its fishing and boating.

GUERNSEY STATE PARK a few miles south of Glendo is on the shores of another reservoir fed by the North Platte River. High bluffs surrounding the park block the wind, helping warm the water.

HOT SPRINGS STATE PARK on the edge of Thermopolis offers a preview of Yellowstone Park thermal activity, in terraces and mineral cones. However, these hot springs can be used for bathing, in several indoor and outdoor bathing pools and a state bath house.

KEYHOLE STATE PARK between Sundance and Moorcroft has a view of Devils Tower, along the shores of Keyhole Reservoir. Nearby Newcastle boasts the only hand-dug oil well, Accidental Oil Company.

SEMINOE STATE PARK is surrounded by sand dunes, miles of sagebrush and thousands of pronghorn antelope. Near Sinclair and the "miracle mile" of the North Platte River, famed for its trout fishing, this is on the edge of the Red Desert.

SINKS CANYON STATE PARK is on the Popo Agie River, which vanishes into a cave in the canyon wall to reappear in a crystal clear trout-filled pool. It is on the edge of the Shoshoni National Forest.

Old Faithful in powerful eruption

The "high country" holds unending enchantment for one of the state's most skilled outdoor photographers, Ron Mamot, whose work appears in The Wind River Rendezvous and other publications of St. Stephens Indian Mission Foundation. He is also office manager and foundation bookkeeper.

Several of Mamot's wildlife photos appear in this book, including the mule deer at rest (opposite page), the magnificent elk fight on pages 4 and 5, and the Indian-mountain montage on title page. For other Mamot work, see photo credit appendix.

As a hunter with both rifle and camera for most of his life, Mamot speaks strongly for conservation policies that will protect the high country, a habitat "essential for the lifestyle of these animals and the final sanctuary so needed for the human spirit." Beyond every ridge is the lure of an unusual picture and this opportunity is, to Mamot, one of the reasons why his state is wonderful.

Ron Mamot hunts with long-lens camera

Wildlife Leaps Into Sights

European royal shooting parties zeroed in their guns on Wyoming game and terrain over a century ago, and adroit management has turned hunting into big business today for people from all walks of life. In a typical year, deer hunters will have 60 percent success, elk hunters 30 percent, and antelope hunters 90 percent.

Two major waterfowl flyways cross Wyoming, Central and Pacific, with geese and ducks vee-ing their way both north and south. Wild turkeys crash the underbrush, and a bird hunter can rustle up pheasant, mourning dove, chukar and Hungarian partridge, and four species of grouse—sage, blue, ruffed and sharptail.

Big game licenses are issued by a lottery system, with numbers regulated by shifting game levels. Generally, antelope areas are open from September through October, deer and elk from September through November. All are abundant, with half a million stately pronghorn antelope, more numerous than anywhere else on the continent; over 3,000 mule deer were counted one quiet twilight on five miles of Powder River bottom. Whitetail deer inhabit the Black Hills area.

The variety in topography also results in variety in wildlife. On the prairies and grasslands, hundreds of antelope can be seen from the highway, as well as prairie dogs, jackrabbits, eagles, coyotes and deer. In the only national elk refuge, up to 10,000 elk are fed each winter. In the high mountain craigs, bighorn sheep climb surefooted.

Almost everyone hunts in Wyoming—that is to say they enjoy their abundant wildlife, whether it is from a gun sight, a camera lens, or the lens of an appreciative eye. Wildlife experiences delight backpackers, photographers, birdwatchers, hikers, hunters, fishermen and motorists. Campers may hear the haunting of a great horned owl, the bugle of a bull elk, and most certainly the chameleon cry (or yip, or wail, or symphony) of the coyote.

The best places to see large varieties of birds and mammals are riparian areas, next to water. In the state are 340 species of birds, 78 species of fish, and over 100 species of mammals. Trumpeter swans and great blue herons, muskrats and beaver, moose and bear, all offer constant surprises from the mountains to the prairies.

And a sure sign that spring is on its way in the Laramie Plains is the first seagull of the season . . . how far from an ocean? The California gull nests in Wyoming on Bamforth Lake, Ocean Lake, Yellowstone Lake, and near Casper. More than 4,000 of them fly in ordered confusion onto a greasewood-covered island in Bamforth each spring. In their fourth summer, chicks hatched here will return to breed.

In ecosystem management, the Wyoming Game and Fish Department strives to maintain a system which has been developing since the beginning of time. Today demands are increasing to maintain and produce wildlife that can be observed and enjoyed by the non-hunting public, while continuing to meet requirements of hunting and industrial development. Maintaining these ecosystems, on which all life depends, requires minimizing detrimental impacts of man's activities.

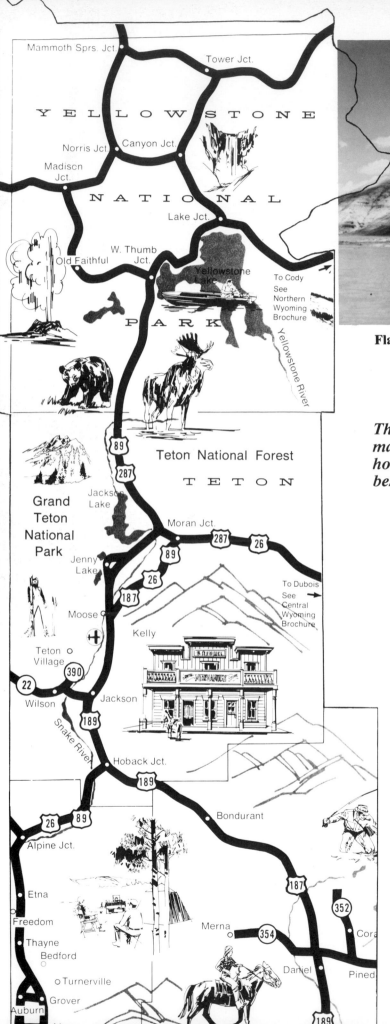

Flaming Gorge is called the "fishing hot spot of America"

Through towery chinks that time has made
man sees with awe
how puny have his efforts been
beside these chasms eons have inlaid

Canyons Were Born in Fire

Born in fire and ice, Wyoming's great canyons cut through 60 million years of earth history to add an intellectually stimulating dimension to driving. Some gashes are cut over 2,000 feet deep.

In Wind River Canyon, geologic eras exposed in the 2,500-foot walls are labeled so the motorist has a guide to cataclysms of the past. Triassic red beds enfold the road, entering from the north, and rise to a complete section of Paleozoic formations. Farther on, Precambrian crystalline rocks and overlying Cambrian sediments were separated in time by two billion years. Faulted arches, spires and majestic walls make this a memorable ten miles.

In Yellowstone Park, exploded in volcanic fire and then frozen in the Ice Age, the powerful Yellowstone River tunneled rock layers as it gushed from glaciers.

Seven ages of geological history are painted on walls of the winding Wind River canyon.

...nd Ice, Carved by Lashing Floodwaters

Volcanoes first belched forth fiery clouds of gas, dust and rocks. Lava lapped at the slopes of mountains.

Thermal activity which causes the park's 10,000 geysers, bubbling pots, and hot springs comes from an enormous volcanic eruption 600,000 years ago. Heat from the molten rock reservoir remains relatively close to the surface throughout northwestern Wyoming—in other words, the earth has a thin skin which erupts in many places, from Ft. Washakie and Thermopolis to Mammoth Hot Springs.

The walls of Ten Sleep Canyon probably were carved by glaciers grooving off the spine of the Big Horn Mountains.

Farther north, Shell Creek Canyon and Tongue River Canyon are only two of many inspiring folds in the Big Horn range. Every mountain range in Wyoming is similarly grooved and faulted into canyons narrow or wide, starkly rock-faced or wooded in easy slopes. Big Horn Canyon, now a national recreation area as is Flaming Gorge, is another example with walls 2,000 feet high.

But the canyon phenomenon does not end with the mountains. They are found throughout the state where rivers have flooded, changed course, receded and gushed anew to cut the land into a watershed network. Many are quiet, secret canyons draining from distant mountains that rise in dream-shadowed layers. Rivers like the Green, the Platte and the Powder each have created webs of canyons through their badlands.

These are the canyons where the echo was born. Sound bounces off the walls to ricochet in memories of solitude and grandeur.

Snowmobiles have opened up large tracts of wilderness not previously accessible to visitors, and can be rented at most resorts in the state

The aurora borealis plays the winter sky like a battery of celestial searchlights. The silent spectacle is fleshed out by the sounds of wind, coyotes and owls, sometimes the great white owl of the north. Winds whip across Wyoming with wintery blasts; heavy snows re-contour the land, and winter becomes a joyous, calculated risk in this high country where not a day of the year has been without falling snow somewhere.

The beauty can be wondrous, the potential for outdoor sports endless—but danger rides the land. Conditions can change rapidly, and what started out as a sunlit trip on dry roads may shift abruptly to a blinding blizzard, or an ice-sheathed highway polished by hurricane-force winds. Equally insidious are surface winds which create hypnotic ground blizzards at road-level. Accelerating wind currents can whip this into a full-blown blizzard in minutes.

Roads are closed before they become impassable, by a prudent Wyoming Highway Department. Steel gates bar the highway behind snowplows which then traverse closed sections to assure no motorists are stranded between closed gates. Warns Keith Rounds of the Highway Department, "If a motorist goes around one of the gates, the best thing that can happen to him is to be picked up and fined—the worse, to be stranded under adverse conditions."

Violating road closure signs endangers lives. In one May storm, which dropped five feet of snow on U.S. 16 over Powder River Pass, blinded snowplow operators found themselves dodging drivers "just looking around"; two plows running side-by-side on a blocked road saw an oncoming vehicle just in time to pull apart enough for it to shoot through. Exhausted deer struggle from deep snow onto newly plowed highways and refuse to move. There is always a possibility of flash flooding—chances of flooding depend on weather conditions, sudden warming followed by rain being one scenario for high water.

Chinook Rips Away Cold

Abrupt rises in temperature in mid-winter, as much as 60 degrees in a few hours, are blown in by chinook winds. Snowbanks three feet deep are blasted to oblivion by this dry wind. No other phenomenon in this land of meteorological mysteries is more distinctive.

Chinooks bare grass for starving animals, often the salvation of stockmen, but their velocity can be awesome and destructive. They have been clocked up to 140 miles an hour. A Casper newspaper cartoonist once showed kite-flying contestants flying anvils, bathroom sinks and lamps, instead of kites. On the wind-swept plain near Medicine Bow, the Federal Bureau of Reclamation tested the world's largest wind turbine; it had a blade the length of a football field.

Named for the Indian tribe, the chinook is born high in the mountains when winter storms stack up behind the

Thermal water, left, created Thermopolis; above, steel gates close highways in storm, but chinooks are born high in the mountains

Continental Divide. As the storms crest the mountains, the wind comes crashing down the eastern slope like water breaching a dam. It increases in both velocity and temperature as it descends. Chinooks can peel off shingles, down power lines, and blow buildings apart.

Snowmobiles Open Backcountry

Snowmobiles and four-wheel-drive vehicles opened winter's wonderland to recreationists, just as they made life easier on ranches and farms, in the oil fields and the mines. Winter excursions into the high country are now available to anyone astride a snowmobile. Winter camping and mountaineering combine with touring to bring backcountry scenery and wildlife into the experience of many. Guided ski and snowshoe tours explore Yellowstone and Grand Teton National Parks.

To escape the resort crowds into the solitude of hidden mountain bowls, cross-country adventurers shoulder back-packs and leave structured skiing behind. Like the mountain men of old running winter traplines when the fur was prime, such people take survival into their own hands and meet winter scavengers on skis or snowshoes.

Dry packed powder of dozens of ski areas, 13 designated ones, can be relied on December through March— and even into June in some locales. Some ski resorts are elegant and expensive, others featuring family style skiing on a budget. Ski touring and cross-country skiing over hundreds of miles of snowy expanse are popular with every income level; skis racked on top of cars moving into deep-snow country is a common winter highway sight.

Wyoming Ski Resorts

The Jackson Hole ski area, served by three resorts, has become nationally known with a 4,139-foot vertical rise, the largest in the U.S. Ski schools at the Teton Village, Targhee and Snow King resorts attract Olympic-caliber instructors; their chairlifts operate year-round, in summer for breath-taking views of the Teton Mountains. Sanctioned NASTAR competitions are held.

Home of the University of Wyoming Cowboys ski team, the Medicine Bow resort in the Snowy Range is a mecca for ski touring and snowmobiling, with a network of trails over frozen lakes and through the forest. The Cowboys, training in this deep snow, are a perennial NCAA powerhouse.

In the Big Horn Mountains, resorts of Antelope Butte and Meadowlark are favorites in north central Wyoming. Next door to Yellowstone Park's east gate, Sleeping Giant caters to skiers in the Shoshoni National Forest. On Casper Mountain is the resort of Hogadon Basin, and over in the southwest corner of the state is Eagle Rock at the foot of the Uintas, America's only major east-west mountain range. White Pine in the rugged Wind River Mountains offers vast tracts of wilderness for cross-country skiers and snowshoers, overlooked by the state's tallest peak, 13,804-foot Gannett. Up Pine Creek Canyon in western Wyoming is the newest ski center, Pine Creek, with a 1,200-foot chairlift.

In cross-country touring, skiers weave trails among snow-shrouded pines

17

*Who squired the glacier
woman down the sky?
She ran the neighing canyons
all the spring.*
— Hart Crane

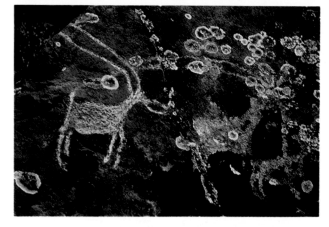

Above, Dinwoody petroglyphs; below, Queen Elizabeth II visits with Sheridan County Sheriff Bill Johnson on Wallop Canyon Ranch

Events in Wyoming

JANUARY
•Wyoming State Winter Fair, Lander, last weekend.

FEBRUARY
•"Snowstation" Winter Carnival, Saratoga. Second and third weekends with snowmobile and nordic skiing first weekend, interstate chariot race finals the second.
•Winter Festival, Pinedale, late month.

MARCH
•State Championship Chariot Race, Pinedale.

APRIL
•Pole, Pedal and Paddle Races, Teton Village, second Sunday.

MAY
•Annual Old Time Fiddle Contest, Shoshoni, late month.

JUNE
•Woodchoppers Jamboree, Encampment, Father's Day.
•Mustang Days, Lovell, late month.

JULY
Fourth •Lander Pioneer Days rodeo, Cody Stampede rodeo, Guernsey Old Timers barbeque and rodeo.
Mid-month •Arapaho and Shoshone tribal pow-wows and sun dances, Ft. Washakie.
•Statewide rodeos and festivals, including Laramie Jubilee Days rodeo. Sheridan WYO Rodeo, Boysen Pike Fishing Derby, Grand Teton Music Festival.
•Green River Rendezvous, Pinedale, second Sunday.
Late-month •Cheyenne Frontier Days, Cheyenne, nine days of rodeo, U.S. championship chuckwagon races.

AUGUST
•Gift of the Waters Pageant, Thermopolis, first week.
•Wyoming State Fair, Douglas, second to last week.

SEPTEMBER
Labor Day weekend •Mountain Man Rendezvous and Black Powder Shoot, Ft. Bridger.
•Cowboy Days rodeo, Evanston.
Third weekend •Oktoberfest, Worland.
Mid-month •One Shot Antelope Hunt, Lander.

'something soft and wild and free . . .'

. . . one can breath this air only on the bright edges of the world, on the great grass plains or the sagebrush desert . . . release the spirit of man into the wind, into the blue and gold, into the morning.   —Willa Cather

19

Deryl Beckel, above, played with this German brown trout for 45 minutes on the North Platte's "miracle mile"; it weighed 21 pounds, two-ounces

Dick Moffatt of Gas Hills tags pike, left, at annual Boysen Pike Fishing Derby

Fish biting the year around

A trout rising to a dry fly is an exquisite pleasure for millions of anglers each year in Wyoming, because it takes consumate skill to set the hook and land this prize of sports fishing. Over ten million fish were harvested in 1983 by four million fishermen on 13,500 miles of streams in Wyoming.

Resident fishing by men and women, old and young, is so popular that it's a surprise to learn 60 percent of these fishermen are from out-of-state—except to southeastern anglers who have coined a special name for Colorado fishermen flocking to Wyoming waters . . . "greenies", for the license plates they see in the bushes near favorite spots. The state fish warden, Don Dexter, once chided them by urging better fisherman distribution and reminding them that these 60 percent contributed 75 percent of state license revenue.

The Wyoming Game and Fish Department is unique in being not only self-supporting, but a profit-making agency. Fishing revenue in 1983 was $129 million; for every 73 cents spent, the return was $12.87. The department's net profit for the year was calculated at $6 million.

In the clear, cold streams, trout challenge fly and spin casters—rainbow, brook, cutthroat, brown, golden and mackinaw. A record golden trout was caught in

Cook Lake, 11 pounds, four ounces. Other trout records are continuously being set. Bass, walleye, crappie, perch, sauger, ling, channel catfish and bluegill are found in warm water lakes and reservoirs; northern pike, illegally introduced into Keyhole Reservoir, now are encouraged 18 miles northwest of Moorcroft.

Walleye pike are carniverous to trout and their puzzling spread in the lower section of the North Platte River threatens the fabled trout fishing there. Biologists were surprised when this pike-perch showed up in the 1960's in Seminoe Reservoir. A small reservoir in Colorado, which washed out in 1962, released walleyes that may have migrated. They spread to Glendo, and then heavy runoff in the spring of 1973 sent them into Kortes, Pathfinder and Alcova Reservoirs. Biologists now are trying to manage trout and walleyes as cohabitants of the same fishery.

So many prime trout fishing areas exist—and no one wants his private Shangri-la publicized—that state Game and Fish publications are the best guides; also, local fishermen sometimes will reveal their secrets.

At Soda Lake in western Wyoming, some of the best brown and brook trout fishing is available. The lake also provides virtually all the brook and brown eggs needed by hatcheries for planting in waters throughout the state. Stocking has been going on since 1948.

Rushing mountain streams like the one above, abound with trout and make this a fly-fisherman's paradise (although bait is not forbidden)

Gangly moose enjoys a gourmet meal from a mountain pond in photo at right

The Blacks Fork-Smiths Fork drainage is one of the lesser-known prime fisheries in southwestern Wyoming, in both Blacks Fork to where it passes under Interstate 80 below Lymon, and in Smiths Fork to just below the town of Mountain View. Flaming Gorge and Fontenelle Reservoirs, as well as the Lower Green River are more well-known in this area.

Jackson Lake in the Snake River drainage of northwestern Wyoming is a picturesque fishing spot in Grand Teton National Park, with cutthroat and brown trout near the surface and larger, trophy-sized lake trout in deeper waters. Mountain whitefish are also caught. Initial stocking occurred here in 1890, when the U.S. Fish Commission introduced brown and lake trout into Shoshoni and Lewis Lakes; by 1906, Jackson Lake fishermen's creels contained 15-pound lake trout.

The cutthroat, so named because of the reddish brush streak under the lower jaw, is the only trout native to Wyoming. It has always been present in all drainages west of the Continental Divide and in the Yellowstone, Madison, Big Horn, Tongue and South Platte drainages east of the divide. The Wyoming Game and Fish Department is attempting to extend the range of the many strains of native cutthroat, whose fine spots distinguish it from other cutthroat and, in a lake environment, may be almost obscure except in the tail area.

*Canyon perspective: From the rim a boat looks
like a dragonfly, but from below the 2,000-foot
Big Horn Canyon echoes history's voices*

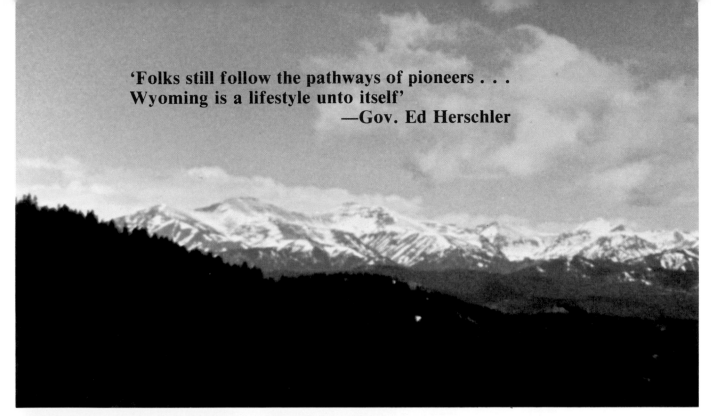

'Folks still follow the pathways of pioneers . . .
Wyoming is a lifestyle unto itself'
—Gov. Ed Herschler

Thermal springs hiss on icy-cold Firehole River

This is Wyoming high country, which packers claim is "so cussed tall that you got to lay on your back and look up twice to see the top of it." They say, too, you can breathe more and get less air, walk farther and cover less distance, take a quicker bath, and spit farther than anywhere else in the United States.

Author of **The Elk,** *John Madson, wrote of the high country: "If a man is to keep safe from falling, he can never aspire toward some incredible height and stand there alone, and consider the smallness of valleys, and how far they lie beneath him."*

Snowy peaks of Wind River range, top photo, conceal clear streams and wildlife in hidden canyons, like browsing mule deer, left

2. LAND USE VARIES

Though most dialogue on public land use occurs between recreationists and ranchers, the economic reality is this: Recreation is bigger business in Wyoming than agriculture—and mineral production is six times bigger than either. Federal bureaus administer 48 percent of Wyoming land, and 72 percent of the minerals.

Most federal land is administered by the Bureau of Land Management under a multiple-use mandate. The U.S. Forest Service, National Park Service, Bureau of Reclamation and Fish & Wildlife are also trustees of federal land in the state. The BLM collects annually more than $114 million in Wyoming, 87.7 percent of this in mineral leases; Wyoming receives half the mineral proceeds.

Recreational usage—fishing, hunting, camping, photography, hiking, backpacking, horseback riding—is allowed on leased lands. This use increases significantly each year, as the growing number of outdoor people require access through intermingled private lands, safety planning to minimize hazards, as well as other services. Land trustee agencies are required to attain the widest range of beneficial uses.

Land with unusual qualities, such as the Cloud Peak Primitive Area, can be withdrawn from other purposes. Lush green meadows, glacial moraines and snowfields which rise to Cloud Peak's 13,175-foot summit caused these 136,000 acres in the Big Horn National Forest to be set aside in 1932. This includes all of the higher peaks—Innominate, Black Tooth, Woolsey—and respresents the principal hydrologic divide between the Big Horn River to the west and Powder River to the east.

Grazing management is rooted in a history that saw extreme overgrazing, 1.5 million cattle in 1885 and six million sheep by 1909. Today there are 2.1 million each of sheep and cattle. Shifting economic conditions cause these figures to fluctuate, as many operators shift back and forth between sheep and cattle. The Taylor Grazing Act of 1934 was passed to correct early destructive grazing practices.

In Wyoming are 210,000 acres of public land which are designated as commercial timber—lodgepole pine, ponderosa pine, Douglas fir and Englemann spruce. Annual harvest is about five million board feet.

Fire is an ever-present threat during annual dry seasons. An average of 73 fires a year are reported, with some 3,200 acres burned. Lightning causes 60 percent of the fires, man the other 40 percent.

In the historic disposal of tracts to states and individuals from territorial days title to surface and subsurface was often separated. In conveying title, the federal government reserved rights to the underground minerals on millions of acres of land which passed into private ownership, thus the federal ownership of 72 percent of Wyoming minerals. The state leads the nation in production of bentonite and trona, vies for first in uranium, is third in coal mining and fifth in production of oil and natural gas.

Biologists borrowed a century-old ranch technique to improve stream habitat when they began transplanting beaver. Two examples of how beaver labor rehabilitates streams are Currant Creek and lower Sage Creek in the Salt Wells area. Willow growth had been lost and extensive streambank erosion existed. Beaver moved onto the Currant Creek Ranch were supplied with aspen for dams and to supplement their winter food cache. In two years the willow returned, streambank erosion stabilized, and the water table rose to allow growth of other vegetation and aquatic life.

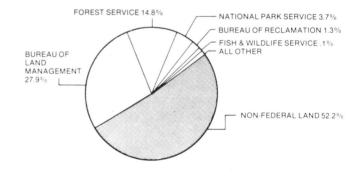

FOREST SERVICE 14.8%
NATIONAL PARK SERVICE 3.7%
BUREAU OF RECLAMATION 1.3%
FISH & WILDLIFE SERVICE .1%
ALL OTHER
BUREAU OF LAND MANAGEMENT 27.9%
NON-FEDERAL LAND 52.2%

Wild turkey habitat is protected by public land management policies

Landmark rock wall crests the Big Horn Mountains on highway 14

Wild Horses Now Protected

"Wild horse" programs create mixed feelings for old-timers who used to round them up by the thousands for dog and fox food. Most of the free-roaming horses in Wyoming are left-overs from this old cannery market. The BLM manages 10,000 wild horses in the Big Horn Basin, central and southwest Wyoming, under the Horse and Burro Act of 1971.

A lucrative market for fine riding horses existed at the turn of the century. In a single year, 20,000 Wyoming horses went to Africa during the Boer War. British, French and Italian governments paid $175 per gelding. The U.S. cavalry sustained this market through World War I.

After the military markets folded and ranch mechanization occurred, the market shifted to one of canner horses, the price dropping to one-dollar a head. Chappell Brothers, CBC, ran 56,000 brood mares in a three-state area, including 10,000 in Wyoming's Red Desert, to supply their plant in Rockford, Ill. Col. W. H. O'Connell, a horse buyer, told of these drives, of horses "dying on the way to the railroad for lack of water . . . my boys' faces were black with tears streaming down."

For two decades, from the early 1920s to 1940, Chappell Horse Plant killed 42 horses an hour, making 17 by-products that included Ken-l Ration and 80,000 cans of fox food a day. "Ship more horses" was the daily telegram O'Connell received; he shipped one trainload of 50 cars out of Sheridan.

O'Connell had driven jerkline freight from Moorhead into Montana, and once rode for Spear Brothers. He later built the Miles City Livestock Sales Yards, selling 1,951 horses there in 1936.

When CBC closed its huge operation, many bands of wild, scrub horses remained on the ranges. They ate twice as much as a cow, chased cattle and sheep off waterholes, and added nothing to tax rolls. The genetic odds were against producing anything but thick-bodied hammerheads. Said one rancher, "Some were crazy, inbred to the point they didn't recognize a fence. We saw them run along fences until they cut their throats and bled to death."

Excess animals today are rounded up by helicopters and driven into traps, where they are loaded onto trucks and taken to Rock Springs. Here, brands are checked and "slicks" go into the Adopt-a-Horse program.

Chart at right shows recreation usage in Wyoming

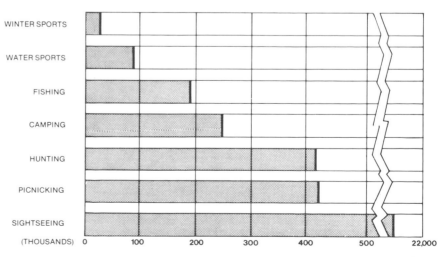

25

Wyoming energy at work . . .
Power for the nation

Shovels digging coal, left, stoke huge generating plants like the one above to produce electricity for eastern markets

Power throbs eastward on huge transmission lines, as antelope graze beneath

Pumps like the fancifully painted one here suck Wyoming's fortune from oil domes

MINERALS BRING $6 BILLION ANNUALLY IN STATE'S BIGGEST BUSINESS

CRUDE OIL—120.9 million barrels produced in 1983, reserves of 808 million barrels.

NATURAL GAS—10 billion M.C.F. production, with reserves of 3.7 trillion cubic feet.

COAL—108 million tons mined in 1983, with reserves of 290 billion tons underground and 260 billion stripable surface coal.

URANIUM—3,022,650 tons, with 35% of known U.S. reserves.

BENTONITE—2,183,865 tons annual production, 65% of nation's output, and reserves of 90 million tons.

TRONA (SODA ASH)—10,542,417 tons annual production, with reserves estimate at 67 billion tons.

OTHER MINERALS—Also mined in Wyoming are Gypsum, Feldspar, Vermiculite, Jade, Limestone, Crushed Stone, Sand and Gravel.

'If your town faces energy impact, Dial a God—and hope the line isn't busy'

3. AS MINERAL FORTUNES RISE, BOOMTOWNS MUSHROOM

Wyoming has been in the vortex of a boom-bust centrifuge for over a century, and this is not likely to change. Cheyenne was the first boomtown in 1862, ballooning in months from zero to 6,000 people; within a year it "busted," back to 2,305.

The state is a vast storehouse of energy, and market fluctuation is the nature of such commodities. Circumstances thus sealed Wyoming into a perpetual boom-bust fate.

Ghost towns from every mining era whisper their stories—Friendly, Welcome and Mineral Hill of aborted gold rushes; Encampment, of a copper boom; Monarch, Sunrise, Deitz, Cambia and Acme, of coal mining; Spring Valley, Edgerton and Savageton, of life in the oil fields; Johnstown, a soda boom. The boom-bust process is ceaseless; Acme died as Gillette boomed in the 1970s, both affected by coal.

The Department of Energy estimates that each new resident associated with energy development will need services "minimally" costing $7,000, or $140 million per synfuels facility.

Since state and local governments benefit from in-creased taxes, industry argues, they should pay impact costs. The reality is that the tax dollars from a new mine or a new plant do not begin rolling in for several years. When 1,000 new people move into a rural community, the local government must find—immediately—100,000 gallons of water per day, an additional two miles of sewer lines, $175,000 worth of sewer treatment facilities, six miles of streets, 102 street lights, 1.8 policemen, 6.5 other new employees, 4.8 elementary classrooms, 3.6 high school classrooms, and funds to keep everything in operating order.

Wyoming Senator Malcolm Wallop tried to solve the problem in the context of his no-tax philosophy when the Hart-Randolph energy impact assistance bill was re-structured in the Senate as a loan bill. The bill died, however; constitutional debt limits would have barred many states from using it. A broad collection of other federal measures have yet to deal adequately with energy impact.

Sen. Wallop pointed out that a federal grant program is justified when, as so often happens in Wyoming, population increases occur in one jurisdiction, but the

ROCK SPRINGS RULES FOR COPING WITH BOOM IMPACTS

Rock Springs city government, heavily impacted during the 1970's by run-away growth, developed a strategy for dealing boom problems. Besides the need to provide immediate services for a population that doubled within three years, there was the question of where to get the money to pay for them. The following steps were taken:

1. A one-cent county-option sales tax was imposed;

2. City government was re-structured, departments of planning and engineering added;

3. Community development replaced Urban Renewal, both federal programs, but implicit in the former was local authority;

4. A planning concept was adopted which emphasized short-term planning, rather than long-term, and geared only to items which could be handled without outside help;

5. Cooperation rather than isolationism was stressed between state, county, school districts and cities;

6. City officials worked closely with state officials, in arranging joint powers loans and highway projects;

7. Economic independence became the objective in all areas, locally generated funding and control.

Instant towns spring up with today's mobile housing, some methodically planned as in Gillette, above

development is across the border in another state or county, providing no additional tax base at the point of impact.

An environment impacted "can be bettered, but only if we stop seeking recognition of a single symbolic program and begin focusing our attention on a number of less glamorous and less visible but infinitely more effective means," Wallop wrote.

No one worried much about social impacts in the early boomtowns. Some disturbed misfits killed themselves, others were beaten up or driven out of town, and some were hung from the nearest tree. Those were "ragtown" days, tent living for many.

Today the mayor worries when local headlines say, "Sheriff Arrests Double, Trailers Increase 1500%, Counseling Caseload Jumps 100%." Times have changed, and many innocent bystanders are affected.

In Sweetwater County, the 1970 population was 18,400 and by 1980 it was 40,100. Rock Springs and Green River both had high crime rates, their community nursing services never had full staffs, and government employee salaries were not competitive with energy-related jobs. In Casper whose "boom" has been spiraling for over 100 years, medical services are still inadequate; one family was traveling over 350 miles for a child's care because they couldn't penetrate the local office of a busy specialist. Rawlins in Carbon County and Douglas in Converse were similarly jarred by a late 1970s boom—as they had been several times before.

Meanwhile, impacts at Gillette in Campbell County and Wheatland in Platte County were leveling off.

Boomtown people are often rootless, wearied by their constant moving, emotionally drained. Social isolation increases family violence, child abuse and neglect, assault, suicide and robbery. Drinking may be the only socialization or recreation available. In Carbon County, for example, newcomers experienced about 33 percent of total alcohol-related problems when they were but 12 percent of the population. Just across the Colorado line in booming Craig, assaults increased about 900 percent and in 1979 there was a 58 percent increase in child abuse.

A 1977 slaying at Reno Junction is symbolic: Two ranchers, Harry Reno and Jack Putnam, were gunned down in the Long Branch bar by a mine welder whom one of the victims had clubbed with a pool cue; the welder, Jesse Collins, was sentenced to spend the rest of his life in the Wyoming State Penitentiary.

Gillette lay for sleepy decades on a billion tons of coal. It had cut its milk teeth as a brawling early-day cowtown, stirred only slightly by an oil boom. Then the nation began fighting air pollution; Campbell County's low-sulpher coal soared in price. Population boomed and between 1974 and 1978, admissions to the state mental hospital rose by 61 percent; the population had grown by 62 percent.

Just as the city of 10,000 geared for trebled population by 1975, the Sierra Club got a court injunction against opening the area's four new coal strip mines. This halted the boom symptoms: acres of mobile homes on dirt strips, overcrowded schools, inflated food prices. When the injunction was lifted, it resumed with all the earlier frenzy.

The Northern Wyoming Mental Health Center made a stress study two years later, when 44 percent of Gillette's people lived in mobile homes. Seventy-two percent were from out of state, and three of ten planned to stay less than five years. The study showed people drank too much, exhibited frequent criminal behavior, often suffered from the blues—and 73 percent would not look for help.

Gillette was fortunate compared with "Sin City U.S.A.", Rock Spring. Notorious for its lurid life, Rock Springs was call "Tin City" by the Governor of Colorado, "Sin City" by east and west coast press, and became a by-word for rampant crime. Visiting Idaho students found school classes being held in bars. The chief of police shot and killed an undercover investigator inside a police car in 1979; two years later he was acquitted.

"If your town faces energy impact," the Rock Springs mayor said wryly, "Dial-a-God—and hope the line isn't busy."

City officials refused to take all the blame for the delinquency of their town. They claim to have made every reasonable effort to plan for impacts, but did their planning based on false projections they allege were deliberately given out by industry to deceive competition.

Arapaho students Velma and Patricia Dewey confer with UW Law School Dean Peter Maxwell

Pius Moss, Arapaho

Indians didn't vanish, as was hoped by realists and prophesied by romantics. Instead, they thrived and multiplied, no one knows how. They were starved, brutalized, and treated as nonpeople. Even today, old prejudices fetter attitudes and decision-making.

4. INDIANS SURVIVE

All outdoors is a church to Indians . . . the plants, the sky, the earth, the animals, so teaches Pius Moss, culture instructor at the St. Stephens Indian School and consultant at the University of Wyoming. As an educator, he works to instill knowledge and pride of Indian ancestry, in addition to the conventional subjects.

Arapaho Indians, who share the Wind River Reservation with the Shoshone Tribe, considered religion as all of life—and singing was the form of prayer. "They always sang to fit the situation," explains Moss. "When the want was mild, they sang; when the want was strong, they might cry. When passing a place where death occurred, they sang; the place where life was taken was revered, rather than the place of burial."

Moss, a descendant of Arapaho Chief Black Coal, constantly exhorts Indian children in the words of his ancestor: "Learn all you can, for this is the new way. The old way of our life is gone."

Living in harmony with nature is a keynote to the Indian way of life, as is sharing, cooperation and respect.

These are among the principles taught today on the reservation. Patience, life oriented in the present, and a family-centered society are values held in esteem.

Awareness of self, of others, of culture and tribal history are part of Moss' comprehensive philosophy.

"Individual freedom was a matter of survival to Indians. They taught by example and advice, never by force. They always held a tremendous respect for each other.

"Nature is all living things, people, animals and plants. The Indian respected the animals that furnished him food, clothing and shelter, only taking what he needed for survival. He respected herbs for their medicinal value, other plants for their fruit, trees for material for shelter."

Without respect, Moss insists, the whole value system is meaningless. At the core are respect, honor and esteem—"respect for those older and wiser, for an honest person, for other people's property, ideas and feelings, and above all respect for self."

Northern Cheyenne youths enjoy Cloud Peak wilderness

Here lived and loved another race of human beings, beneath the same sun that rolls over your heads . . . the Indian of falcon glance and lion bearing, the theme of the touching ballad, hero of the pathetic tale, is gone.
                                                           —Charles Sprague

Indian self-government provided the pattern for American colonists trying to rid themselves of the divine-right-of-kings system. Indians practiced democratic self-government long before European immigrants arrived in the western hemisphere, exercising sovereignty from time immemorial. These values and characteristics are maintained on today's Wind River Reservation, and continual effort by both tribes is made to strengthen their role in daily life.

The status of land, not regarded as something which could be "owned," has necessarily changed with imposition of federal laws. This viewpoint and Indian way of life has been dramatically altered over the past century, but attitudes of interdependency and harmonious existence in the universe have been retained.

Shoshones and Arapahoes elect separate tribal councils, with joint meetings held as needed. Neither tribe accepted the 1934 Indian Reorganization Act charter provisions; thus neither has written constitution or by-laws.

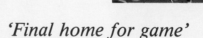

Willie LeClair, Shoshone

'Final home for game'

"Amid the special beauty and seclusion of the High Country is our final territory for big-game hunting—the last connection with the old Indian way of life," declares Willie Le Clair, Shoshone.

Shoshones, whose province on the Wind River Reservation is the mountains, have been anxious to pass a game code. Non-Indians may obtain fishing licenses for angling in over three dozen lakes and rivers.

Adds Le Clair, "Maybe with developed game codes, the great animals can continue to roam. Without such a closeness to the true and complete world of nature, our children will have lost much of their Indian heritage."

His family hunting camp is located in the St. Lawrence Basin along the North Fork drainage of the Little Wind River, a short trail ride to Ft. Washakie. To the north is Paradise Basin, a remote refuge for big game animals—"for the native Americans, the most beautiful land on earth."

Legend of lost band

Gem-like Lake DeSmet is sacred to Cheyenne Indians, as the home of a band who lives everlastingly in its cavernous depths. As late as the 1940s, vision-seekers from their reservation in Montana fasted on its shores. Prayer cloths were often offered by others traveling by.

The legend of the lost band has been told as a bedtime story to generations of Cheyenne children.

Long ago when the people separated into small bands for seasonal hunting, and berry-picking, Cheyennes kept track of each other whenever possible. A certain band was known to be in the area, and another group followed the tracks of horses and travois, hoping to catch up with the first band.

At the edge of Lake DeSmet, which is called "Ma-xe ne han-ee-va," the tracks continued into the water . . . dogs, horses, travois, men, women and children. Puzzled, the second band circled the lake looking for more tracks. There were none. The first group of people with all their animals and traveling gear had vanished in the waters.

Sometimes at night, you may hear the sound of Indian music coming from the water, of children playing, and of dogs barking. In the morning, you may see children's footprints along the shore. This happened long before white people came to Wyoming.

Since Texaco Inc. acquired Lake DeSmet, there has been development along its shoreline and the lake has been enlarged. This is perhaps why Cheyennes seldom go there anymore for religious retreats.

One respected medicine man who customarily received his spiritual instruction from this lake explained that an ordeal which had to be endured was the attempt of evil spirits to detract him from prayer. During one such fast, he was besieged four times by such problems: Lightning struck very close, with thunder and rain drenching him; however, he remained in his prayerful position. Next, a big eagle attacked him four times from the air, grazing his back with its talons. The third attack was by a black stallion, which halted its charge so close that dirt from its hooves sprayed the worshiper. The last attempt to deter him came from the water itself, as it rose over his body, receding only when it reached his lips.

Lake DeSmet was named by a group of Assiniboines, Minnetarees and Crows, with whom the famous priest was traveling in 1851. Wrote DeSmet, "We arrived

Paul Warren in fancy-dance dress with trophy he won dancing

'It's really a turtle'

An Arapaho story tells of the "Medicine Wheel" on top of the Big Horn Mountains being, rather, the outline of a turtle, used as late as 1800 as site of the sacred "Majestic Lodge" ceremony of an exclusive Arapaho clan.

The legend was told by the late Thomas Shakespeare, as passed down to him by his great-grandfathers, Eaglehead and Scarface. He said they were among the last members of the "Majestic Lodge" who offered worship on top of Medicine Mountain.

Arapaho were known for their placements of stone, and often erected cairns as monuments or symbols. One of their regular campsites on the western slope of the Big Horns was at "the tall trees," where the creek drops down out of Tensleep Canyon. From here, the "great trail" headed northward by way of Medicine Lodge Creek, climbing through the forests to the peak, where the elevation offers a vast view.

It was here, according to Shakespeare, that the cairns and some spokes were built to represent the turtle, the sacred life-source in Arapaho tradition. This is what white people named the Medicine Wheel, of such mysterious origin that even the Crows say only that it was "built by people who had no iron."

The turtle faces northwest because there is no direct way in life; its tail symbol is brief, for this represents the past that is brief and death which is short. At the center is the hub, as the center of the life-circle, the symbol of Mother Earth. All the trails (the 28 spokes of stone) lead from the hub outward, yet all terminate within the life-circle; also from the hub, the headwaters, run the streams in every direction, returning to the "great waters"—the sea and their beginnings. The entire structure is regarded as "the life monument of the people."

Twenty-eight old men, after much ritualistic preparation, took their seats at the rim of the ceremonial circle. More than simply age was required of participants, for each must have won special powers from the natural kingdom established by the Great Spirit.

August 25 quite unexpectedly on the borders of a lovely little lake about six miles long, and my traveling companions gave it my name. Our hunters killed several wild ducks."

Another Cheyenne legend deals with rocky cliffs of the Big Horns, and the song derived from it is still sung sometimes at sun dance time.

A young girl who was very much in love bade goodbye to her sweetheart, as he left with a war party. Enemy warriors managed to box the Cheyenne party against a rocky cliff from which there was no escape. The young man was killed.

Eventually the grieving girl married another man. In traveling with her village, camp was to be made one day near the spot where the tragedy had occurred. This was pointed out to her, as the other women began setting up tepees, gathering wood, and making preparation to cook. They did not notice the girl's absence.

Suddenly the villagers heard singing. Looking up, they saw her dancing at the very top of the formidable cliff. She was singing a song whose essence is, "I have finally found him." She danced to the edge of the rocks, fell off and was killed. Humiliated, her husband instructed those who picked her up, "Do not make my lodge sad with her body, take her to her own people."

*'Mile wide, inch deep.
Too thin to plow, too thick to drink.
POWDER RIVER, LET 'ER BUCK!'*

River flows sedately by Gwyn Collins homestead

5. POWDER RIVER
LIVES ITS LEGENDS

Powder River in flood runs a mile wide between ramparts of scoria and gumbo seamed with coal. Side creeks flow so full and fast that water ridges up in the middle, bouncing from side to side. Early ice breakup, heavy mountain snow melt, "gully-washers" and three-day rains—occurring singly or in combination—cause this split personality in a river which wanders shallow and deceptively harmless much of the year.

The storied river, where some Wyoming ranches have existed for four generations, is like a wealthy dowager aunt—both irascible and amiable, genial giver and despot, or just cranky and comfortable. Powder River is life-giving to fields and cattle and sheep. It also can exterminate them in a moment's madness, or suck them slyly into its depths.

This unique river flows sand and silt 30 inches deeper than its water depth. The sub-channel of flowing sand creates a true silt concentration of unmeasured levels.

Dr. John Watt, a biologist who lived his entire life on the river, read flow meters for the U.S. Geological Survey showing 50 percent silt in samples taken from the water; this did not take into account the difference between the "upper flow" and the "bottom flow", which is animated quicksand. Even his 50 percent figure from the upper flow long was doubted in Washington, D.C.—"a big-shot came out to prove I was lying," he grinned. The test sample drawn for his visitor was poured into a glass; next morning it was more than half full of silt.

Fine clay soil and shallow, mile-wide valley cause the channel to be fickle and sinuous in its northern reaches. "You meet yourself coming back," said one man freighting its ice with long string-teams. In flood, these tight bends might be sheered off and recontoured, entire gumbo banks moved to the opposite side of the valley. A field taken from a farmer at Lieter might be deposited on another man's meadow at Moorhead.

Drains 350 Miles

In its 350-mile run, the Powder has more cartographic complexities than most rivers. For instance, there are two North Forks, two South Forks, a Middle Fork and the Red Fork. Four branches originate in the Big Horn Mountains—Middle, one South, and both North Forks. Red Fork starts in the foothills to the south. The southernmost South Fork starts 75 miles farther south in the Rattlesnake Range near Hell's Half Acre and the town of Powder River. Some 50 miles north of the Wyoming line, the combined waters flow into the Yellowstone River, on to the Missouri, and the Mississippi.

Tributary names are clues to early lifestyles on the drainage: Crazy Woman Creek, Gray Cabin Draw, Remington (for the rifle), Hanging Woman, Dead Horse, Baking Powder, Dead Man's Draw (horse thief killed there), Dry Creek, Fortification, Wildcat, Bitter Creek. Other creeks and draws are named for ranches or people: Three-Bar, Circle Bar, P K, Bradshaw, Barber, Ivy, S A, 76. Still others are named for wildlife.

'Bogs a Saddleblanket'

Quicksand in the Powder can bog a saddleblanket, insist old-timers. Its bars still shift with deadly stealth, and are eyed just as warily by today's riders as they were by those of a century ago, when the river's quicksand first found its way into folklore. Upstream flash floods bury in silt formerly safe rock crossings. Those who know the river's habits advise: When your horse drops from under you, you'd better slide off and help or you're liable to leave him there.

The famous western photographer L. A. Huffman wrote in 1878 of a crossing at the N-Bar ranch:

The herd is pouring into the water, the point coming out on the opposite shore. Powder is a treacherous, dirty stream. Going or coming with cattle, the cowboy never hesitates whether it be high or low, full of driftwood or easily fordable. He hops into it with his horse herd or herd of cattle whenever or wherever he strikes it. Sometimes he gets into quicksand, abandons his struggling horse, and gets ashore if he can.

However, cattlemen were neither so blithe to the danger nor so heedless of their animals as Huffman suggests. In reality, "the Powder" was carefully scouted before each crossing, no matter how many safe crossings had been made at a site, because of the continual shifting of the unstable river bed. Bogged cattle and horses were painstakingly dug out of the sands. Lucille Kendrick White described this chore as one involving shovels, boards and ropes:

Railroad looks like suspension bridge with pilings gone, 1923; below, 1978 flood cut road

"You cannot rope an animal and pull it out of quicksand, as you can from mud. It will pull them apart—or at least break their legs. You must dig them out."

Geologists rate the Powder as a dry river. Even so, there have been many attempts since 1940 to dam it for industrial purposes.

Ranchers answer such "nonsense" with facts assembled over a century: a draw filled with 19 feet of silt in 40 years, a flood that left only two feet showing of 15-foot-high posts, eight inches of silt washed in by one storm and dragged out by the next, six successive banks built up at the mouth of Clear Creek, deltas built up in tributary draws. If the dam were 250 feet high, it would fill with quicksand in less than 22 years; the protection buffer (half the height of the dam) would be gone in 11 years.

Another problem cited is the rate of evaporation— 3½ feet of water per square foot per year, according to Watt. The normal flow is not enough to sustain the evaporation. Watt's mathematical calculations show that "sand becomes the continuous phase, and the water becomes the dispersed phase."

'The Land Heals Self'

Private irrigation systems operated successfully from the turn of the century. None, however, was so quixotic as the system designed by George Brundage after he saw a water wheel and centrifical pump at the 1904 world's fair. With his brother, Doc, as a partner, he built a five-foot rock dam and ditches, pumping water under the river bed to a ditch on the north side. It then irrigated a flat by gravity flow, returned to an overhead pipe, and crossed the river again to the Grey homestead,

Skeptics said the only practical thing it accomplished was to give the mailman a pipe to shinny across when the river was high or the ice going out. The system irrigated only 30 acres. Even George realized it was too costly. He sold out to Doc, and Doc went broke. The mailman, however, did use the overhead pipe for many years.

'It is with rivers as it is with people: the greatest are not always the most agreeable nor the easiest to live with.'
—Henry Van Dyke

A Lozier hunting party packs into Wind River Mountains for big game

6. GAME AND FISH
IS BIG BUSINESS

Rams at rest in high country

Grumpy moose and haughty pronghorns glare from trophy walls all over the United States, symbols of high adventure in Wyoming. Abundant game still lures hunters, as it has for more than a century, deep into canyons, up stark peaks, and onto the high plains. Continuing popularity has produced a stable hunting business and promoted creative game management.

Record heads in all species—moose, elk, bighorn sheep, pronghorn antelope, bear—have been taken from the game-rich Wind River Mountains since the Box R Ranch was established at the turn of the century. Irv Lozier followed his father's and grandfather's game trails and blazed some of his own up to 13,300 feet, in guiding hunters from this cattle ranch sprawled at 7,600-foot elevation. It is one of 65 to 90 guest ranches in the state.

As with many such ranches, the Box R's early entry into the guide business was a response to urging of an eastern hunting pal. Carl Rungius, noted wildlife artist of 1900, coaxed the first Irvin Lozier into the business—"my grandfather packed him around the mountains," explained Irv, who is past president of the Wyoming Guides and Outfitters Association.

An average of 255 hunters and dudes each year take white water trips on the Upper Green River, hunt fall and spring, fish countless mountain streams and lakes, pack into the high country, and even help with Box R chores if they like. In early days, most out-of-state hunters came from the west; today, as many come from the southwest and from California. Meat packing plants in Pinedale, butcher, package and ship the successful hunter's meat; a taxidermy shop works artistry on trophy heads and ships them.

In search of bighorn rams with their great curling horns, Lozier and other Wyoming outfitters soon learn the caliber of their hunters. Mountain sheep hunting is considered among the most grueling big game hunting in

the world, a fine ram's head America's most prized trophy. To locate a mature ram, the hunter must be in top physical condition, willing to ride, climb and search rugged terrain for days or even weeks. The difficulty of sheep hunting is part of its mystique.

Fortunately for Lozier, the nearby Whiskey Mountain area in the Wind River range is one of the most heavily populated bighorn wintering areas on the continent. It is one of the main sources of transplants for other states. Even so, though it is common to sight ewes, lambs and young rams, the older rams are difficult to locate. About 200 are harvested each year.

More plentiful are the ungainly moose, said by Indians to be the final large animal created from leftover parts of other animals. Wyoming Game and Fish plans a 1,446 annual harvest of this creature known to Europeans as elk and to Shoshone Indians as black elk. (Our elk is technically wapiti.) Both moose and elk frequent mountain meadows. Most hunters get their moose; most do not fill their elk licenses, with only 24 percent elk success even though nearly 17,000 are harvested annually.

Guided hunting parties find ample herds of deer and pronghorn antelope (which also isn't really an antelope). Over 80,000 of each species is shot each year. Lozier also takes his hunters in search of bear—brown, cinnamon and black. In 1985, six spring hunts were scheduled.

Bighorn sheep favor isolated rocky terrain such as Whiskey Mountain slopes, most heavily populated wintering area on the continent

Hunters savor glacial scenes of remote peaks, where game thrives in natural state

Mule deer with its horns in velvet seeks protective cover on edge of clearings

"Wild game is an inherent feature of our mountainous regions . . . destroy the birds and animals of our mountains and plains, and no artificial substitute will ever compensate us for this loss," wrote the Wyoming State Game Warden in 1905, Daniel C. Nowlin. He laid the groundwork for today's state Game and Fish Department, created in 1921.

On this philosophical base, wildlife managers have built the department into a successful business enterprise which nets several million dollars annually. Beyond this, hunters and fishermen spent $223,034,620 in 1983 for their sport. No data has been collected on proceeds from other outdoor activities. Game and Fish spent $17.2 million in 1983, and took in $23.4 million. It employs 400.

Before Wyoming was a state, the territorial legislators realized conservation was needed if the abundance and varieties of fish were to be maintained. A Fish Commissioner was authorized in 1879. The first State Game Warden in 1899 was Albert Nelson of Jackson.

It was Nolin, however, who spurred state officials with the thought that conservation might be good business. Before his appointment as Game Warden, he served in the fifth state legislature, urging passage of game laws.

"When the last buffalo had been slaughtered, we made it a felony to kill one," he said acidly. "Shall we await the final disappearance of our elk, deer and antelope before we provide for their protection?"

The new state's need to develop its natural resources was a reality he understood, too, and he pointed out, "Thinking men everywhere are beginning to realize that the utilitarian spirit of today may be pushed to such extremes that all things which may be exploited into ready cash will be marred, crushed or exterminated to satisfy present greed, with no thought of those to come after."

Thus it is that the Wyoming Game and Fish Department works with industrialists and developers, minimizing harm to wildlife—and, in the process, bringing the state huge profits.

Elk Went by Sled

Transplanting of game from areas where they are too numerous into other areas where there are none has been occurring since 1910, when Nolin supervised removal of a carload of yearling elk from the Jackson Hole herd. These were turned loose in the Big Horn Mountains, with great effort: "The road to St. Anthony, Idaho (the nearest rail point) was never worse, part snow and part mud. Teton Pass was covered by several feet of snow, necessitating the use of sleighs to Victor, Idaho, where the elk were transferred to wagons." His son Bruce, who also headed the department for six years, repeated the plant in 1928, using four-horse teams and sleds to reach the railroad and unloading between Buffalo and Sheridan.

The Whiskey Mountain wintering area is one of the

Mountain goat numbers climbing

High in the cliffs of the deepest canyons, the nimble mountain goat is thriving in a land not native to it. There are about 75 goats in the state, with an annual harvest of 15.

Many goats winter on the east and south slopes of the Beartooth Mountains, in the Clark's Fork Canyon, and in the canyons along Littlerock, Bennett and Line Creeks. The slopes around Deep Lake appear to be one of the major summering areas for this bearded resident of high, rugged terrain.

The majestic animal moved first into the Beartooth Plateau from Montana plantings. Care is being taken that they not intrude on the native bighorn sheep ranges. The shaggy white goats generally prefer the stark terrain near or above timberline.

Ron Klotoske

'The time is not remote . . . when parks and breathing places will be rated for their true value, when those fortunate enough to own homes in Wyoming will bless nature for the rugged mountains and rough canyons— even for the desert places.'
—Daniel C. Nowlin

This fawn has out-grown its spots

continent's main sources of bighorn sheep transplants. Population of this Wyoming native range is about 7,000 animals, with 350 licenses sold each year; 193 were harvested in 1982 and this has been increasing each year. They are most numerous in the Wind River Mountains, and sheep trapped near Dubois were released in Utah and in Idaho in 1982. Mature rams are hunted, ewes and lambs transplanted in over-stocked herds.

Included in Game and Fish work is planting shelter-belts, monitoring new industrial development, enforcing game laws, protecting endangered species, and verifying wildlife damage claims. Largest amount paid out in the past ten years for wildlife damage was $319,336 in 1976; state law allowing ranchers reimbursement for damage is part of the good-neighbor policy of the department—elk and deer can demolish haystacks quickly in a hard winter. Only nine other states pay for wildlife damage.

Chief Game Warden Rex Corsi, concerned about Wyoming's rapid growth in 1980, wrote that man's manipulation of the environment may destroy the basic needs of conditions he cherishes: "If we want wildlife to thrive, we must retain natural environments and properly reclaim those we disturb."

Cooperation Pays Off

This century-long effort to come to terms with industry—in some cases, impacting heavily an area—is one with which Game and Fish lives daily. In some cases,

mining pits have been turned into bass lakes. The state's pronghorn antelope appear to co-exist amiably with oil wells and mines. Domestic livestock and big game share the mountains, forests and plains.

Bob Oakleaf, a nongame bird biologist, says, "In ecosystem management, we are not attempting to build a new system—but rather to maintain ones that have been developing since the beginning of time.

"Elimination of humans from an ecosystem is not possible. We are part of the ecosystem. What is possible is to guide activities in development so that detrimental impacts are minimized and functioning ecosystems are maintained. All life ultimately depends on this."

State residents had indicated in one survey that they would like more effort given to preserving nongame wildlife. Greater sandhill cranes, once endangered, now number about 15,000 in western Wyoming. The only known population of the black-footed ferret is at Meeteetse and biologists are trying to increase this to make new transplants.

Environmental protection is a significant part of the fish division effort, according to its chief, Joseph R. White. Streams straightened for industrial use may be ruined as habitat for fish. In Fontenelle Tailwaters, for example, it cost $800,000 to restore habitat by placing large boulders in 29 miles of stream and creating a spawning facility. Stream channel alteration proposals thus are monitored carefully. A harvest of 10 million fish each year returns an estimated $129 million to state coffers.

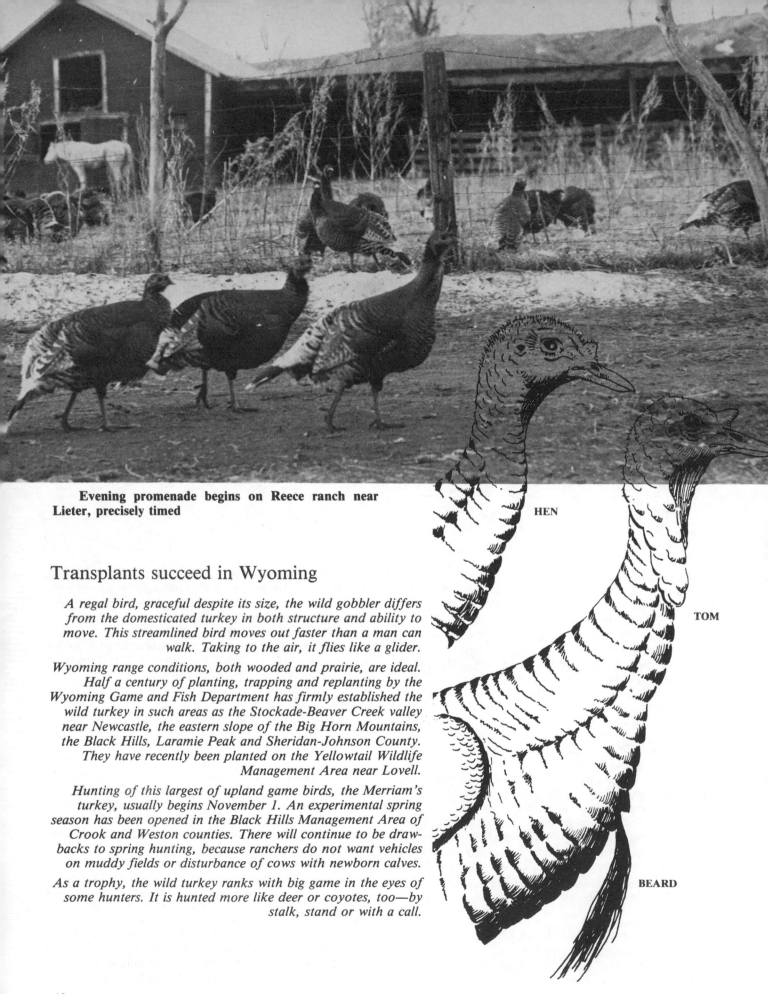

Evening promenade begins on Reece ranch near Lieter, precisely timed

Transplants succeed in Wyoming

A regal bird, graceful despite its size, the wild gobbler differs from the domesticated turkey in both structure and ability to move. This streamlined bird moves out faster than a man can walk. Taking to the air, it flies like a glider.

Wyoming range conditions, both wooded and prairie, are ideal. Half a century of planting, trapping and replanting by the Wyoming Game and Fish Department has firmly established the wild turkey in such areas as the Stockade-Beaver Creek valley near Newcastle, the eastern slope of the Big Horn Mountains, the Black Hills, Laramie Peak and Sheridan-Johnson County. They have recently been planted on the Yellowtail Wildlife Management Area near Lovell.

Hunting of this largest of upland game birds, the Merriam's turkey, usually begins November 1. An experimental spring season has been opened in the Black Hills Management Area of Crook and Weston counties. There will continue to be drawbacks to spring hunting, because ranchers do not want vehicles on muddy fields or disturbance of cows with newborn calves.

As a trophy, the wild turkey ranks with big game in the eyes of some hunters. It is hunted more like deer or coyotes, too—by stalk, stand or with a call.

HEN

TOM

BEARD

FLOCK INSTINCT GUIDES WILD TURKEY BEHAVIOR

A young tom struts through the feeding hens, shining in the early sun like polished metals, bronze wedded to blue steel. An older tom's red wattles quiver in a challenging gobble; he erects his fanned tail, spreads mammoth wings—and the rush is on, flashes of irridescent colors in a flurry of feathers.

This moment is magic in remote badlands where wild turkeys have adapted to a harsh environment. It is a scene played throughout the state today.

The "pit! pit!" alarm—or placid "keow-keow" of a feeding flock, if you are lucky enough to creep upon them unobserved—now sounds from one corner of Wyoming to another, as plantings since 1935 have thrived in most areas. The first plant was on Cottonwood Creek near Laramie Peak.

Though some ranchers protect the birds and do not allow hunting in an effort to firmly establish flocks in areas that probably never were native for turkeys, local seasons are open to hunters in fall and spring.

A gregarious bird, the naked-headed wild turkeys of Wyoming feed in flocks—and the entire flock moves when one is alarmed. They can move swiftly, in streamlined bodies weighing 12 to 20 pounds.

Silhouetted against a Wyoming badlands sunset, turkeys fill bedroom tree

Their Timing Is Precise

Built-in timing and orderly habits make their sunset promenade to the winter-bare cottonwood roosts an impressive sight, as well as humorous.

On the shortest day of the year, at precisely 4:15 p.m., you can notice a restlessness among those turkeys feeding in the alfalfa field across the frozen reservoir. A few begin a noticeable surge across the stubble. Up along the ditchbanks, turkeys at the scattered edges of the flock show no sign they have gotten any signal. They continue to peck in the stubble, their bodies hunched back in balance over the fulcrum of their sturdy legs.

The restless group, however, is gaining reluctant followers. Their movement now has taken on a sense of direction. They walk slowly at first, gaining momentum, toward the east end of the reservoir.

They now begin a stately promenade along the same route they have followed for hundreds of sunsets, until they reach the barren trees where each has established his nightly roost on a particular limb.

If they are spooked along the line of promenade, the turkeys will detour briefly and begin to feed again—but not for long. That built-in clock keeps ticking. Presently, they will regroup and retrace their steps to the point at which they were startled. If the coast seems clear, they resume their interrupted promenade toward the big trees.

On arriving at the roost, the first birds will peck for a few minutes around the base. Their sense of timing tells them the moment has not yet arrived to take to the air. More birds assemble, fanning out some distance from the roosting tree. Others move on up the ridge to a second bedroom cottonwood.

Turkeys Rev-up for Flight

Suddenly, from a wild rose thicket 100 yards away, a turkey takes to the air—revving up, gaining altitude in a long diagonal flight, rising almost leisurely to the desired height. He settles on a branch, silhouetted against the sunset, then hunkers sideways until he reaches his special spot. It is part of the evening ritual, signaled from the depths of turkey metabolism.

Other barred wings drum the air to gain altitude. Once having attained 10 to 15 feet of altitude, they seem to have enough momentum to glide upward the 50 feet or so necessary. It is now clear why the first arrivals just peck around the cottonwood base. They must move some distance away from the roost in order to fly into it in their customary pattern. Few rise straight into the air.

The wild turkey, meleagris gallopavo, was native in the U.S. as far north as central Colorado, but not west of the San Francisco Peaks and Santa Catlina Mountains. As such, it figured in early white man's history in America as the Pilgrims' thanksgiving bird.

Yearling toms are likely to have visible beards in the spring, and beards of gobblers may reach from 4 to 12 inches by the second fall. The gobbler has longer leg spurs than the hen, its wattles larger and more brilliant, and its plummage more irridescent than the female's. Wild turkeys have acute hearing, are sharp-eyed and extremely alert. They move fast and decisively when startled.

Locating the birds is easiest in late fall and winter, after the deciduous "bedroom trees" have lost their leaves. They can be seen then at twilight—graceful big birds at rest on gnarled tree limbs, silhouetted in fading sunset. Another magic moment in Wyoming wilderness.

Eliminating beaver caused flooding and erosion, so ranchers aided their comebacks by shifting beaver to coulees that needed new dams

Man lives in eco-system of exacting species mix

The world of nature is a chain in which each species affects all others; if one link is removed, the chain no longer works without some repair. Thus, when the first white man came into Wyoming to trap beaver, he set in motion a reaction felt all the way to the Gulf of Mexico.

The flat beaver tail no longer thwacked the water in ponds dammed by the industry of this first conservationist of the north country. Flood waters rushed unchecked, eroding the fragile land and multiplying flooding and erosion mile by mile. The beaver, prized for hats and coats, became an endangered species.

One of the first conservation efforts in Wyoming was by ranchers who captured live beaver and moved them in barrels to locations where dams were needed to stop the fine gumbo soil from running away.

The list of other creatures nearly eliminated by man is part of Wyoming territorial history—the buffalo, the wolf, the mountain lion, black-footed ferret, whooping crane and elk. Many other species later suffered drastically from man's depredations. Even streams were altered, the loops bridged by dredging to open more bottom land to farming; increased velocity caused flooding, erosion, and eliminated fish habitat.

Only a few people—besides Indians—in early Wyoming understood the intertwined relationships between land, air and water creatures with the earth itself. Much of the destruction occurred before statehood. The hide hunter's wasteful practice of taking only the skin and leaving the carcass caused sharp increases in predators such as wolves and coyotes. Carrion-eating vultures followed the carcasses northward into Wyoming.

The need to maintain and re-stock fisheries first

Tusk hunters nearly eliminated regal elk from forests

Elk regally pushing underbrush aside with their giant horn racks were threatened with extinction, paradoxically, by the Benevolent and Protective Order of Elks (B.P.O.E.). For two teeth, ivory and agate-eyed—the pair of tusks each possesses—thousands of the huge animals were slaughtered and left to decay in forests early in the century when bull tusks brought $50 a pair.

Long before the B.P.O.E., Indians had regarded these tusks as special, dresses, shirts or vests decorated with elk teeth being worth many ponies. But the Indians wasted no other part of the elk in obtaining the prized gem-teeth.

Poachers in 1905 in Jackson Hole were organized under Charles Isabel, who served six months in the Uinta County Jail for poaching and ultimately was threatened with vigilante justice after over 500 elk had been killed in the "hole" for their tusks. Mop-up operations which continued through 1907 included the confiscation of a wagonload of empty beer barrels found to contain elk scalps and teeth.

In 1909, the Wyoming legislature acted with a law setting a prison term of up to five years, the basis for the "wanton destruction" law still on the state books.

Masked raider nearly fell to man's range poison work

Rare black-footed ferret

A masked terror of prairie dog towns, the black-footed ferret, exists in only one known place in the world, the Meeteetse flats. The weasel-like creature was thought to be extinct, a victim of widespread prairie dog poisonings. It eats the charming prairie dog which denudes and pocks vast areas of rangeland.

One night in September in 1981, a dog at the John Hogg ranch killed a black-footed ferret. Lucille Hogg, thinking it unique, took it to a taxidermist, Larry La Franchi. He identified it and called the local game warden, Jim Lawrence, who contacted the U.S. Fish and Wildlife Service. Thus began an on-going project for the Wyoming Game and Fish Department: the black-footed still lived, 88 of them, most on the historic Pitchfork ranch.

Landowners, industry and the various wildlife agencies began a cooperative effort to study, maintain—and, possibly, propagate and/or transplant—the almost-extinct ferret.

caught the attention of legislators. This was soon expanded to include game and all wildlife, as a few people who understood ecology began campaigns to restore balance and to stop further depredations. Hunters of elk for a pair of teeth, ivory tusks, left dead elk to rot in the forest and were the first targets of Wyoming conservationists.

Even pronghorn antelope were scarely to be seen by 1916. Moose declined in such numbers that by 1923 there was only half of today's 7,700 count. Bear and other fur-bearers once were hunted without restraint.

Perhaps the most obvious example of what happens when man meddles with nature is the rabbit-coyote syndrome. Campaigns against both created a see-saw range war for many decades. In defending their livestock, stockmen caused the near extinction of the wolf and intended to do the same with coyotes and bobcats, when nature gave them a depressing lesson in ecology: rabbits over-ran the ranges. Wholesale rabbit hunts were launched, as thousands upon thousands of jackrabbits and cottontails nibbled grass to the roots and gnawed the bark of other cover. With this new abundance of rabbits, coyotes and bobcats again increased—so the range war had to be fought on two fronts.

Had control efforts been tailored to individual areas—and total elimination not been the goal—compromises with nature could have been reached sooner. Effective local programs cannot be designed in the halls of the U.S. Congress, where the politically powerful took their predator problems.

The Wyoming Game and Fish Department has met an increasing list of challenges throughout the years: over-killing of game animals, shrinking habitat, transplanting species to areas where they had been killed off—and, in some cases, where they had never been. Game counts were started, hunting managed in order to control

game populations.

The excitement generated when a colony of black-footed ferrets was found a few years ago is typical of today's concern for the ecosystem. The ferret was thought to be extinct, a victim of depression-born poisoning of prairie dog towns. Though not endangered, the eagle certainly was threatened by a recent fad to wear eagle-feathers in hats. Efforts with the once endangered whooping crane have resulted in a gratifying come-back of this majestic bird.

Bobcat Fur Now Prized

Game and Fish biologists now talk of management programs for the bobcat, as prices for the spotted fur skyrocket. If over-trapping depletes breeding stocks, the animal is in trouble. It may be time to control harvest and areas trapped, suggests Douglas M. Crowe of Game and Fish. Will people care? "Because of his nocturnal habits and extreme secretiveness, I fear the bobcat's welfare suffers . . . out of sight, out of mind."

The Wyoming bobcat justifies the expression "meaner than a wool sack full of wildcats." It is bigger here than in other states—25 to 26 pounds for the male, with upper limits reaching 35 to 40 pounds. California's heaviest was 31 pounds, the average 16.4; males in Massachussetts, New Hampshire and New Mexico average 21 pounds.

Stress has been placed on keeping wildlife in as natural a condition as possible, totally dependent upon its own natural instincts and physical characteristics for survival. Artificial feeding is not a substitute for natural habitat and death is natural, emphasize Game and Fish officials. What is working so successfully in Wyoming is the practice of providing the habitat for wildlife and then allowing it to live in a wild condition.

Sage grouse, right, and prairie grouse (or chicken), below, dance in strutting grounds like open area occupied by pronhorn antelope in photograph

Moonlight dancer struts
in grouse courtship ritual

The thrum-thrum of the grouse to his lady-fair is spring ritual on the prairies of Wyoming, copied in dances by Indians of many tribes. More than 100 cocks may spread their tails, inflate air sacs, and "drum" for moonlight dancing on a windswept ridge, exposed knoll or sagebrush flat used year after year.

The sage grouse is the most numerous of several species of grouse, most of the 150,000 harvested annually in the state being sage. Blue and ruffed grouse are mountain forest birds, which dance singly rather than in the group display common among sage, sharp-tailed and prairie grouse.

During the full moon of April, most of the mating takes place in a nuptial group of hens surrounded by guard cocks. Dominance of males is based on bluffing, strutting and fighting, which sometimes draws blood. Rapid beating of wings produces a swishing sound, a resonate plopping sound added by vibrating membranes of the air sac. During the peak of strutting, the entire routine may be repeated as often as 12 to 15 times a minute.

Courtship display begins between sunset and darkness, continuing throughout the night. An hour after sunrise, the dancing comes to a close and the grouse fly away. An increased number of cock dancers appear on strutting grounds in late April and early May, when yearling males are allowed to join the courtship display. Most of the breeding has been completed by that time.

Sometimes the cocks turn to the left, sometimes to the right. Two cocks may face each other and glare for minutes without moving. The white tips on spread tail feathers shine in the dark, a reminder of the white tips on feathers of some Indian dance bustles. Antics of the grouse are copied in Indian Prairie Chicken dances, with prairie and sharp-tailed grouse not as spectacularly costumed as the sage—but much better performers.

Those interested in observing this phenomenon can contact local Game and Fish Departments for locations of sage grouse strutting grounds.

Mountain grouse, blue and ruffed, move down the mountains in the spring and upward to higher elevations in fall. They need conifers for winter cover and food. The fall movement coincides with the first heavy frost or snowstorms, which restrict or eliminate berry and fruit food supplies. They then feed on buds, shoots and leaves of both deciduous and coniferous vegetation.

Favorite haunts are edges of clearings and along the openings near streams and springs. Open glades in the forest with heavy cover all around them usually attract these birds. During mild weather they roost in trees, in snow banks in winter. They normally feed from daylight until noon, then go to a sheltered area to dust and rest. In mid-afternoon they resume feeding until dusk when they go to roost.

Blue grouse frequent sagebrush as far as 500 feet from the nearest trees, ranging in open grasslands on wooded fringes. Ruffed grouse frequent small creeks rather than ridges; they are never far from water and like ravines with willow, dogwood, chokecherry, service berry and other fruit-bearing shrubbery. In the timber, they favor second growth areas.

A total of 27,661 hunters pursued grouse during the 1982 season, resulting in $1.8 million in expenditures in the state. Partridge and pheasants are other common game birds in Wyoming, although grouse hunting is by far the most popular.

Antelope neared extinction

Lonely Wyoming highway driving is enlivened by thousands of pronghorn antelope grazing, playing, traveling, or hung up in fence barriers. This state supports over half the world's population, 517,030 in 1982-83; it once may have numbered 50 million from Canada to Mexico.

Wyoming's largest herd, 26,000, is in the Pumpkin Buttes area 45 miles west of Gillette. There are 49 other herds, decreasing in size to 1,000. Once threatened by extinction, its habitat cut by 75 percent in 1919, game management officials began lobbying the legislature to allow them to manage. At that time, it was rare to see an antelope.

Antelope are curious creatures, and knowledgeable hunters know that if they spook a herd, it will return to spy on them. Thus, the flash of white tail poof over a butte does not mean you will never see them again. Wait, and they will peek curiously around the butte from the other side.

This comic of the prairie is not really an antelope at all, and has no close biologic relatives anywhere in the world. Fossil forms have been found in rocks 20 million years old. It is the only animal with a hollow horn branched, shed, and grown anew each year. It is also the swiftest of American quadrupeds. When killed, it must be skinned immediately, or at least the hind leg glands removed, to avoid too-strong taste to the meat.

Antelope population fluctuates in direct proportion to the adversity of each winter. In 1927, no permits for hunting were issued, where the previous year 500 were issued. In 1952, 41,000 were harvested. In 1974, the harvest exceeded 40,000. In 1983, 100,000 permits were issued.

Antelope and sagebrush flats seem to go together, sagebrush being peculiarly digestible to antelope. The stomach capacity is only half that of a domestic sheep and antelope can subsist on browse unpalatable to most mammals. Sagebrush eradication, warn biologists, also can eradicate the antelope, the sage grouse and the mule deer.

Antelope inhabit very dry country and, if they required much water, could not long survive. They need less than a gallon a day. They do not perspire, and lose little evaporation from mouth or nose. Their kidneys concentrate urine. They eat snow in winter, and they time feeding to obtain the most moisture.

One of Wyoming's 3,000 bear in tree perch

EAGLES SURVIVE WITH ELEGANCE AND POWER

Eagles soar on Wyoming's windstreams with an elegance and power that has made them symbolic to as divergent civilizations as ancient Rome, the American Indian, countries of Mexico and the United States of America.

Both golden and bald eagles are common throughout the state—but eagles fall prey to predator poisons, coyote traps, and rodeo cowboys willing to pay $125 per feather to decorate a hat. The eagle is the largest of the hawk family, a carnivorous predator responsible also for plucking newborn lambs into the air.

Roosts in Jackson Canyon and Little Red Creek, both near Casper, have been documented by the Audubon Society as winter refugees between late September and March. Tagged Canadian eagles, normally solitary and mating for life, soar into windy canyons in groups about an hour past sunset. On windless days, they fly directly to the roosts they have selected.

Dude ranches extend season if hunters guided

Dude wranglers saddle thousands of horses for visitors at Wyoming ranches every year, most in the western mountain regions. Some are working cattle and horse ranches that take guests as a sideline; others are elaborate and luxurious dude ranches with traditions that encircle the globe.

The number varies from the 55 listed by the Wyoming Travel Commission to as high as 90. Some ranches which cater primarily to hunters are also sometimes dude ranches—and vice versa. With the increasing popularity of winter sports, many now are open year-around. Traditionally, the season is May through October, with an extension for those outfitting big-game hunters.

Guiding and outfitting out-of-state hunters is a long established business in Wyoming, direct descendant of the old-time mountain man's sideline. Some guides make trophy-only hunts. Game variety is wide—bear, mountain goat, bighorn sheep, moose, elk, deer, antelope. Upland bird and waterfowl hunts also are guided.

Dude ranch activities are many—pack trips, general riding, swimming, fishing, hunting rocks and artifacts, hayrides and rodeos. Facilities may include movies, game rooms, whirlpool baths, arts and crafts. Cross-country skiing and snowmobiling are winter activities at year-around ranches; guests at some can be helicoptered into wilderness areas.

UW shoots a basket at New Mexico game

Trout Strike on Wind River Indian Reservation

Boysen derby pays off on pike lips

Up in the high country, trout are popping bubbles on dozens of lakes as they rise to feed on mosquitoes, larvae and other goodies. "They'll take almost anything you pack in," says veteran outfitter Edward Le Clair Sr. of Fort Washakie.

Fishermen come from all over the world to pack into the Wind River wilderness. Guides here take no hunters, since they operate within the Shoshone-Arapaho reservation and the tribes do not allow hunting by outsiders. In the misty mountains to the west, streams and lakes abound with trout—brook, rainbow, Mackinaw, cutthroat, California golden, rainbow, German brown.

"We use fly hooks and lures—no live minnows or salmon eggs. We don't want trash fish from discarded bait," Le Clair says. "This is one of the cleanest set of lakes you've ever seen."

The tribes have opened a total of 40 mountain lakes to non-tribal members. They bear names like Sonnicant, Upper Heebeecheeche, Little Moccasin, Wykee, Tigee, Pie and Paradise. The tribes also control fishing in the Wind River Canyon, from the tunnels downstream to the "wedding of the waters" at the canyon mouth, where the river's name changes to Big Horn. A tribal fishing license is required. This is also true to cast a line into Dinwoody lakes and streams, Washakie Dam upstream, the Big Wind River above Boysen Dam, and downstream from the confluence of the Popo Agie and the Little Wind River.

Reservoirs such as Boysen, Ocean and Cameawhait are under the jurisdiction of the Bureau of Land Management, and a Wyoming fishing license is required.

Fishermen troll in luxury, drop dry flies into fast streams, or fish jewel-like mountain lakes. Whatever the preference, it is an area to stimulate geologic interest as well. It stretches from the sheer rock-walled canyon, through mineral-rich desolation . . . into the snow-capped and forested mountains beyond.

Each year thousands of sportsmen are introduced to this area during the annual pike fishing derby on Boysen Reservoir. The gala begins the previous weekend for sponsors, who literally put $10,000 into the fishs' mouths.

Symphony orchestra rehearses, left, while a new student has family help, above

7. UNIVERSITY LEADS IN RESEARCH

The University of Wyoming has integrated its trio of mandates—to instruct, research and serve people of the state—until it now plays a major role in economics as well as in futuristic discovery. Researchers probing a wide range of subject matter, from sheep disease, rattlesnakes and sagebrush to climate, oil shale and the stars, attracted $13.7 million in outside funds in 1983-84. The state legislature budgeted $195.2 million for the university's 1985-1986 biennium budget; a century ago, it was $5,000.

Skills of the UW "think tanks" are recognized far beyond the windy Laramie Plains where they labor most of the year. Their research is regional, national, spans the globe in some cases—and probes the universe itself.

A list of 1,000 endangered species is under study by Wyoming biologists on all National Park Service lands—Wyoming to Ohio, Michigan to Missouri. UW researchers cooperate with other countries, as in designing an isotope mass spectrometer with British scientists. Climate research takes them to Antarctica, and they will be probing space with design of an imaging infrared camera for a telescope to be flown into orbit in 1988.

They share international health concerns in cancer research, brain function and aids for the handicapped. Water and acid rain are significant in-state as well as beyond. Oil shale experiments, development of synthetic fuels, and other mineral research are of both regional and national consequence.

Seven colleges, plus School of Extended Studies and Graduate School, academically comprise the university, which occupies 79 major buildings on 780 acres. Four farms near Laramie and five agricultural substations add 5,253 acres. The UW investment is over $370 million. A 50,000-watt stereo radio station beams to Wyoming, Nebraska and Colorado listeners. One of the two major computer facilities operated by the state of Wyoming is located on campus for instruction, research and data processing; the other in Cheyenne is used by all state agencies.

Fine arts collections of sculpture, paintings and artifacts, as well as an herbarium, mycological and zoological collections, anthropology and geology specimens are used in instruction—and displayed to the public in many campus museums.

New clues to the origin of the solar system are emerging from a remote sensing project of the physics and astronomy department. And one professor, Robert D. Gehrz, has been appointed to assist in development of the world's largest telescope on the extinct Hawaiian volcano, Mauna Kea, by the University of California. Planetarium shows take place on campus every Wednesday evening in the biological sciences building.

High-tech equipment is used today even in the physical education department, nucleus of UW's broad spectrum of sports. A biomechanics laboratory puts motion analysis on a precision level: camera, video system, an X-Y digitizer interacting with a microcomputer, a 16mm movie camera exposing up to 10,000 frames per second. The geology department helped buy the latter camera, and also uses it in particle studies.

Teleconferencing has extended UW instruction throughout the state. Courses are being given and credits earned by site-bound students via telephone lines; the system is designed so that students can even talk back. The university outreach program long has offered an extended degree program for teachers throughout the state.

'We live within a frame-work of erosion which ticks away constantly' —W.C. Knight

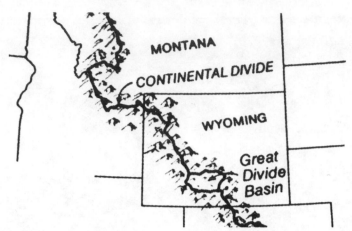

8. GEOGRAPHY OF WYOMING

Eons ago the earth's crust buckled to expose the backbone of the Rocky Mountains diagonally across Wyoming. Erosion of wind and water gullied the steeper slopes into a network of miniature gorges and cliffs, mushroom-shaped pinnacles left when soft shales eroded. The plains were trenched by rivers. Isolated mountains rose abruptly, island-like.

In examining the state's geography, it is important to note that change occurs all the time—entire hillsides sluffing along the west side of U.S. 25 are visible south of Sheridan. Some flooding rivers change their channels annually. Thus the face of Wyoming is mobile, some features erased while new ones are formed.

It is this process which geologist W. C. Knight described as important in the transportation of soils, "The arid regions of Wyoming, chiefly tertiary and cretaceous plains and tablelands, receive very little rain. Soils loosened by great earth cracks are transported by the wind to the broken country, the distant hills and mountains.

"We live within a framework of erosion. The question is whether we accelerate this process—or whether it goes along at about the rate it has always done, regardless of what we do."

Basic terrain is determined by the Continental Divide which passes south over Togwotee Pass, Union Peak, and a triple-divide peak, Three Waters Mountain. Drainage from here is not only to the east and the west, but southward to the Green River and subsequently to the Gulf of California. Just south of Yellowstone Park is Two Ocean Lake, where the mountain man Osborne Russell reflected, "Here is where a 12-inch trout, by swimming hard, can actually cross over the mountains." With an average elevation of 6,700 feet, Wyoming is second highest state, just 100 feet under Colorado's average height.

The great divide, with many mountain ranges extending from it, determined numerous basins and smaller "holes" or secluded valleys richly grassed. The Laramie Basin in southeast Wyoming is over 7000 feet above sea level, buffeted by constant wind gusting off the Medicine Bow range. Wyoming Basin located southcentral at a lower elevation contains rough country trenched by the North Platte River and its tributaries. Canyon country marks the periphery of the Green River Basin of the southwest. Bridger Basin butts against the Uinta Mountains.

Big Horn Basin is ringed by a horseshoe-shaped complex of mountains, a grassland 125 miles by 100 miles where temperatures are extreme and rainfall only 7.75 inches a year. Temperatures of 114 in the summer and 50 below zero in winter are recorded. It grades into a true plains environment in the north, grasslands in the west and south, and near desert to the east on the dry slopes of the Big Horn Mountains. The Owl Creek Mountains meet the Big Horns on the south, and the Absaroka range forms its west boundary.

The Black Hills of Wyoming attracts more rainfall than the plains it borders. Flora is unique, with heavy stands of oak, quaking aspen and ponderosa predominate. This is an oasis environment well-watered from numerous small streams, offering winter protection for wildlife and cattle. A large part of the Black Hills is in Wyoming.

Major mountain ranges such as the Big Horns, Absaroka and Wind River are steeply dissected, their slopes layered with grass and brush above and below timberline. The ramparts of the Wind River Range become the Absarokas, and Beartooth Mountains. Jackson Hole is rimmed by the Teton range and ranges of the Bridger Teton National Forest. Gallaten, Madison and Gros Ventre ranges also rise in that section of the state.

Thus many features add variety to Wyoming topography—canyons cut through sheer granite walls, geological faults, deeply eroded sandstone formations, and dune areas.

Thunder National Grasslands take up about one-third of Wyoming east of the Big Horn and Medicine Bow Mountains. This open plains area is punctuated by uplifts like the Rochelle Hills, Pumpkin Buttes and the Pine Ridge escarpment running east from the northern Laramie Range. The Hartville Uplift runs north toward Lusk from the North Platte River. Another "hole" here is Goshen, eroded 100 or more feet below the high plains. Buttes, brushy canyons and steep scarps offer livestock protection from bitter winter winds.

This is a land of majestic solitude—immense color-streaked cliffs, red canyons that look black with brush in the bottom, and vast expanses of open rolling prairie. Only the dull ring of a hoof striking stone, or the clatter of sliding shale as the horse climbs, breaks the quiet for a rider. Possibly a faint stirring of grass is detectable as a rattlesnake slides for cover. Otherwise, silence.

Parts of Wyoming once were under the sea, and there are many areas where fossils can be discovered. In northeastern sections, leaves of lost ages are imprinted in shale and giant fern stems three feet in diameter are found.

Such isolated igneous rocks as Indpendence Rock on the old Oregon Trail offer mute testimony to the boiling cauldron that once was Wyoming. Sinks State Park, where the Popo Agie River disappears, Hell's Half Acre on U.S. 26 from Casper, and networks of mountain caves indicate age-old action of underground water.

Part II

Wyoming Today

470,000 People

Apple dunking, Old South Pass City; Laying line out for trout, above; H. E. McIntyre, Casper, baits for pike; Skiing the Big Horns; Floating Clear Creek; Mrs. Tom Penson, Sheridan, with cedar art

Find joy in ice wonders, in a rushing stream, Boysen Lake in a pontoon—or in a fossil fern, bottom photo

People at play . . .

Even Powder River quicksand is enjoyed with caution, for fabled river "flows" sand three feet below water bed; Jeff Seeley, Jimmie Gibbs play in it

1. LIFESTYLE MOLDED BY LAND AND SKY

Wyoming is a mosaic of lifestyles, people whose daily lives may differ radically but hold in common challenges and values that are unique. They have had to be self-reliant, whatever their role in life. And all are caught in a web of life that combines flora, fauna. climate, topography and historic events.

Writers tempted to define this culture often draw puzzling stereotypes: "a society alternately the reproach and marvel of mankind", "a new phase of Aryan civilization", "unprecedented environment producing a temperament volatile and mercurial . . ." One explained it in ethnologic and physiographic terms: "intelligent, progressive and self-adaptive types of mankind arise in elevated upland or semi-arid environments"—Henry Fairfield Osborn. Louis Atherton wrote in favor of the rancher as the arbiter of culture, pointing to his influence and efforts to dominate the environment.

It is simpler to say that those who enjoy living here have learned to roll with the punches, to accept the unchangeable and to function within its terms.

Lifestyles do not stereotype readily. Some mountain men were Indians. Cowpunchers became sheep shearers. A homesteader might have been also a freighter, a miner, a cowboy and sailor. Lawmen became shopkeepers, bankers and ranchers. Cattlemen became sheepmen. Historically, social life was paradoxical, as well. Had one lived in early Wyoming, social life might have included a trappers' rendezvous, a country dance, the opera, or an English salon. Wyoming had them all.

The contrasts remain. Today, Wyoming has Basque dances high in the mountains, Indian powwows and sun dances, concerts ranging from honky-tonk to symphony, sports of all types and, yes . . . even a mountain man's rendezvous. The queen of England, the oil rigger, infamous mobster and famous author all walk the same streets. A ragged little old woman once dropped $5,000 cash in the snow in Sheridan and got it back; she runs her own cow outfit. A motorist switched on his CB radio after the second flat tire on a lonely road; his plea was answered by a concert pianist scanning the band for other humanity. Texas trail drivers now ride 18-wheelers, still moving herds of Wyoming cattle around the country.

Lines are drawn loosely in this state, the edges blurred between occupation, social status and personal goals. Land and sky help shape lifestyle, here where skies are awesomely wide. You may be able to see for 100 miles— or no farther than your nose in a winter blizzard. People watch the skies, both for vital signs and for pleasure . . . just as they did 10,000 years ago. The difference is that new stars sparkle in the night sky, as satellites bring the world into the most isolated dwelling.

Some pioneer principles remain in the lifestyle . . . hospitality and friendliness, "never judge a person by appearances," a traditional respect for privacy, the family-centeredness of most lives, the tolerance or "hands-off" another's affairs. Most are "private people", concerned first with survival for themselves and their families. Harsh weather is a great leveler, and produces caution that infuses all areas of life.

"Wyoming, with its open ranges and outdoor life, can never have the same ideas or ideals as those of states where the entire population has been lambed in sheds," said P. H. Shallenberger, Lost Cabin sheepman. This is as apt today as when he said it in 1927.

One of the most forbidding spots, Buford at the top of the divide between Cheyenne and Laramie, is exhilarating to a new family from New Jersey. When winds reach 85 miles an hour and wind-chill temperatures drop to 70 below zero, Betty Reeder and her son, Robert, light coal oil lamps and switch on the electric generator. Robert and his wife, Joanne, keep fires burning from semi-truck-loads of stored wood. Betty's mother Ruth, though, dislikes the roaring blizzards that pack windows in snow four months of the year; she'd like to go back

'People aren't lambed in sheds here'

Fine registered Herefords are auctioned in ranch sale

where they came from in 1980, but no one else agrees with her. Robert is postmaster, and the whole family runs Lone Tree Junction store, bar, gas station and refuge for stranded motorists.

The impact of terrain and climate on personality can not be overstated. Undoubtedly this creates quixotic contradictions in people, causing them to be quick to react to abruptly changing conditions. It has made them resourceful, scornful of both the faint of heart and the pessimist. Typical is the Buffalo college editor who hitched a ride with the Jersey milk truck, the only vehicle moving through a blizzard, to meet a deadline in Sheridan.

This is a state that can elicit sudden wonder . . . at a triple rainbow arching the sky, hills washed in the sepia tones of a tintype, badlands backlighted by sunset, or clouds boiling up like geothermal steam from purple mountains. Nature has twisted the earth into deep, dark canyons, lofty spires, mesas, mountains, prairie and desert. Someone once said Wyoming was built with the debris left over from creation of the world. It may as well have been the apex of creation . . . and the Creator looked at a work upon which he could not improve.

Land's Gifts Cherished

The largess of the land has a value to its people beyond mere utility. Things of earth and time . . . twisted cedar, arrowheads shot from bows thousands of years ago, fossils of ancient seas . . . these hold charm for Wyoming's people. Many are amateur archeologists fiercely protective of these curious relics of the past. Others take renewable resources and fashion objects of art: cedar polished into gleaming lamps and tables; giant sagebrush from southeastern Wyoming, a special art form; diamond willow, traditionally made into canes, also becomes table legs and lamps.

Wild game and native fruits intrigue local cooks, both men and women. With one in four residents being hunters, people take pride in finding new—and old— ways to prepare the game. Dried meat recipes abound, ranging from the Indian method which requires skill to slice it thin enough, to oven-dried and smoked-in-a-barrel

jerky. Elk meatloaf, meatballs of venison, mooseburgers, antelope sausage, stews galore and other exotic main dishes are found on Wyoming tables.

"Experiment with your game," advises a Hoback Canyon cook, Margaret Feuz. "Don't soak it in vinegar or milk or anything else. Cook it like you were preparing a rare dish . . . add spices and sauces, bouillon or onions."

The piquant flavor of chokecherries is prized, just as it is by Indians who still pound the berries or grind them to dry into patties. Other cooks generally make jams, jellies and pancake syrup of them, while Indians make pudding or sweet "gravy". Wild plums, buffalo or bull berries, wild currants and gooseberries also are native fruits so distinctive in flavor no "storebought" product can compare.

Memorable People

Wyoming is its people in all their varied dimensions, people of today building a rich heritage for those of tomorrow—just as those who are now history did for the present. A few of today's memorable people would include the following:

• Clarence Bulkley of Buffalo, a rancher who continues to ride and break horses even though one leg was amputated because of cancer; when he broke his remaining leg, hospital attendants found oats sprouting in the other boot.

• Jack Anderson of the Wind River Canyon, a trapper and cowboy who built his own cabin in 1926; four of his six children died in a fire there in 1931, memorialized by Anderson in a scholarship fund which will pay $2,000 yearly to each of three students.

• The late Al Stevens of Thermopolis, who decided to go straight after packing a machine gun in his trombone case as a big-time gangster; Stevens returned to his home state, received a Wisconsin pardon with the help of Wyoming's governor, and became a vocal proponent of law and order (Stevens actually did play professional trombone with national name bands—when he wasn't pulling "capers" with "name" gangsters).

Al Thomas chops corn for silage

•Pat Hamilton of Parkman, the female rodeo coach at Sheridan College who has trained over 350 rodeo cowboys and a significant percentage of today's Wyoming professionals; she's an anthropologist with special interest in jade—when she's not helping with ranch work or critiquing "her" champions like Wally Badgett of Ashland, Mont., Chris LeDoux of Kaycee, or Bill Pauley of Miles City, Mont.

•Nick Eggenhofer of Cody, dean of western illustrators who died in March, 1985, after illustrating more than 50 books and thousands of western pulp magazines.

•La Vere Gardner of Afton, still guiding deer hunters at age 82, born at the base of the Salt Creek Range and a wool grower during the stringent 1930s; he only lost his temper once at a hunter, when a horse four times rubbed off a loaded moose—"by the time we got back to the truck, neither of us was talking to the other."

•Bill Utzinger of Casper, shipping tycoon and third-ranking among U.S. trapshooters who has hunted the Absaroka wilderness since 1925 for bighorn sheep; "not everyone could take it, you get up there in one of those 100-mile winds . . . a fellow with me came across the high divide between Wiggins Fork and Emerald Creek on horseback. The trail is only three feet wide and it's a thousand feet down . . . poor old Charlie was off his horse and crawling on his hands and knees. I couldn't talk to him 'cause the wind was blowing too hard. When we got across and he learned we would have to go back that way to return to camp, he said, 'I won't go. You have to find another way out.' Well, I had to go clear down into the forks of Wiggins and Emerald."

Wyoming lifestyle lives in the 90-year-old woman who drops her dry-fly furtively into a secret trout hole, the professorial escapee from Hollywood who feels free not to entertain, teenagers buzzing snow-clogged roads at 40 below zero in four-wheel-drives, a radio engineer rescued by helicopter from a mountain-top shack after wind heaped snow against a door mistakenly built to open outward—ordinary people embracing both the commonplace and the unexpected, being themselves. This is Wyoming lifestyle.

Alan Simpson

Long-tall Simpsons stride into politics

The name Simpson has moved in state affairs since Wyoming was born. In re-tracing his father's footsteps to Congress, Senator Alan Simpson also embellished a voters' trait of maintaining continuity. He is majority whip in the U.S. Senate.

Milward Simpson, the gentleman from Jackson who called opponents "my splendid opposition," served a term as governor, in the U.S. Senate, and many terms in state legislature. For two decades he was booster and builder for the University of Wyoming, its education and sports, as trustee and board president.

His son, Peter K. Simpson, directs the prestigeous University of Wyoming Foundation and has served in the legislature. Milward earlier obtained the money to build UW's Coe Library and to endow the School of American Studies.

The tall Simpson boys—fourth generation Wyomingites, "young but never small"—had seven-foot beds upstairs with a ceiling too low for Alan, 6'7", and Peter, 6'4". Late home one night, they climbed a repair scaffold to their room, congratulating themselves next morning that neither parent seemed aware of their late entry. Two weeks later, returning from church, Simpson searched in vain for his house key. Al asked if he could help. "Why don't you go back there and climb up that scaffold like you did two weeks ago," replied Dad. "You could not pull one over the Old Man," Pete says ruefully.

He bribed his sons and four basketball teammates with a quarter a Sunday to sing in the church choir—guild women had to alter choir robes. One of the boys decided they deserved a raise after several weeks of faithful vocalizing. Simpson: "You guys all look like a million bucks, but you still sing like two bits."

Wit and humor were decisive in father and son political fortunes, according to brother Pete. Others credit Milward Simpson's enthusiasm and zeal—as governor, successes included: creation of Dept. of Revenue and Division of Mental Health, an underground water code, increases in state salaries, and school funding, voting machines and a civil rights bill (always careful of fine print, he voted against the federal civil rights bill later as a U.S. Senator).

"My county is sopping wet and the saloons run wide open. Juries will not convict if it means a jail term," Simpson reported in 1927, then a state legislator. In 1955 as governor, he had to intervene in Jackson to close gambling, obtain the resignation of the Teton County sheriff and suspend four liquor licenses—not a popular action with the Jackson Hole tourist industry.

Sen. Alan Simpson, a member of the Senate Judiciary Committee, received his Juris Doctorate in law from the University of Wyoming. He returned from service in the army's "Hell on Wheels" 2nd Armored Division in Germany to serve in the Wyoming State legislature for 13 years. On the national level, he authored immigration reform legislation.

Wyoming Senator Wallop won't follow the herd

Government? "We don't need it in our daily lives," snorts U.S. Senator Malcolm Wallop, a staunch defender of state's rights.

"People's view of the obligations of government in the west is quite different than in the east . . . conventional wisdom is not always very wise. We don't need to react to the intrusions in life that haven't occurred."

He forsees a reassertion of "the independence that was necessary to settle the west," in which he is well-grounded; his grandfather, Oliver Henry Wallop, bought the Canyon Ranch in Big Horn in 1885, the fourth son of the British Earl of Portsmouth who had a choice of going into the clergy, to India with the army or leaving England. Oliver Henry came to Wyoming.

British ties have remained strong in family tradition, and the Queen of England was hosted at Canyon Ranch, in 1984 by the senator's sister, Lady Jean Porchester, wife of the queen's racing manager. Winston Churchill's mother, Jennie, fished here in 1882; a Wallop cousin, she became the mother of Winston Churchill.

In fact, Oliver Henry, after riding "hell bent for leather" all over Wyoming and Montana collecting horses for the Boer War, did become the Seventh Earl of Portsmouth and sat in the House of Lords—until he was ousted for keeping his U.S. citizenship. He also served in the Wyoming legislature.

Malcolm remembers his grandfather riding from the ranch into Montana to the Cascade Mountains, and trailing back horses gathered. In Big Horn, the wild range horses were bucked out for polo—because the British buyers required them well enough broke to ride the length of a polo field. Wallop and his Scottish cousins, William and Malcolm Moncreiffe, shipped 20,000 in one year. "The Boer War started polo," says his grandson, who doesn't play; the field remains in weekly use as possibly the oldest in the U.S.

One son, Gerard, returned to England to become the Eighth Earl of Portsmouth, while the senator's father, Oliver Malcolm, remained to ranch in Wyoming.

Oliver M. Wallop and son, Malcolm

Senator Wallop's battles in Congress for Wyoming have been in the tradition of state senators since his grandfather's day. As a lifelong conservationist, he finds himself sometimes in the paradoxical position of opposing today's conservation movement. Water policy issues, for example, have elicited the acid comment: "Our experience is different than your concept."

Then, the contemporary confusion linking party politics to the far right conservative movement is another source of pique. He cites federal intrusion in education, the requiring of student transport to out-of-town events on school buses. This is fine, he says, if they don't have to travel more than an hour; Wyoming students often must drive for hours, or even a full day, to sports events—the issue is one of human comfort, and being anti-busing is "not a conservative reaction."

Typically as independent as his constituents, he resists traveling with the herd: "It's like driving sheep—one jumps off a cliff and the next 700 are right behind."

A conservation easement to all Canyon Ranch land bordering the forest was given for public use by Oliver M. Wallop. The ranch remains a monument to the fiesty elder Wallop.

WYOMING POPULATION % Increase		
1870	9,118	
1880	20,789	128.0
1890	62,555	200.9
1900	92,531	47.9
1910	145,965	57.7
1920	194,966	33.2
1930	225,565	16.0
1940	250,742	11.2
1950	290,529	15.9
1960	330,066	13.6
1970	332,416	0.7
1980	469,557	41.1

Politics hinges on state's rights

One theme runs firmly through a century of Wyoming politics—defense of state's rights. Both today's U.S. Senators, Alan Simpson and Malcolm Wallop, carry on in Washington D.C. this resistance to federal intrusion in state affairs. Both are Republican and both well grounded in Wyoming affairs, of families here before statehood was granted in 1890. Gov. Ed Herschler, a Democrat and the longest tenured governor in history, has guarded fiercely state's rights for more than a decade.

With a grim consistency, whichever their party, statesmen have lined up behind this issue. This has required special vigilance, since the federal government owns vast natural resources within state borders. An electorate of independent voters demand control of their own affairs; their elected representatives have carried out these wishes for nearly 100 years.

People at work they enjoy . . .

Upper photo, Natrona County leads state in wool production; above, University of Wyoming professor John Ravage, Casper engineer Tom Norman plan satellite-linked TV

Above left, Jim Hall makes guitars in Sheridan; left, Eunice Sonnamaker builds houses; above, state legislature is lobbied to protect water

Welcome is extended by the Indians to the White man to travel to our Indian village (Lander) and stop many days to visit. When he becomes hungry he may travel to the forest and hunt elk. When he kills his elk it should be brought back to the Indian village where the Indian and White man visit while a hearty feast is prepared and eaten.

'When someone dies, Indians stop everything as this is an important event . . . the white culture has much to learn'' —Pius Moss

2. RESERVATION TODAY

In a complex framework of tribal and federal government, 5,951 Shoshones and Arapahoes operate ranches, oil wells, schools, and ventures of daily life on the beautiful Wind River reservation. It is complex because their lives are bound by state, county and federal laws—plus the differing rules of two tribes. They are masters of bureaucratic alphabet soup.

These two tribes, once enemies on the plains, were located on the same reservation over a century ago. Their land base then was whittled, chopped up, parceled out to the public, and poorer portions restored. Oil and gas wells were drilled in the 1940s; thirty years later it was discovered tribal royalties had been siphoned off by the oil companies in a system of fraudulent production figures.

Three times, vast and key areas were ceded. The word "ceded" came to mean "forced to concede", as a land area once over 44 million acres shrunk to one million. Ink on the 1868 treaty, which reduced the reservation to three million acres, was hardly dry before another million acres was carved off because of gold discoveries, the Brunot Cession Treaty of 1874. In 1904, it looked as though a dam on Wind River could make the desert bloom, so still another million acres was "ceded". The Riverton Reclamation Project immediately was occupied by non-Indians. In 1939, 1.47 million acres of non-irrigated land was returned, as were mineral rights on the rest in 1958.

Because they are different nations, each "sovereign," Shoshones and Arapahoes have separate governments, or general councils, which elect business councils of six members each. A joint business council of both tribes meets each Wednesday, following Tuesday meetings of separate councils. The joint council has no authority with either tribe. To complicate matters, both tribes chose to remain "unorganized" without constitution or by-laws in the wake of the 1934 Indian Reorganization Act. This means there is no chairman or president; a chairperson for the day is elected from the floor.

Over this system—and controlling the purse strings—are federal employees of the Bureau of Indian Affairs (BIA). They still function under an 1880 congres-

Shoshone Jodie McAdams prays in sign language at Gift of Waters pageant

sional act mandating them to "civilize and christianize" the Indians. Even though Indians received all rights as citizens in 1951, every tribal action must be ratified by these BIA bureaucrats.

Such a system of government creates the kind of problem that rose in 1984 concerning hunting on the reservation. The Shoshones felt game should be "managed", and restricted hunting curtailed. The Arapahoes didn't agree. The BIA sided with the Shoshones. A lawsuit against the BIA was filed by the Arapahoes, on the grounds that the BIA "trustee" was not looking out for their tribal interests. At this writing, it has yet to be resolved.

Life isn't easy for the bureaucrats, either. One recent BIA superintendent complained that he couldn't even leave Fort Washakie without the approval of both tribes—and they often disagreed just to be contrary.

Despite all this, the reservation is a beloved homeland, full of human warmth, rich tradition, progress and modern technology. It is a place to which those who leave feel compelled to return. Driving across miles of dry sagebrush flats, the snow-capped mountains beckon. The streams and rivers rush blue and clear toward the dam

White man is invited also to stop at night and camp so that early in the morning he can travel and fish in the streams and see many beautiful lakes and mountains. Should it storm, he may hurry and return to the Indian village to visit until the sun comes out.

—Interpretation by H. D. DelMonte

Branding time on the 300,000-acre Arapaho Ranch on the slopes of the Owl Creek Mountains is a huge job involving six sub-ranches, 30 cowboys, and up to 10,000 cattle.

Most of the cowboys are Indians here. They sleep in the hills under the stars during branding, moving through the 25 square mile ranch to brand, castrate and dehorn the year's calf crop. In the photo above, Mrs. Pete Hemley cooks in a tent for the hard-riding crews. Each cowboy needs eight or nine horses, in order to change horses at least twice a day.

In its 45th year of operation, the ranch west of Thermopolis used to be Pitchfork range. It was bought jointly by the Arapaho and Shoshone tribes, but is operated solely by the former. Registered Quarter Horses also are bred.

Map shows land area carved from the Wind River reservation by various treaties

now built across Wind River. By the time the water reaches Boysen Reservoir, it takes on the clay color of desert buttes and barren gumbo hills. This is arid land, despite the rushing snow-fed streams.

There are few jobs on the reservation, and unemployment is 68 percent or more; in one recent recruitment, nearly 1,000 people show up seeking 17 jobs. A police force of about 25, patrols 324 miles of roads. Police and tribal court, called the Court of Indian Offenses, operate as BIA agencies. Death rate from disease and accidents is still high; the reservation accidents are not included in the state traffic fatality toll. In the Indian Health Service clinic, medical standards have never been high; doctors come and go like yo-yos, many just out of medical school paying back government service for educational funding.

Education is one catch-basin for large numbers of unemployed, as well as being considered critical for the future of both tribes. In addition to the on-reservation population, many more tribal members live in adjacent areas to give Wyoming a total Indian population of 7,125 by 1980 BIA figures.

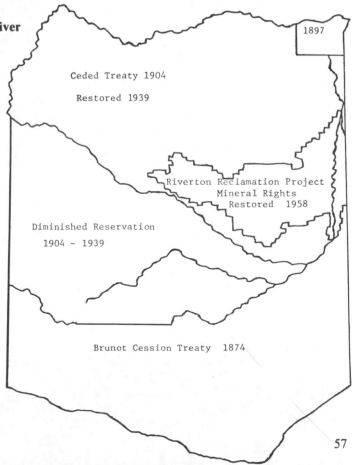

1897

Ceded Treaty 1904
Restored 1939

Riverton Reclamation Project
Mineral Rights
Restored 1958

Diminished Reservation
1904 – 1939

Brunot Cession Treaty 1874

Grandfather holds the child aloft. "I name you Wa-he-ne-ba," he pronounces, passing her around the circle to seal her recognition as one of the community, accepted for the loving concern of all present.

This is an Arapaho naming ceremony, an ancient custom still observed on the Wind River Reservation. The child, now with an Indian name that means "Singing Peppermint," is Adene C'Hair, daughter of Wayne "White Star" C'Hair and his wife, Mary Ann "Nightingale Woman." They have three sons who have also been thus formally presented: Brent "Walking in the Mountains," Leo "Night Horse," and Steven "Buffalo Bounce Back."

This ceremony, in which relatives and neighbors are seated on floor mats, is much more than a naming. It is a dedication of the child, acceptance of parental and community responsibility, and prayer for the four stages of her life—to the east for the beginning-of-life, the south for teen years blessing, the west to petition a happy adult life,

and the north for a blessed final stage.

Grandfather, John Anthony C'Hair, acknowledges human dependence upon the Great Spirit and prays for blessings through the entire circle of the child's earth existence. His Indian name translates to White Sun.

'the reservation is a beloved homeland, full of human warmth, rich tradition, progress and modern technology'

Arapaho girl studies at St. Stephens, upper right, while a pool tournament player, Jack Badhorse, takes a shot, right

Shoshone girls at Episcopal boarding school wore uniforms; now four are public schools

Main Street of Riverton, the instant city born of an irrigation project

3. CITY AND TOWN

From the largest, Casper, to the smallest family-run post office, a vitality and civic pride characterize Wyoming's cities and towns. Each is distinctive in its way, possessing a special slice of history, a piece of natural wonder, or a purpose for being that is like no other.

City builders were sensitive from the beginning to the benefits of tourism. Wealthy easterners and Europeans began coming to Wyoming even before the Indians were subdued. Pilgrimages to the two national parks, Yellowstone and Grand Teton, shifted into high gear with the auto. Many cities like Jackson and Sheridan grew hand-in-hand with tourists who invested in the state. For tourists, Cheyenne built its rodeo into "the daddy of 'em all", largest in the world.

Superlatives abound. Thermopolis has the largest mineral hot springs anywhere, 27 minerals mixing and healing. Green River is the "trona capital of the world." Douglas is home of the jackalope, a taxidermy whimsy with deer antlers grafted on a jackrabbit. Cheyenne has the world's only museum dedicated to first edition postage stamps. The first commercial moss agate deposit in the U.S. is near Guernsey. Cody was born in the superlatives of a master showman.

Once called the world's wickedest city, Cheyenne was surpassed in this respect by Rock Springs—and in population by Casper. Cheyenne's population of 58,429 is occupied now with affairs of state radiating from the gold leaf dome of the Capitol building. Warren Air Force Base, formerly Fort Russell, maintains 200 of Strategic Air Command's Minute Man III missiles; a military base for more than 111 years, it began as a cavalry outpost. Wyoming State Museum houses a full scope of state history. But for nine days a year, state affairs take a backseat to rodeo during Frontier Days; in Old West

Museum, memorabilia of the first rodeo in 1897 is featured.

Nearly every major oil company has exploratory offices in Casper, more than 400 such companies and their affiliates. Four interstate pipelines either originate in or pass through Casper. As the hub of the oil and gas industry for nearly a century, Casper had its first refinery by 1895.

A recent boom in uranium, coupled with expanding coal and oil production, pushed Casper into first place as Wyoming's most populous city. Agriculture and tourism are also important, with five convention centers; Hogadon Ski Area and other facilities on Casper Mountain entice tourists. Hunting and fishing are ideal in Natrona County, which also leads the state in wool production. It seldom rains, and the 20.48 inches annual precipitation come primarily from a snowfall averaging 137.6 inches.

Tiniest towns are each significant, too—like Buford, population 5; Crowheart, population 10; Ten Sleep, 320; Midwest, 825. On the U.S. 80 divide between Cheyenne and Laramie, Buford is a haven for winter motorists buf-

MAJOR WYOMING CITIES 1980	
Casper	59,287
Cheyenne	58,429
Laramie	24,410
Sheridan	15,146
Rock Springs	19,458

Treasures of the old west can be found at auctions around the state

feted by high winds. Parkman across the state used to have 27 saloons, now has only one—a refuge for snow-bound motorists near the Montana border. Midwest throbs with oil field life. Ten Sleep, a ranching communi-ty, was "ten sleeps" (or nights) between old Indian camps on the Platte and Clarks Fork Rivers.

In Buffalo are the Basques, the "chosen people" who trace ancestry to Tubal, fifth son of Japheth, son of Noah; prominent sheepmen, many speak the Spanish, French and Basque languages of their native Pyrenees Mountains. A biblical name is Eden settled by Men-nonites, the "Eden point" arrowhead named for its valley rich in archaeological artifacts. Another of biblical origin is Goshen County, Wyoming's farming center; this fertile valley of the North Platte has more cultivated cropland than any other county: wheat, sugar beets, potatoes, beans, corn and hay.

Civic Pride Runs Deep

Racing through Buffalo on a fine black horse, white beard flowing, Robert Foote mobilized the town against invasion, a symbol of the staunch civic pride ever present in Wyoming towns. Robert Foote was the "Paul Revere" of the Johnson County War, a respectable Scottish mer-chant defending a town accused of harboring half the enemies of the early cattle barons.

Born as a stage-stop on the Overland Trail, Rock Springs plays a leading role in the nation's energy pro-duction. Lives of its 19,458 people center on coal mining and railroads in the heart of gem-rich Red Desert. In the 108-mile stretch between Rock Springs and Rawlins, are found Turritella agates (agatized shells), jade and petrified wood. Here, too, is the Great Divide Basin where it never rains—if it did, the entire region would turn into a huge lake, as it is a "hole" in the Continental Divide that drains to neither ocean, only into itself.

"East of Eden" are heaped enormous sand dunes, reaching from Eden more than 100 miles to the Seminoe Mountains. Strong winds from the west and the desert-like environment dominate lifestyles in such towns as Farson, Eden, Wamsutter, Red Desert and Superior.

Rawlins, like many southern Wyoming cities, had its origin in Union Pacific Railroad track-laying camps. As a stage stop on the gold trail to South Pass City, Rawlins got so wild that vigilantes lynched and skinned Big Nose George Parrott; as a warning to other outlaws, they made a pair of men's shoes and other articles of apparel from Parrott's skin. Cattle, sheep, coal, uranium, oil and gas are principal industries. The Wyoming State Penitentiary is in Rawlins.

Third largest city and Wyoming's academic center is Laramie, population 24,410. The state's only four-year college, the University of Wyoming, now dominates what once was a railroad tent town. Evanston grew out of an-other rail point, riotous Bear River City; with 6,421 peo-ple, it is Uinta County seat. Worland, about the same size and Washakie County seat, became a major trade center because of the railroad—but Worland once had a prob-lem; the UP ran its tracks on the opposite side of the Big Horn River. Settlers waited until winter, gathered all their belongings and moved Worland to the rail side of the ice-bound river.

Tourist Wealth Helped

Sheridan and its satellite communities of Story, Big Horn and Ranchester long have been focus of wealthy and prominent tourists. At the Sheridan Inn, "house of 69 gables", Presidents, generals and show business luminaries have been guests throughout a century.

Sheridan also is a trading center of the no-man's land of northeastern Wyoming and southeastern Mon-tana—areas too far from the capitals of either state to feel kinship. Sheridan always has been their city—the trade, shipping and banking center, the place where ranch wives moved in the winter so their children could go to school. Close to rich coal beds extending into Mon-tana, it also has experienced periodic mining booms.

Mining, wheat and "zebra stone" (onyx) are diverse features of the Wheatland, Chugwater, Guernsey and Glendo areas. Wheatland Irrigation District comprises 55,000 acres; iron ore from Hartville and Sunrise mines is the most prominent mineral. Milk from herds of dairy cows is moved to the Denver milk shed.

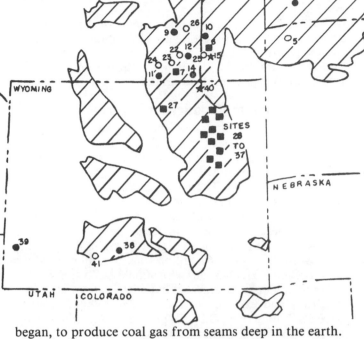

'If we're going to have a slurry pipeline, I'd much rather Oahe water be used than the Madison Formation'

—Gov. Ed Herschler

4. A DECADE OF MINING FRENZY

National and international events of the 1970s nearly turned this state into a vast crucible of energy production, as investment frenzy surpassed reason and reality. Sixty-four huge power plants were on the drawing boards—where most of them stayed. Population projections, had they been realistic, would have changed the face of Wyoming.

Three events caused all the excitement—and, indeed, much development: (1) the Arab Oil embargo of 1973; (2) passage of the national Clean Air Act; and (3) issuance of the North Central Power Study. The Clean Air Act put a premium on Wyoming coal, which is low enough in sulphur to allow many industrial plants to meet air quality standards without adding costly scrubbers. The 1971 Power Study targeted Wyoming for massive development.

A fourth event, entry of the U.S. into nuclear power production, created Wyoming's uranium industry. And a fifth—which proved untimely—was establishment of U.S. Synthetic Fuels Corporation, a federal funding entity to promote syn-fuels development.

The Exxon U.S.A. president, Randall Meyer, glowingly foresaw one and a quarter of a million people living in the Powder River Basin of Wyoming, compared to half a million in the entire state now, all working to achieve a goal of 15-million barrels of syn-fuels per day within 30 years. Other population forecasts added in all mineral production and were much higher.

Predictions like this began to frighten people. Skeptics reminded that bigger doesn't necessarily mean better, as they watched the boom begin: 13 new coal strip mines in Campbell County, 64 gasification plants planned in a three-state area with most in Wyoming, boomtowns advertising the state as "sin cities on the prairie," newcomers in company pickups roaring past stranded motorists.

Two experimental projects on coal fracturization began, to produce coal gas from seams deep in the earth. Energy alternatives of sun and wind power were tested, 58 large windmills installed near windy Medicine Bow. Velocity and consistency were studied in the hope of supplementing hydroelectric power with wind-generated power. Technical problems developed with the generators and, under the administration of President Ronald Reagan, wind projects received low priority.

The world's richest deposits of high-grade oil shale, containing 1.8 trillion barrels of oil, were tapped—the Green River Formation in southwestern Wyoming, northwestern Colorado and northeastern Utah. New technology made it possible to extract oil from what Indians once called "the rock that burns." Six federal tracts were opened to leasing, but there were no takers in Wyoming; development began in Colorado, but stalled in Utah's courts.

Conventional oil drilling increased 28 percent in 1977, and the "Overthrust Belt" was called "the most promising new oil and gas frontier." Crude oil had peaked at 141 million barrels a year in 1970 from 12,000 producing oil and gas wells.

Water became a major issue, with at least five pro-

FEDERAL MINERAL ROYALTY RETURNS TO STATE					
1973	1974	1975	1976	1977	1979
19,412,664.95	33,392,196.84	34,450,233.27	49,433,821.66	58,971,484.29	70,000,000.00

These funds are distributed as follows:

Foundation Program 37½%	Highway Commission 26¼%	University of Wyoming 6¾%	Counties for Roads 4½%	Cities & Towns 7½%	Impact Assistance 7½%	School District Construction 4%	State Highway 6%

posals received in the State Engineer's office to mix Wyoming water with Wyoming coal and move it to market in slurry lines. Other water demands were made for power plants and synthetic fuel facilities. This water would be drawn from underground flow in the Madison Formation, the state's principal aquifer. Residents also depend for their own water supplies on this hydrologic system.

Gov. Ed Herschler secured support of the four other governors of the Old West Regional Commission to study the alternative of piping water from Oahe Reservoir in South Dakota to the slurry lines. Slurry pipeline proposals ultimately went down in defeat.

State Production Figures

Meanwhile, fortunes of the state rose sharply. A total of $5,852,764,024 in minerals was produced in 1981. Bentonite and trona production led the nation. Wyoming and New Mexico traded places for first and second in uranium production. The state was third in coal, fifth in both crude oil and natural gas.

Production in 1979 included 4.4 million tons of bentonite, 65 percent of the national output. Trona, or soda ash, was being mined at the rate of 11.7 million tons a year, with reserves at 67 billion tons. Uranium production reached 5,512,345 tons with 90,600 exploratory holes being dug. Coal was shoveled out at the rate of 68.8 million tons and expected to rise to 200 million; reserves were 550 billion tons. Oil wells pumped 126.6 million barrels, with 900 million in reserve.

The state's 37½ percent share of federal mineral royalty payments went up to 50 percent in 1977, and Wyoming's U.S. Senator, Frank Barrett, was paving the way for an increase to 90 percent. Income from federal royalties doubled to $70 million within two years of the 1977 increase. The federal government owns 72 percent of the minerals in Wyoming.

Cities serving as "bedroom" or shopping centers for miners began adding up the profits, basing figures on a rule that a dollar is spent 11 times before it leaves a community. Sheridan housed miners earning $15.7 million a year; most worked in mines across the Montana line. Many of these mining companies had offices in Sheridan, while still others bought supplies and equipment there—Decker Coal Company at the rate of $3.5 million a year, for example.

Things were looking so flush that John T. Goodier, chief of mineral development in the state Department of Economic Planning and Development (DEPAD), verbally slapped the hands of all agencies instrumental in slowing down production. This included licensing and regulatory agencies, severance taxation, protection of health and safety. "It is counter-productive," he said, "to cause industry any delays for these purposes."

Goodier also advised, "It would be to the state's benefit to enhance the industrial development program in an effort to broaden the tax base against the time when some of these depletable mineral resources are no longer available."

Not everyone agreed. Fearing that Wyoming's agricultural economy and way of life would be destroyed by increasing energy development, ranchers from Sheridan, Johnson and Campbell counties organized the Powder River Basin Resource Council. They lobbied success-

fully for a strip mine bill, an industrial siting act, and the Surface Mining Control and Reclamation Act which forbid mining alluvial valley floors. They raised questions about syn-fuels plants and coal-fired plants. Construction of a coal-fired plant in Tongue River Canyon was cancelled. Plans for five others were dropped. Funding for two syn-fuels plants was stopped; another company withdrew its application.

Perhaps to offset activities of the Powder River Basin Resource Council, as well as to handle their own public relations, nine companies formed the Wyo-Mont Industrial Association in Sheridan. The Wyoming Coal Information Committee formed in Casper, and the Rocky Mountain Oil and Gas Association was based in Denver with 700 members.

Estimates Exaggerated

Estimates of Wyoming's own use of power by the North Central Power Study indicated it would be 2,340 megawatts by the year 2000, more than double that of 1985. It identified 42 sites in Wyoming of strippable coal, each capable of supporting a 1,000 megawatt or larger coal-burning generating plant.

Both state and national energy need projections turned out to be unrealistically high, and failed to consider effects of energy conservation. By 1981, Great Plains States were producing more than 8,000 megawatts of power that wasn't needed, the equivalent of five and a half Wheatland-sized power plants.

Power generation plans were trimmed. Syn-fuels turned out to be too costly. Eight uranium mines closed in the wake of the moratorium on licensing of nuclear plants, putting 5,000 miners out of work. A 1982 "clearance sale" by the U.S. Dept. of Interior, including 1.2 billion tons of coal in Campbell County, turned sour when it was revealed that Interior had lost $60 to $100 million on the sale. The boom once more was leveling off.

The North Central Power Study, which caused industry to begin building huge coal gasification plants, based its power estimates on a population growth rate of 6.5 percent a year until the year 2000—somewhat less than the historic national average, but still with tremendous implications for suppliers of low-cost power supply. U.S. history has shown electric consumption to double every ten years, equivalent to a rate of 7 percent.

Cheapest method of transporting coal is as electricity via power lines. Thus, by the early 1980s, Wyoming prairies had sprouted six multi-megawatt plants such as the ones near the highways at Gillette and Wheatland. Some two dozen more were planned, when it became apparent that the Powder River Basin electric production was producing more electricity than could be sold. Each 1,000-megawatt steam plant operating 24 hours a day, 365 days a year, would generate 8,760 million kilowatt-hours of electrical energy. Size of planned plants ranged upward to 10,000 megawatts.

Water Scarcer Than Coal

Coal to feed these plants lies near the surface in abundance. What is not so abundant in Wyoming is water. Water requirements for cooling these monstrous thermal plants whose furnaces reach 1,500 degrees temperature are enormous. Water is needed for wet-tower

Once a sleepy cowtown, Gillette has come into wealth, and is alive with culture

CAMPBELL COUNTY COAL MINING

Fourteen coal mines in Campbell County produce over 80 percent of the state's total coal. Production was 94.5 million tons in 1984 and expected to rise to 95 million tons by 1986. The county also leads the state in total assessed mineral valuation, with oil and natural gas produced in quantity.

Arco's Black Thunder mine led all producers in 1984 with 21,200,000 tons. Kerr McGee's Jacobs Ranch mine, also in Campbell County, was second with 15,900,000 tons. Black Thunder is expected to increase production in 1985.

Favorable weather in 1984 caused a surge in production, and some mines broke all existing records for stripping overburden and removing coal. Of the total coal industry employment of 5,336 people, over half—2,738—worked in Campbell County.

Production in 1984 from other coal mines in this county was as follows: Amax's Belle Ayr and Eagle Butte mines, 13.4 million tons each; Arco's Coal Creek, 1.7 million; Black Hills Power & Light's Wyodak mine, 2.9 million; Carter's Caballo, 8.1; Carter's Rawhide, 9.35; Frontier Coal's Fort Union, 0.3; Kerr-McGee's Clovis Point, 1.5; Sun's Cordero, 10.3. Operators of five mines planned to increase production in 1985.

Most Wyoming coal lies in seams near the surface, so that it can be recovered by machinery working above ground after shallow overburden is removed. All but two of the state's 30 mines are open pit; only one in Carbon County and another in Sweetwater County are underground mines.

Power plant for Tongue River Canyon was cancelled; above, Wyoming power travels east

cooling and the cooling pond to dissipate heat from condenser cooling water. Reservoirs were built, others were expanded. Underground water was tapped. Conservationists worried about chemical leaching from plant discharges.

The Laramie River Power Station in Platte County, for example, is a 1,500 megawatt plant with water supply impounded in Grayrocks Dam on the Laramie River.

Loss of stream habitat for fish concerned the Wyoming Game and Fish Department. A cooperative agreement was negotiated with Basin Electric Power Cooperation, acting for the Missouri Basin Power Project. Public access was insured, and releases of water by the company to maintain flow is expected to provide a more stable flow than existed in the past. Sediment will be retained in the reservoir, and large mouth bass stocked when the reservoir fills. Fisheries biologist, Mel Oberholtzer, noted the severe changes occurring on a previous quiet agricultural area, both on the environment and social aspects,

but expected "these impacts will be mitigated as people take advantage of recreational opportunities at Wyoming's newest reservoir."

Syn-fuels a Costly Program

The development of synthetic fuels plants is a different story, based as it is on federal subsidies. Texaco and Mobil both proposed large syn-fuel facilities near Buffalo. The U.S. Dept. of Energy estimated Mobil's gasoline production technology would result in 40,000 barrels of gas a day with water requirements of up to 15,000 acre-feet a year—and it would emit 9 to 14 tons a day of sulfur oxides, 5 to 8 tons of nitrogen oxides, and 21,000 tons a day of carbon dioxide. Air pollution of syn-fuels plants would be extensive even with emission controls in operation.

In addition, Texaco and Transwestern Pipeline wanted to build a major industrial complex at Lake De-Smet that might include an ammonia plant, a 1,500 megawatt power plant, transport facilities, power lines and pipelines. Tri-State Generation and Transmission Association proposed a 1,500 megawatt power station. Together, these facilities would pump an estimated 19 tons a day of particulates and 80 tons of sulfur dioxides into the surrounding air. This is near Cloud Peak Primitive Area in the Big Horn Mountains.

The case of Hampshire Energy's two-billion-dollar syn-fuels project, however, emphasizes the folly of the government's syn-fuels program—which has turned out to be one of the most expensive ways to cut dependence on foreign oil.

Hampshire got a $4 million DOE grant in 1980 and began hiring consulting firms to develop a host of Wyoming permit applications for Campbell County. When this effort appeared to be built on flimsy foundations, these applications were rejected, financial support from U.S. Synthetic Fuels Corporation was cancelled, and Standard of Ohio withdrew backing. Hampshire than went to SFC for $1.3 billion in loan guarantees. This project was placed on indefinite "hold" in 1984.

NINE COMPANIES PRODUCE BENTONITE

Wyoming produces 65 percent of the nation's bentonite, a soft-textured clay that can absorb three times its weight in water. Over 200,000 acres are permitted for this purpose. Annual production in 1980 was 3,584,713 tons, with mineable reserves at 90 million tons. The table below shows Wyoming bentonite companies and their annual production.

American Colloid	908,371
Aurora Industries	446,929
Baroid/N.L. Industries	472,624
Benton Clay Co.	116,300
Dresser Minerals	608,328
International Minerals	110,756
Kaycee Bentonite Co.	405,263
Southern Clay Products	9,659
Wyo-Ben Products	506,483
Total Tons	3,584,713

Modern Prospectors Find Vast Uranium Deposits

Rain washing over granite millions of years ago picked up particles of uranium. These remained dissolved in the water as it percolated underground, until chemical conditions caused them to solidify. Areas where they dropped out of the underground action are called "roll fronts", the uranium deposits of today.

From these roll fronts, uranium is extracted and atomic energy created. The uranium yellow cake that leaves Wyoming can build the mushroom bombs dropped in Japan to end World War II—or it can be used as a powerful source of peacetime energy. U.S. officials hoped nuclear power would replace the need for other non-renewable resources.

When the Atomic Energy Commission began looking in 1946 for domestic sources of uranium, it guaranteed a market and tempted prospectors with bonuses. Since uranium had been known in Wyoming since 1918, people bought Geiger Counters and went hunting. The uranium they found varied from high-grade in eastern Fremont County to low-grade in the Pumpkin Buttes area—and what they found was 35 percent of this nation's known uranium reserves.

This new boom was a repeat of old times in Wyoming. A complex pattern of land and mineral rights resulted in litigation. In the Pumpkin Buttes of Campbell County, the U.S. Dept. of Interior withdrew 65,343 acres from public entry, then re-opened it; ranchers organized a mining district with procedures later ruled illegal. Thousands of claims were filed in every county in the state.

Paying uranium deposits in Crook County's Black Hills were exploited immediately by Homestake Mining Company, leading gold producer of the hemisphere in Lead, S.D. The Lucky Mc strike in Gas Hills, eastern Fremont County, was made in 1953 by Neil McNeice and Lowell Morfelt. Strikes were made in Shirley Basin and Crooks Gap, and in northwestern Carbon County. The boom was on and prices rose, from $8 a pound to more than $50 by 1977.

As in all federal minerals programs, there were hitches. Temporary buying stations had been set up by the AEC, price guarantees extended through 1966. But in 1957, a cutback was ordered and authorization of all new mills cancelled. Only one mill in Wyoming had been completed, with one other under construction. Gov. Milward Simpson led a delegation to Washingotn, D.C., assisted by Senator Frank Barrett, to demand more mills. The AEC authorized seven, three at Gas Hills, two at Shirley Basin, and one each at Crooks Gap and Riverton. An old mill in Shirley Basin was re-opened, four were under construction in the Red Desert and three in Powder River Basin.

Uranium 'Milled' in Ground

Higher prices warranted mining of lower-grade ore, and mine shafts went to 900 feet underground. In situ acid-leaching methods were used, dissolving the uranium solids and bringing them to the surface in liquid form: chemicals are injected through as many as seven wells, the uranium solution retrieved through a control well.

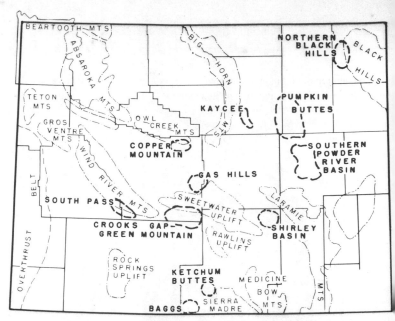

Map shows uranium mining areas in state

As over 90,000 exploratory wells were drilled in a single year, Converse County landowners became concerned about mine de-watering and improperly abandoned exploration holes. They joined with Pumpkin Butte ranchers to strengthen state regulations on drill hole plugging, sealing and enforcement requirements.

More than 99 percent of the ore becomes mill waste and tailing, a slurry of sand and sand-like material, when uranium is extracted from the ore during milling. Thus, a mill may generate 1,800 metric tons of tailing solids per day slurried in 2,500 tons of waste milling solutions—all bound to produce ecological impacts, according to the Wyoming Game and Fish Department. Reclamation efforts, thus, were complex.

Chemicals powerful enough to dissolve uranium leaching into ground water supplies presented problems that quickly alerted Game and Fish and conservationists.

Industry Causes Own 'Bust'

By 1981, the price of uranium dropped to $25 a pound, caused partly by accidents at nuclear plants and partly by an over-optimistic industry. Thousands of workers were laid off. Uranium towns of Jeffrey City and Shirley Basin virtually became ghost towns.

However, the Wyoming governor's ad hoc Uranium Study Committee reported that industry's cataclysmic collapse was not fully legitimate. It was revealed that the trouble actually started when the industry began to speculate in a market that didn't exist. Workers were imported to mine ore that hadn't been sold, in the hope that when the price shot up stockpiles would be ready to mill. Instead, the market for yellowcake declined. The governor's committee said production levels had remained stable—but industry's miscalculations caused unemployment of thousands.

The Powder River Basin, Shirley Basin, Red Desert, Gas Hills and Crooks Gap have abundant low-grade reserves. Three mines in Converse County, two in Johnson, one in Carbon, two in Sweetwater, several in Fremont, and one in Natrona comprise a partial list of recent mine developments.

Minerals of vast interest

Wyoming's shining mountains issued a siren-call to seekers of gold, silver and diamonds—but her fortune was to be in less glamorous, more pedestrian minerals. About 325,000 ounces of gold was produced before efforts were abandoned; no silver deposits rich enough to warrant mining were discovered. A few small diamonds, less than 2 millimeters in size, were found in Kimberlite pipes near the Colorado border.

The "chink-chink" of oil pumps, the roar of coal blasting, and the squish of trona and bentonite dust translate into riches beyond the wildest precious-minerals dreams. Mineral production accounts for the state's historically low unemployment rate—3.69 percent in 1974 when the national rate was 5.67, and 5.8 when the national rose in 1982 to 9.8 percent. When the average U.S. worker earned $175.83 per week, the average Wyoming worker earned $192.58; this escalated proportionally as wages did.

Trona Deposit World's Largest

The world's largest deposit of trona is found in Wyoming's Green River Basin, precipitate from ancient Lake Gosiute which once covered 15,000 square miles. Only two other mines, in California and in Kenya, are in operation. This state produced 93 percent of the naturally-derived soda ash in the U.S. More than 30 individual beds of trona underlie an area of about 1,300 square miles.

There are an estimated 50 billion tons of mineable trona, plus up to 40 billion more tons of marginal trona.

Re-discovery of these beds in 1938 were of worldwide importance, as nearly all soda ash had been produced synthetically up to that time. Trona is used primarily in glass making, as well as by the chemical industry, in soap and detergent manufacture, water treatment, pulp and paper production, photography, and petroleum refining. The soda had been mined marginally as early as 1880.

With only one U.S. synthetic plant still in operation, in New York state, Wyoming mines steadily increase production. A significant European market also is developing, as synthetic plants shut down there. The mining is done with costly machines in tunnels 800 to 1,600 feet below ground, in beds up to 12 feet thick. More than 3,700 workers receive annual contracts averaging $17,500. Value of 1983 production was $104,500,003.

Mountain Fuel Supply Company found brine rich in trona, while drilling an oil and gas test well. Westvaco, predecessor of FMC Corporation, sunk a 1,500-foot shaft into the main trona deposit in 1946, and built a pilot refinery at the surface. FMC began producing soda ash in 1950, with Stauffer Chemical coming on line in 1962, Allied Chemical in 1968, Texasgulf in 1975, and Tenneco Oil in 1982.

Bentonite Has Many Uses

Wyoming possesses much of the nation's reserves of high-swelling bentonite, and is first in production. When wet, bentonite will swell to as much as 15 times its original volume, thus is important to seal oil wells and carry

Oil, Gas Still Mainstays Of Energy Production

Oil pumps like giant feeding grasshoppers suck the black gold from pools deep in the earth, feeding it into six Wyoming refineries and many others out of state via pipelines. It is Wyoming's single most lucrative industry.

In addition to royalties, the state received 39.5 percent of its property taxes from the oil and gas industry. Other mineral properties bring about 10 percent. Wyoming is the only state which pays in full for its federal reclamation projects.

Production by the year 2020 may drop to 60 million barrels of oil annually from the 1970 peak of 155.7 million, it is estimated by Professor Don L. Stinson, head of the Mineral Engineering Department of the University of Wyoming. About 130 drilling rigs are in operation in the state.

The rich oil domes visible even from the surface are leveling-off in production—but assessed valuation has increased steeply. The artificial federal designation of "new" and "old" oil affects this, "old" oil being from wells in production prior to 1973. "New oil" prices were set at $11 a barrel, old at $5.50.

The state produced 118.8 million barrels in 1981, 120.9 million in 1983, and has been a major producer throughout this century. Largest oil producing regions, in order, are: Powder River Basin, Green River Basin, Big Horn Basin, Overthrust Belt, and Wind River Basin. The first well was drilled in 1884, and decades before that, pioneers oiled their wagon wheels with petroleum oozing to the surface.

cuttings to the surface, as a binder in the metal casting industry, and in pelletizing taconite iron ore. It was first used in manufacture of cosmetics.

Long before white people ventured into Wyoming, Indians used bentonite as a bleaching clay and washing agent. Pioneers used it as an emergency substitute for axle grease, as a curative pack for inflamed horse hooves, and as waterproofing for roofs of dwellings.

Considered wind deposits, volcanic ash blown east from Idaho and western Wyoming, the bentonite beds occur in the Big Horn Basin, the southern Powder River Basin, and along the western edge of the Black Hills. Six counties are major producers, with 57 percent coming from Crook County and 27 percent from Bighorn County. Johnson, Weston, Washakie and Natrona counties also produce significant quantities.

Deposits are at the surface or covered by shallow overburden, thus all is surface mined. After trucking to the mill, the bentonite is broken into small chunks, screened. and conveyed through a dryer. The clay is then pulverized.

Iron Ore Mines Closed

Iron ore mining died in Wyoming in a single decade, depression in the steel industry snuffing out century-old mine operations. U.S. Steel Corporation closed its Atlantic City mine in 1983. Colorado Fuel and Iron Corporation closed the Sunrise Mine in 1980, and United States Aggregate shut down its Albany County operation in 1971, the year production peaked at 5.4 million tons.

The state's iron ore industry began in 1870, when hematite was mined north of Rawlins for use as a paint pigment and as a fluxing agent in an early day ore smelter. Commercial mining began in 1901 when a pit was opened near Sunrise in Platte County; the Sunrise Mine changed to an underground operation in the 1930's.

Three types of iron-bearing deposits have been mined in Wyoming. Magnetite (iron oxide) was mined in Albany County for heavy aggregate in ship ballast between 1963 and 1971. Hematite (hydrated iron oxide) was mined at Sunrise, and taconite from Atlantic City was produced by U.S. Steel for use in its Geneva, Utah steel foundry.

Natural Gas Worth $1 Billion

Natural gas, today a prized heating source, once was worth so little it was burned in dramatic flares that night-lit the oil fields. Settlers drilled artesian wells, lit cigarettes, and the water caught fire. It is plentiful, and today is worth one billion dollars. Wyoming ranks sixth in production and seventh in reserves.

Processing plants remove impurities, which themselves are important by-products—ethane, pentane, sulphur, hydrogen, heluim, nitrogen and carbon dioxide. Propane and butane are the fuel gases.

Natural gas occurs both in association with oil and alone. Early production came from Wind River and Big Horn Basins. Today, the Green River Basin leads in natural gas production, followed by Wind River and Powder River Basins.

Gypsum, Jade Also Mined

Gypsum and jade are two other minerals mined commercially in the state, both a result of this state's cataclysmic geologic history. Gypsum is found in Permian, Triassic and Jurassic red beds, jade in Precambrian metamorphic rocks in the southern Wind River Mountains.

Most valued of jades, light apple-green nephrite, has been found only in Wyoming and five other places in the world—China, Turkestan, Siberia, New Zealand and Alaska. Jade occurs as pebbles and boulders, varying in color through dark green and black.

Most gypsum, used in ancient times for carving, today goes into the manufacture of wallboard, cement and plaster. It is precipitated primarily from sea water, but may be deposited in saline lakes or hot springs; it often occurs, too, as a product of volcanic activity. Current mines are in Albany, Big Horn and Park counties.

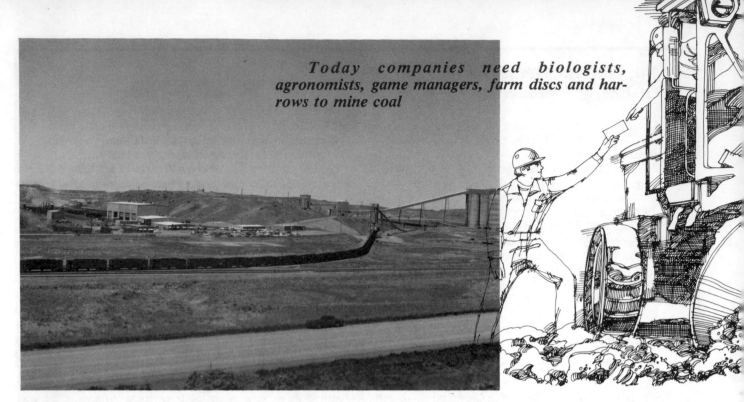

Today companies need biologists, agronomists, game managers, farm discs and harrows to mine coal

Modern Coal Mining Differs Vastly From Early Days

Computers swing today's dragline buckets into the coal seams. Complex engineering is required to design mining plans. A single piece of equipment may cost millions of dollars, each coal mine a billion-dollar enterprise. Thus new technology and new laws have changed vastly the nature of coal mining since the blast-and-load days in Wyoming.

"Wyoming has enough coal to supply the nation for 50,000 years," predicted early geologists. Its coal helped develop the west, in providing ready power for west-moving railroads. However, conversion to diesel locomotives had a devastating effect, and production dropped to two million tons by 1960; 4,000 men were dropped from the payrolls.

Low sulphur emission standards were formulated a few years later, and Wyoming coal's low sulphur content pushed it to the top of the market. Production was predicted to go to 200 million tons by the year 2000. State proceeds were running about $35 million a year. Wyoming reserves are estimated at 900 billion tons, of which 24 billion lies in stripable beds 10 to 200 feet thick without much overburden.

The coal industry today employs thousands of people, pays millions of dollars in taxes, and is meeting social and environmental responsibilities not imposed early in the century. Just in applying for a permit, a company must deal with more than 30 governmental agencies. It takes about ten years to put a new mine into operation, as much as four of those years obtaining permits.

Mines in 1983 operated at only 50 percent capacity, but in 1984 a total of 130 million tons were mined. Wyoming is the third highest coal producing state in the nation, behind Montana and Illinois. The Wyoming Geological Survey estimates that existing mines have reserves of over ten billion tons with a little over four billion contracted for sale. A new city, Wright, grew up on the eastern Wyoming prairie, designed and built by Arco for its Black Thunder mine employees. The flow of cash into existing cities affected by mining had doubled in some cases, by 1985.

Stricter conservation laws caused two new sciences to develop, land reclamation and hydrogeology.

The interaction of soil, moisture and climate with vegetation and wildlife became important to understand. In order to reclaim the land, restoring it to its original condition as the law required, mining companies had to know more about the ecology. They began hiring soil experts, biologists, game managers and agronomists. They conducted their own experiments. Farm drills and harrows were added to the list of equipment needed to mine coal.

Not much was known about the underground water system before 1970—except that coal seams act as water aquifers, or stream channels. In arid eastern Wyoming, lowering the underground water table could be disastrous. The science of hydrogeology refined existing knowledge and sought ways that miners could avoid upsetting underground water flow. Instead of leaving huge dirt piles (the overburden) behind, operators now must reclaim the land; previously this had meant dumping it back in the holes where it came from, thus plugging the hidden stream channels.

All of the nation's largest coal miners have huge western coal reserves, much of it in Wyoming—Peabody, Consolidation, Westmoreland, Island Creek and Amax. Conoco owns Consolidation, Occidental Oil owns Island Creek. Other major oil companies also have leased billions of tons of coal as a cushion against energy competition: Texaco, Gulf, Shell, Atlantic Richfield, Carter-Exxon and others.

'Somehow agriculture will survive these hard times.'

'Digger' Moravek—'Whoa, back up'

5. RANCHERS TAKE STEPS TO PROTECT LIFESTYLE

Grassroots interest in preserving a rural lifestyle in Wyoming rose in the 1970s, and by 1985, a firmly rancher-directed body worked on several public-issue levels as the Powder River Basin Resource Council (PRC). Ten allied local groups and a consumer advocacy organization also emerged to watchdog agricultural concerns.

As conservative as ranchers usually have been, PRC researched issues such as industrial siting, hazardous waste disposal, agricultural economics and new developments in energy production. It took an active role, within a framework of pro-development, to guard the state's natural resources from damage and to promote agriculture. Headquarters are in Sheridan, with temporary offices opened in other locations as issues demand. It is the only non-state-funded organization overseeing mining and water quality laws.

Former chairman Gerald (Digger) Moravek helped set the conservation note to PRC work with a "Whoa, back up" posture toward an attempted raid on Wyoming water for coal slurry pipelines.

He recalled small-scale range water conservation efforts of the past, stock water ponds and range pitting. "Could their concept be expanded to meaningfully increase ground waters?" he asked. "They could reduce both local and mainstream flooding and (prevent) the long-term siltation of 27-plus dams proposed by the Wyoming legislature."

In "pitting," oil conservationists and range management people gouged small depressions in the prairie which caught and held run-off waters, substantially increasing grass production. Many stockmen ran feeder ditches from stock reservoirs to channel run-off water gently so that it soaked into the ground. Both techniques are low-technology and low-cost, Moravek reminded, "neither grandiose nor glamorous."

And this is what the work of PRC has been about—low-key but tough on violators of Wyoming resources. Groundwater being polluted in Cody by the Husky Oil Company refinery, and in Laramie by Union Pacific Railroad's tie plant, was an object of PRC testimony in hearings and in public education events.

In 1984, PRC helped make technical assistance funding a reality for ranchers suffering severe erosion along the North Platte River near Torrington. Two years of higher than normal spring run-off, coupled with faulty dam operation, resulted in some farms losing as much as one foot a day; diversion dams and ditches were destroyed, several bridges damaged.

Said the PRC chairman, Richard Cross of the Boot Ranch, "Wyoming has a strong agricultural base. Somehow it will survive these hard times . ."

PRC helped put a damper on the rush to build power plants, as well as wildcat efforts by several firms to grab federal funds for syn-fuel development. They just weren't needed, it was noted—and the facts bore out this argument.

Allied organizations include the Goshen-Platte Protective Association, Crook County Landowners Association, Converse County Landowners Conservation Association, Pumpkin Buttes Landowners, WYOBRASKA Landowners, Story Oil Impact Committee, Park County Resource Council, and the Western Nebraska Resources Council. PRC also organized a consumer advocacy group in 1983, United Wyoming Residents.

Winter doesn't change but it's easier to cope

"Hard winters? Son, I was on the Chugwater in 1911
. . ."

"Shaw! I recall a cold snap, January 1923, froze the words right out of your mouth . . ."

On many a long winter's night on Wyoming ranches, old timers sit by the fire topping each other's tales of hard winters. It all began with 1880-81, for that was the first hard winter detailed in ranch history. Other giants in winter hardship bluster through the pages of history—1883-84, 1885-86, 1886-87, 1903-04, 1906-07, 1908, 1918, 1920, 1943, 1959, 1964, 1978 . . .

But 1964-65 took some of the sting out of the old-timer's blizzards. Children eating popcorn in the corner now could top their fact and fiction. No longer was any tall winter's tale beyond belief of even the littlest skeptic.

This was the year cows ate boxes, and winter lasted seven long months. Snowy owls flew in; Lapland longspur and snowy bunting flocked down from the alpine tundra. And the antelope began mass migrations.

On November 13, snow began to fall. From that date until the end of March a series of blizzards, snowstorms and cold snaps—each seemingly designed to top all the rest—swept across Wyoming. November's storm to remember came on Thanksgiving Day, the 26th. This was followed by severe blizzards on December 16, 17, January 31, and March 14. Winds blew intermittently between times. Some areas recorded 148 days of constant snow cover. With the broken land leveled by snow, there was no protection for cattle, sheep or wildlife.

One truly horrifying blizzard, unmatched in memories of old timers, brought the equivalent of 83 below zero weather; winds of 53 miles an hour swept snow across eastern Wyoming for three days, with the thermometer at 40 below zero on the leeward side of the barn. Animals suffocated in their own breath, as it crusted an icy mask over their nostrils. They froze piecemeal—a loin here, a backside there, and some lived for the flesh to rot away as they struggled for survival. Some places they stood like statues, frozen dead against the fences.

Cattlemen borrowed on their calf crops to buy feed to finish out the long winter. The snowstorms continued through March, with the temperature down to 24 below zero. Rust-colored calves were dropped in the snow—and froze there. More than one rancher spent calving time with his jacknife, slitting teats that had frozen shut . . . so calves that were still walking wouldn't starve to death.

Sheep shearing crews battled snow drifts, and shorn ewes died of pneumonia or went into lambing in weakened condition. Sheep and cattle grazed behind bulldozers that spewed snow into ten-foot drifts, left and right.

Hard Winter May Not 'Kill'

Heavy losses have been reported somewhere in Wyoming nearly every winter. "1905-06 was our hardest winter, but . . . we lost the most cattle in 1916-17," recalls a former Weston County rancher who wasn't there before 1905 and left in the 1930s. A popular belief once was that the winter of 1886-87 "signaled the end of the cattle industry" in the northern high country. None of the assessments were wholly true—and none wholly false.

70

Jean Harriet brands lamb in high camp

Lamb castrated before summer graze

This is because of the spotty nature of disastrous winter storms. They also point out that a hard winter isn't necessarily a "killing" one.

History has no monopoly on puffed-up loss reports, though loss estimates from 1886-87 ranged from an official $5,000,000 to four times that. One ranch reported a 125 percent loss, and the hard winter was credited with saving many reputations—"It never killed half the cattle that were charged up to it." Range managers, anxious to reflect credit on themselves and lure more capital into their operations sometimes reported no more than 2 percent winter loss—when actual average winter losses in early days were 10 percent.

In modern times, losses may be ballooned for income tax purposes. Of the winter of 1964-65, the U.S. Department of Agriculture statistical reporting service commented: "Losses reported at the peak of the storm were greatly exaggerated." Much of this missing livestock had drifted with the winds and was later found. Some of the exaggeration was deliberate, however. False loss reports, deliberate or not, nevertheless have distorted the record and given Wyoming winters a reputation worse than they perhaps deserve.

No telephones in sheep wagons, but modern vehicles ease weather problems for today's stockmen

Sheep herded from lone wagon

In the course of a Wyoming winter, many kinds of snow will fall . . . glittering, crystaline snow signaling an end of a cold snap . . . fine, hard flakes hovering on the ground as spooky as a bronc, shying at the first wind gust to leap easily into a raging blizzard.

Weather-wise Eye the Sky

The winter-wise Wyomingite keeps an eye on the sky, the thermometer, and the ground. When loose snow begins feathering at your feet on a still day, it is ominous. A "ground blizzard" may stir the surface of the snow until the air below your knees coils and swirls and twists with a dizzing fury. It is at this stage that the loose snow can take to the air in minutes, to wrap one in the invisibility of a full-blown blizzard.

Livestock operations, despite modern technology, still revolve around the weather in Wyoming. Statistics mean little in terms of hardship. An easy winter might bring a mid-season thaw that subsuquently freezes a crust of ice on the land—or on top of the snow, impenetrable to hungry, pawing livestock. It can reduce the use of horses to a minimum—like in 1905-06 when all the swales

were full of ice-encrusted snow; ranchers wrapped their saddle horses' legs in gunny sacks all winter-long.

Then it rained. The thermometer dropped to 30 below the next morning. Ice that had cut like razor blades now literally sawed at legs, and gunny sack wraps were useless. Some riders sliced up old boots, and wrapped their saddle horses' legs in heavy leather. One sheepman skinned dead cows to make leggings from the green hides for the teams feeding sheep.

Parts of Wyoming ranch country are in chinook belts, and sudden rises in temperature blow in on wild, warm winds off the mountains. These mid-winter thaws enable more snow moisture to sink into the ground, instead of piling so deep that it must run off in the spring when the earth becomes saturated.

Modern communications and vehicles have greatly improved the stockman's ability to cope with sudden shifts in Wyoming winter weather. In severe situations, hay and cake feed may be airlifted to cattle and sheep. Despite the use of planes, helicopters, snowmobiles and four-wheel-drives, however, a rancher still must give personal attention to his livestock, afoot or horseback.

LEADING WYOMING AGRICULTURE PRODUCTS

+LIVESTOCK: (January 1985)			++CROPS: (1984 production & national rank)		
All sheep and lambs	120,000	3rd	Sugar Beets	654,000 tons	9th
Stock Sheep	740,000	3rd	Dry Beans	759,000 cwt	7th
Beef Cows	630,000	22nd	Barley	10,400,000 bu	11th
All Cattle & Calves	1,365,000	33rd	Potatoes (fall)	520,000 cwt	18th
Chickens	49,000	—	Alfalfa Hay	2,200,000 tons	21st
Hogs	33,000	—	Winter Wheat	7,290,000 bu	29th
			Oats	3,220,000	25th

+A three-day blizzard in late April 1984 cut sheep inventory up to 23%. The same blizzard also caused heavy cattle losses.
++An early September freeze contributed to halve potato production of the previous year; sugar beets have been on a downward trend. Alfalfa and oats production rose.

Cattle gathered for market, above, and, left, grain is seeded and harvested

Ranch products exported While grocers import food

Three factors coincided in the 1980s to curtail the state's third largest industry: agricultural economics, the energy boom, and the rise of national grocery chains. Fortunes of the Wyoming rancher and farmer plummeted, as did those of producers nationwide. Declining economy, a drop in the cattle market, and rising costs caused serious damage.

The state's booming energy development caused land prices to soar beyond the means of those who wished to obtain land for food production. It also took land out of production, threatened water supplies, and deluged some rural areas with people. On the positive side, many ranchers had enjoyed extra incomes from mineral leases for decades; now, some of these sold out for much more than the land was worth as ranch or farm land. Off-ranch jobs at high wages was an alternative benefit for others and a source of supplemental income.

Agriculture income in 1981 was $616 million, ranking it the third most important industry after minerals and tourism. But it was in a declining cycle. Income in 1979 had been $720 million, and by 1984 it was down to $530 million.

The first farm loan foreclosure by the Wyoming Farm Loan Board occurred in 1983. A year later 7 percent were rated severely delinquent. In Goshen County, the delinquency rate was 8.5 percent. The 1983 legislature called for establishing eligibility criteria in loan policies, to give priority to those demonstrating a need for state loans. This was in response to criticism that young farmers with low equity were discriminated against, and that well-to-do ranchers often siphoned off these state loan funds at low interest rates.

Wyoming produces and markets a surprising diversity of agricultural commodities, ranking second in the na-

tion in stock sheep production and third in wool. Sales of cattle and calves account for 67 percent of Wyoming's agricultural economy. Sugar beet and dry bean production most years rank about ninth and tenth nationally. Also produced are hogs, wheat, potatoes, honey, eggs, poultry, milk and cream, barley, corn, hay and oats.

Because of its historic importance, Wyoming agriculture always has had powerful supporters in state government. One of these was Walter C. Ackerman, for ten years head of the Wyoming Land Quality Division.

Gov. Ed Herschler once said of Ackerman, "On more than one occasion he told the mining industry that the coal was their resource of the future—but that topsoil was the resource of Wyoming's future. Much to industry's dismay, he protected the topsoil as though it were gold."

Long Haul Replaces Drive

Marketing costs have always been high, with a thousand-mile trip to market being standard in the case of cattle. The livestock trucking business developed to replace the long trail drive and shipping by train. This lack of nearby markets and of in-state processors was an obvious loss of potential income as population growth rose 41 percent between 1970 and 1980—but Wyoming agriculture wasn't feeding any of these people.

If they want to market to local groceries, producers and processors are forced to ship their products out of state. The three largest grocery chains operating in Wyoming all have their central warehouses in other states. Slaughter and meat processing businesses are impacted by this trend, because it is difficult for them to gain access to the central purchasing and distribution channels. Seventeen went out of business between 1975 and 1983. Only 15 commercial slaughter houses remain, permitted to sell meat to in-state stores.

Within the past few decades, Wyoming has lost several other processing plants. These include a wool scouring plant in Laramie, sugar refineries in Sheridan and Wheatland, a cheese plant in Powell, flour mills around the state, potato packaging plants in Casper and Pine Bluffs, and several feed processing facilities.

Ranchers and farmers are searching for a strategy to increase consumption of their products in Wyoming. They have called for (1) promotional efforts by the Wyoming Department of Agriculture, (2) preference in sales to state institutions similar to the five percent bid preference given building contractors, and (3) coordinated effort between the tourist industry, state agencies and agricultural commodity groups to increase in-state consumption of Wyoming products.

The agriculture products consumed within the state are those purchased by farmers and ranchers themselves—hay, feed grains and seed wheat. Only one percent of the beef and mutton raised here is eaten here. The beef of some 88,000 cattle actually is imported to supply Wyoming's needs; lamb from 15,000 animals is shipped here from out of state. All wool, wheat for flour, potatoes and sugar produced here in Wyoming is shipped elsewhere, while 19,000 cwt. is imported. Over a million and a half cattle are moved out of state on brand certificates each year, 1,549,740 in 1982.

British cameras film Wyoming ranch life

Nostalgia for the "great American west" brought this camera crew from England to film a cattle roundup on the Big Horn Mountain slopes. British Broadcasting Corporation still airs details of Wyoming ranch life for a viewing public whose interest goes back 100 years to early English investments here.

Since the demise of both the cowboy and the Indian was prematurely lamented throughout the world, it may surprise some Europeans to learn that both are still alive and well.

Despite the untimely epitaphs, it will be a long time before the last cowboy kisses his horse and rides over the sunset horizon. Picturesque corrals like the desert one shown in the photograph above still are necessary tools of ranching.

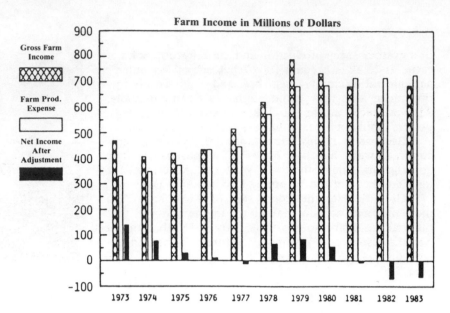

Wide climate variations affect Wyoming's agricultural posture, with moisture ranging from 5 to 16 inches, temperatures from 60 below zero to 115 above, and as few as 30 frost-free days or as many as 130 days

Farm Income in Millions of Dollars

Gross Farm Income

Farm Prod. Expense

Net Income After Adjustment

Hay leads all crops in farming industry

Hay is the leading farm crop in Wyoming, where agriculture is determined by soil ranging from sand to rich alluvial and by wide variations in terrain, climate, moisture in nine major river drainages. Moisture varies from 5 to 16 inches, temperatures from 60 below zero to as high as 115 degrees Fahrenheit. A variable growing season gives some northern and eastern basins 130 frost-free days—but only 30 days in western basins.

For crops other than hay, prime areas are located in the southeastern section of the state, Big Horn and Wind River Basins, where wheat, sugar beets, hay and barley are leading cash crops. Other important crops are dry beans, corn, oats and potatoes. Total value of 1984 crops was $242,377,000, excluding sugar beets; sugar beet value in 1983 was $21 million.

Wheat is the major grain crop, well adapted to the short growing season and usually part of a two-year wheat-fallow rotation. Up to 35 bushels per acre has been produced. Winter wheat production in 1984 was 7,280,000 bushels, spring wheat 792,000 bushels. The 1984 record barley crop of more than 10 million bushels was grown primarily in the Big Horn Basin, contracted to breweries across the country.

The history of sugar beets is checkered by fluctuating prices, war, import quotas, federal support payments, and contract disputes between beet growers and sugar companies. Thus, the smallest acreage since 1955 was harvested in the state in 1983 and 1984, 32,100 acres and 32,700 acres.

Farming Supports Livestock

A goal of early Wyoming farming efforts was to raise feed grain and forage crops to supplement the feeding of cattle, sheep and horses. This is still important as livestock raising comprises 60 percent of agricultural revenue. Oats and corn thus are staples of farming. The 1984 oat crop of 3.22 million bushels was the largest since 1971.

Corn raised for silage has steadily expanded over this century, as irrigated acreage increased. With the decline in the sugar beet industry, much of this acreage was planted to corn. Record crops have been grown in the 1980s, with 6 million bushels produced in 1984 and a total

1980s, with 6 million bushels produced in 1984 and a total acreage of 110,000 acres. This was grown in Big Horn and Park counties and in three counties of the southeast corner of the state—Platte, Goshen and Laramie.

Cyclic Droughts Hurt Crops

Periodic droughts impact crop production heavily in Wyoming. For example, the severe drought of the 1930's caused some crop production to decline by 74 percent. When moisture improved in 1937 for a decade of normal precipitation, increased crop production occurred. Record crops of oats and dry beans were produced in 1947; wheat acreage nearly doubled from 1942 to 1953. Much of this newly plowed ground proved unstable in succeeding prolonged dry periods and was subsequently put back into grass.

Below average precipitation again occurred from 1948 to 1957, with drought conditions extreme in 1954. By 1957, Wyoming agriculture had been subjected to five of the driest years in the state's history, surpassing the drought of the 1930's in length and severity. More productive land was under irrigation, however, and better farming practices conserved what moisture was available, thus effects were not as drastic.

Again in 1977, a lighter than normal mountain snowfall combined with below-average rainfall to hurt dryland crops. Hail storms also damaged crops severely in some areas. Through 1980, drought conditions continued in the northeastern section.

A notable crop year occurred in 1981, with record yields set by alfalfa hay, corn, barley, dry beans and sugar beets. Above normal precipitation in the next two years combined with favorable growing and harvest conditions to set new record yields. The wet spring in 1983, which caused record alfalfa yields, delayed bean planting in many areas and development was later than normal.

Heavy winter kill and disease losses to the 1984 winter wheat crops resulted in some wheat acreage being re-drilled to oats during the spring. Unexpected early fall and late spring frosts also handicap farmers in this high country. Stormy weather, for example, in April and May slowed 1983 planting, and a mid-May blizzard damaged some crops. A winter storm in September then brought a killing frost throughout the state.

Research studies intestinal cattle worms, above, and water use by crops, right

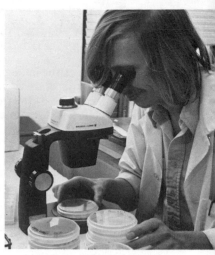

Saving money on fertilizer is object of nitrogen study, above

WATER AND WIND TEAR OUT TOPSOIL BY THE TON

Some Wyoming fields lose over 13 tons of soil per acre in a single irrigation, researchers find. Ways to keep the soil from flowing—or blowing—away are sought in some of hundreds of research projects being conducted in all 23 counties by the University of Wyoming's College of Agriculture.

In the computer printout of such research projects, the profile of the state's third largest industry is traced. Goshen, Park and Washakie counties are sites of weed and disease control research in sugar beets, for example. Experiments with dry beans, potatoes and corn in these and other predominantly farming areas draw the profile with even more precision. Location of disease and nutrition research tells where sheep and cattle production predominate.

Water is of statewide concern, with projects concerning quality, flushing flows, stream loss, water rights and irrigation techniques continuously underway. Rural credit, 4-H leadership, range forage, and mining impacts on the quality of rural life are studied throughout the state.

In a joint project with the Soil Conservation Service, UW researchers examined more than 1,000 furrows in 40 fields to learn how much soil is lost during irrigation; more than five tons per acre per year is unacceptable because the soil is not replaced naturally, yet actual losses range to 13 tons each time it's irrigated. This discovery prompted testing prevention ideas—no-till growing methods, sediment ponds to trap escaping soil, packing the earth, smaller stream flow rates. No-till practices reduced losses by about 85 percent; scientists found it would work with corn, but not sugar beets and other crops.

Biochemists manipulating genetics search ways to save farm dollars now spent on fertilizer. Such plants as alfalfa, sweet clover and legumes long have been known to add nitrogen to the soil. Mountain mahogany and alder do the same in mine and forest reclamation. Increasing the nitrogen fixing properties of crops will reduce both costs and volume of fertilizer required in farming, now as much as 1 percent of all fossil fuels consumed in the U.S. One such project on Goshen County studies the nitrogen content in corn after alfalfa in rotation.

The university's collaboration with agriculture in Wyoming goes beyond research. The state veterinary laboratory was placed under UW's jurisdiction in 1978, and is a diagnostic center for animal disease and parasites. A new microbiology and lab center was completed in 1985. The Agricultural Extension Service network operates from the university.

Weed control and forage nutrition are important research areas which concern both farming and livestock on the range. UW researchers work with both the Wyoming Game and Fish Department and the Bureau of Land Management, as livestock and wild game utilize the same ranges. In some cases, they share similar diseases, parasites and nutritional needs.

Sagebrush which covers so much of Wyoming has been attacked by fire and herbicides in the effort to increase farmland and improve range. This practice, however, might affect soil productivity, climate trends, water and nutrients. Two UW botany researchers study these questions, working with the National Aeronautics and Space Administration (NASA). The sagebrush study has far-ranging implications—related to global effects of carbon dioxide build-up, water capture and utilization.

6. WATER CONTOURS AS IT GIVES LIFE

Water shapes the landscape, and is guarded vigilantly by the Wyoming state agencies. A stream's quality, velocity and contours determine the fish life existing there—as well as, ultimately, the quality of life for an inter-related world.

Wyoming is a unique complex of mountains, plains and badlands sculptured by headwaters of Missouri, Colorado and Columbia River tributaries, as well as that of the Great Basin drainage. And yet water actually is sparse in Wyoming. Thousands of dry creek beds come alive only during local cloudbursts, or in rare years when heavy snow runoff might combine with rainfall.

When man attempts to re-shape waterways, unexpected damage often results. Numerous such examples, plus acceleration of this trend, has caused Game and Fish to take a decisive role in restoring altered channels during the last two decades. At stake is the recreation of 100,000 Wyoming fishermen, and 200,000 from out-of-state. Also at stake is long-term health of the land itself.

Stream channels were straightened by urban developers. "Oxbows" were cut from streams by farmers wanting more hayland. Others tampered with stream flows by trying to reduce stream bank cutting and flooding. Until 1966, however, such activity was relatively minor; then new industrial needs for water started large-scale alterations, and conservationists began demanding legislation to govern re-channeling activities.

'Leave It Alone'

The best way to improve a stream is to leave it alone, decided Murland Morss, foreman of the Fayette ranch south of Pinedale, after that ranch spent nearly $40,000 to un-do a chain of mistakes begun in 1968.

They cut an oxbow out of Pole Creek flowing from the Wind River Mountains, trying to stop gravel filling the bend; this had been caused by Highland Ditch Company's failure to shut down water flow from Fremont Lake during haying months. Morss describes the disaster: "We cut a new channel through the oxbow. That started a chain reaction, dropping the bottom above and cutting the stream bottom below . . . so we made another mistake—we channeled to make a chute in the second oxbow." This increased the water velocity and washed out three other oxbows, a grove of cottonwood trees, and covered a 56-acre hay meadow with gravel.

Fred M. Eiserman

In another example, a landowner decided to enlarge his bottomland pasture and add land for recreational housing. In one afternoon, he destroyed a fine trout stream and a hydrologic process that had taken uncounted years to establish. He lost a well-grassed willow bottom and increased the water speed so that flooding damaged downstream areas.

Inventory Used to Restore

Fred Eiserman, Wyoming fisheries resource manager, has inventoried similar damage throughout the state—the Salt River in western Wyoming, the Wind River near Dubois, the Snake River near Wilson, six streams on the Big Horn River drainage, five alterations in Blacks Fork River, seven in Smiths Fork River, and so on.

Coal mining activities caused channel alterations in Tongue and Powder River areas of northcentral Wyoming. On Tongue River, a total of 4,789 feet was altered, as well as 1,320 feet on its Little Goose Creek tributary. In the Powder River drainage, 1,000 feet of Clear Creek was channelized.

An articulate and practical man, Eiserman has written many tracts on beneficial use of Wyoming water.

"Restraint should be practiced whenever a bulldozer or dragline is used to manipulate a waterway," he writes. "Ideally, no channels should be modified except under the direction of a person familiar with stream hydrology, working with a qualified aquatic biologist."

Boulders and logs have been put back into streams such as Rock Creek in southern Wyoming, to restore lost fish habitat. Game and Fish has many such projects underway, in order to insure continued trout fishing.

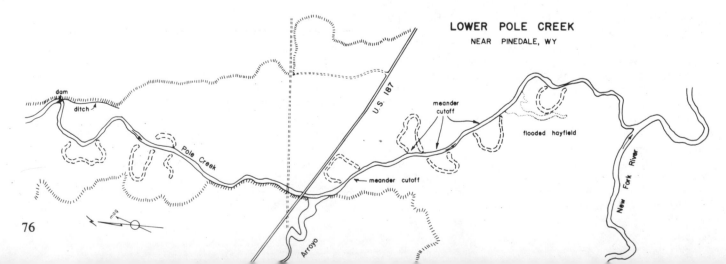

LOWER POLE CREEK
NEAR PINEDALE, WY

dam
ditch
Pole Creek
U.S. 187
meander cutoff
meander cutoff
flooded hayfield
New Fork River
Arroyo

Quality of fishing is directly affected by straightening natural channels

'Take our coal— but not our water'

An issue which shook the state to its grassroots, water for coal slurry pipelines, went down to defeat in 1984 after a decade of political maneuvering. It illustrates how precious water is regarded in Wyoming.

All three major industries—minerals, tourism, agriculture—have water requirements which sometimes are compatible, and at other times conflict. Energy development, based on the nation's need for power, requires water to cool its huge coal-fired plants; it also has other water needs. Without sparkling streams and fishing waters, tourism could not exist. And neither livestock nor crops can be produced without ample water supplies.

So vital is water, Gov. Ed Herschler presented a $600 million program to the Wyoming Legislature in 1982, a program which divided 29 water projects into four planning categories. Several state agencies are involved: Wyoming Water Development Commission, Economic Planning and Development, the State Engineer's office, Game and Fish. Several federal agencies also participate.

The Water Development Commission conducted an inventory in 1984 in Campbell, Crook, Weston, Niobrara and Converse counties—searching for ways to increase surface storage and develop new aquifers. These have been areas of severe water shortages.

The slurry pipelines would have siphoned water from the Madison Formation, Wyoming's major underground water system. It then would have mixed it with coal and sent it on a one-way trip out of the state.

The first proposal came from Energy Transportation Systems, Inc. (ETSI). Several others followed in quick succession, among them Northwest Pipeline Company, Wyoming Water Reclamation Association, and the Little Horn Water Group. Response was immediate and sustained in opposition to taking the water.

A Casper opponent, John S. Moore, pointed out that hundreds of low-yield wells and springs in 80 percent of Crook County, 25 percent of Weston County, and a small portion of Niobrara County get water from the Madison aquifer system—"this area is chronically and

---

HARMONY NEEDED

People who have worked all their lives to conserve nature's bounty are confused by the surge of popular interest. On one hand, they are glad—on the other, they suspect a credibility gap in a movement long overdue but often lacking in understanding. They are wary of its penchant for showmanship and for siphoning of funds.

"Where is the joy that we 'established' conservationists should feel at this hour of awakening?" asks Fred M. Eiserman, Wyoming fisheries resource manager.

Wyoming history is replete with authentic conservationists. The current fad of pasting on politically-tainted labels, then obscuring the meaning—or even reversing it—baffles those who just want to preserve game habitat and a balance of nature.

Eiserman cautions that sensationalism and sentiment are poor guides to the ethics of environmentalism and conservation, which exist on both spiritual and intellectual levels. Citizen and legislative programs are essential, but he doesn't like to see them clouded by over-simplification.

"Environmentalists sing loud, but sometimes they ignore harmony and reach a squeaky, high soprano when they try to upstage the old chorus of conservation tenors."

---

often critically short of water and these low-yield wells are essential to the livelihood of these people."

Gov. Herschler proposed that the water be imported from Oahe Reservoir in South Dakota, mixed with Wyoming coal, and then shipped back out. The governor of South Dakota, William Janklow, testified before the Wyoming Legislature against groundwater withdrawals for slurry lines: "When experts are divided, it is mankind who suffers."

Ultimately the slurry proposals were defeated, Wyoming's latest water crisis averted.

In every era of Wyoming history, tourists have come back to stay . . . and become good neighbors.

World's largest rodeo, Cheyenne

Desert space charms without pollution

The stark beauty of Wyoming deserts contrasts abruptly with forested mountains. Less than seven inches rainfall supports sparse vegetation—or maybe none at all on alkali-crusted slopes and wrinkled gumbo.

Main desert areas are located in the eastern Big Horn Basin and southwest of Rawlins, the Red Desert. These are the most northern of the continent's desert areas. (Many arid plains, it should be noted, are not desert—but rangelands with cured grass rich in protein.) Today some of these desolate deserts teem with mineral activity, particularly uranium.

Temperature extremes and drought led to the evolution of some of the most highly adapted plants in the world—cactus, greasewood, sagebrush. In wash channels, plants may be spaced as though planted, each within its own perimeter of moisture and soil nourishment. Plants also tend to be small and some have roots eight feet long.

The kangaroo rat, long-tailed and nocturnal, burrows in the ground where temperatures are neither as hot nor as cold as on the desert floor. Prairie dogs, lizards, snakes and tortises do the same. Insects are "waterproofed" to avoid moisture loss.

Some so-called desert is actually marginal and contains grass enough among the sagebrush to support elk herds. Range for the desert elk is bound by the Red Desert-Great Divide Basin on the east, Green River on the west, the Jack Morrow Hills on the north, White Mountain and Zirkel Mesa on the south. Desert elk number 400 to 600. During the winter, about 500 mountain elk move onto the western edge of the Great Divide Basin.

The desert has a magic to it. Solitary eagles ride the updrafts. The land has a naked appearance, millions of years of history laid bare. Mute testimony to the desert's long and varied history is seen in petrified wood from primeval forests, agate chippings by ancient inhabitants, a crumbling stage station on the Overland Trail, and the horse traps of yesterday's wranglers.

The desert's greatest asset may be space, vast reaches of fragile space unpolluted by civilization.

7. TOURISM RANKS AS SECOND INDUSTRY

In Wyoming tourists are regarded as friends—not as intruders. This is because many of the people who built Wyoming once were tourists in this cherished land. They invested money, energy and thought to develop this unique state; they were elected to positions of public trust. In every era of Wyoming history, tourists have become good neighbors.

Tourists today bring more than $735 million into the state economy each year, hundreds of thousands enjoying hunting and fishing, three million a year gazing in awe at the Teton Mountain range. Hunters from out of state created the guide business, taxidermies and custom slaughter houses.

Wonders such as Yellowstone Park's 10,000 thermal features, the grooved lava spire of Devil's Tower, and ancient archeological treasures are to be found nowhere else in the world. Bighorn sheep, bear, elk, moose and the continent's largest antelope herds exist here side by side with huge energy complexes. Ranch life is still typically livestock centered, and its action plays publicly in dozens of rodeos around the state.

Unique geological formations abound in widely varied terrain—from spectacular canyons like the Wind River, the Big Horn or the Tongue to sand dunes and barren desert craigs. There are fossil areas and relics of people of another time in the Medicine Wheel, petroglyphs, and teepee rings by the thousands.

An Indian pit house used 5,100 years ago is one of the discoveries of the past decade, when a new law required archeological inventories on land to be mined.

Angler finds peace in Wyoming, while girls find horseback action

Located in the Hanna Basin, it is significant because the oldest previous pit houses in the southwestern U.S. date only to 2,000 years ago. Fire hearths, storage basins, impressions believed to be roof pole holes, and numerous artifacts were found in 1983.

Records of by-gone people who once lived in Wyoming are found in many areas, petroglyphs varying widely in style. Animals, directional signs, and religious symbols are deeply carved. Others are pecked, such as at Torrey Creek and Dinwoody Lakes. At Castle Gardens, a rugged sandstone formation east of Riverton, the designs are carved rather than pecked; this hidden valley of sandstone towers and fantasy shapes contains many petroglyphs, both grouped and singles. Castle Gardens with a picnic lunch offers a day of discovery . . . of ancient hunters and warriors, their shields and symbolic remains.

John Underwood, a rancher on Torrey Creek, wrote his anthropology thesis in 1938 on the petroglyphs pecked on huge boulders on his ranch. A Shoshone legend credits the spirits of long ago with these complex figures. Eyes, hands and feet on ornately dressed creatures are all pecked in detail; most appear to be masked. The solitary grandeur of this accessible area caused Underwood to speculate on Indian legends of the "little people," the "water babies," and the shaministic powers of a place which may have been sacred.

A cave in the Big Horn Mountains trapped long-legged lions weighing 650 pounds, elephants and camels—20,000 years ago, by radiocarbon dating. This sinkhole near Lovell, called Natural Trap Cave, drops 80 feet to a base of mineralized bones of animals that fell in during the Ice Age. The Bureau of Land Management grated it in 1973, after a car full of cavers very nearly became part of the deposits.

Caving is one of the prime recreational activities in this area of Madison limestone formations, and the National Speleological Society has held its annual convention there. Big Horn and Horsethief Caves near Natural Trap have a combined length of 17 miles of mapped passages.

The steep granite outcrops of Wyoming's Scab Creek wilderness were recommended in 1948 to be set aside for enjoyment without intrusion of industry. Located 20 miles southeast of Pinedale on the west foothills of the Wind River Mountain this wilderness was cut by glaciers and streams. As one fishes for cutthroat, rainbow, brook and brown trout, wildlife may stroll by—elk, mule deer, moose, black bear or coyote. A mountain lion or bobcat may watch from hidden cover.

Nearly all federal lands are open to recreational use—and this is half the state of Wyoming. In addition, state public lands include parks and fisheries. The Bureau of Land Management maintains campgrounds, picnic areas and historical interpretive sites. The U.S. Forest Service invites use of others.

'Summit of world,' Grand Teton Park

Canyons of the Tetons echo with Indian legend in this "place where the Maker's work is not yet finished," an Arapaho description. The Shoshone called the snowy peaks the "hoary-headed fathers" and "Teewinot, land of many peaks."

Also known to Indians as "the summit of the world," the Teton range is one of few visible in its entirety, rising abruptly in rocky craigs from the valley floor. They are "new" mountains, their sharp edges not yet worn down. Even today this is an area of earth tremors, of sulphurous steam, of the "roaring mountain," adjacent to Yellowstone National Park.

Says Arapaho historian, Pius Moss, "I have heard the same words . . . 'majesty, splendor, greatness' . . . repeated and repeated. But all the people have used them with a kind of special reverence. And for awhile they have all talked like Indians—quietly."

Grand Teton National Park, created in 1929, includes an area of about 500 square miles surrounded by national forests, the Teton and the Targhee. Over 200 miles of foot trails fan out through the canyons. The park's 160 miles of paved roads is laid out for continuous viewing of the range. Three million visitors a year come here, from Yellowstone to the north, Togwotee Pass to the south, or from Idaho to the west.

Cascade Canyon is a popular hiking terrain, about 30,000 hiking up from Jenny Lake each summer. Waters of the mountains gush over Hidden Falls to the lake nestled at the base of the canyon. Inspiration Point provides a broad view from this elevation. A series of towering scenic spots are visible—The Jaw, Rock of Ages, and Symmetry Spire high over Storm Point.

Curious Bear

Bears Not to Be Fed

This is avalanche and glacier land, too, and Schoolroom Glacier lays off the northeastern edge of The Wall, an abrupt limestone formation stretching southward for miles. This marks the western boundary of Grand Teton Park. Switchbacks in the trail allow repeated views of the glacier.

Vast meadows of wild flowers and wildlife existing in its natural state delight visitors. The alpenglow paints the heart of the Tetons in fantastic sunsets over Elder Brother, the Shoshone's ancient name for the Grand Teton Mountain. The number of hikers to Lake Solitude has become so great that a new name of "Lake Multitude" has been suggested.

The secret wellsprings of great rivers are here in the Tetons—the Green, the Snake and the Yellowstone, main tributaries of the Colorado, the Columbia and the Missouri Rivers.

NETWORK OF STATE HIGHWAYS

Ribbons of asphalt today make the state in all its dimensions accessible safely to the traveler, with 47 rest areas for breaks from driving. Information Centers are located in Cheyenne, Sheridan, Jackson, Laramie and Casper in elaborate rest areas.

Wyoming Highway Patrol now has 130 officers on the highways, linked by a modern communications network. Aerial patrols assist ground vigilance. A biennial budget of $4.25 million maintains this system, in which uniforms and vehicles closely resemble those of the California Highway Patrol; first training in 1933 of the then "special agents" was done by a California officer.

Unlike earlier days, there are no toll roads in Wyoming. Once, however, a toll road led from Soldier Creek Canyon near Sheridan up the Big Horn Mountains; this was used until about 1910.

Wyoming promoters bought a four-horse stagecoach in 1921 and drove it to Omaha behind a four-horse team to promote the first road to Yellowstone Park, the Big Horn Mountains and Custer Battlefield. The stagecoach was loaded with "things to sell for money" to build the road. In Omaha, they were "shot up" by horsemen from the stockyards, feted by the mayor—and shipped their stagecoach back home by rail.

But today the foothills, the mountains, deserts and prairie all readily are reached by motorists in every season of the year.

Part III

History of Wyoming

Quaking Aspen poles of this Indian lodge in Ten Sleep Canyon were erected about 1840

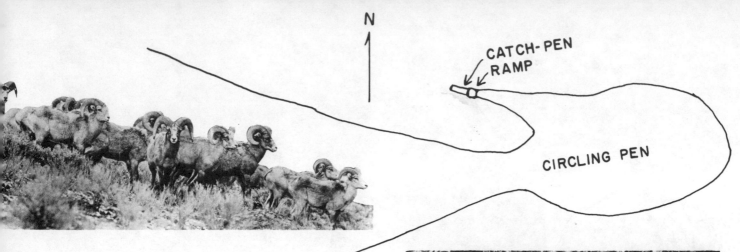

Mountain sheep trap in Big Horns led off circle corral. Drive strategy, as shown in schematic drawing, utilized wings and pocket trap.

1. HUMAN ROOTS DEEP IN WYOMING SOIL

The land that came to be known as Wyoming has nurtured the human race for 11,000 years. On windswept high places, in dry caves, and beneath the sheltering pines evidence remains of ancient drama, of people long since gone.

Stone fragments tell of daily prehistoric routines—if these ciphers could be decoded. Many legends are told of rock circlets, miles-long lines of piled rock, and stone walks from the past. Archeologists have various theories, as do Indians. In fact, however, nobody knows what most of them represent or their purpose.

Anthropologists like George C. Frison, however, have dug into bison kill sites and ancient mammoth meat processing plants to find keys that unlock some of these mysteries. A professor at the University of Wyoming, Dr. Frison is the author of several books and is the foremost authority on life in early Wyoming.

Frison's curiosity was whetted on fossils while growing up on a ranch near Sundance, and he has been applying practical ranching logic to the field of anthropology ever since. He once butchered a buffalo with crude stone tools, to see if prehistoric man really could have done it. And out in the field he often reasons thusly: "Suppose a man and his family camped for a single night . . . very likely a pit would have been dug, a fire built . . ."

Complicating the search into the past is the fact that weather made violent intrusions, rivers changed courses, wind and water picked up the earth and dumped it elsewhere. A single spring flood, for example, has been known to leave Powder River silt eight feet thick. Steep banks where one might trap bison today may have been shallow and meandering in the Late Archaic period. Mammoths were killed in the Big Horn Basin in a steep trap that was then at least 30 feet wide with banks more than 30 feet high; today the same site is drained by a

shallow stream with gently sloping, sodded banks—no place to trap a mammoth. Throughout the ages, constantly changing land forms, climate and vegetation determined human and animal activities.

Big game animals like the moose, mountain sheep and the elk have been here for 20,000 years. Others became extinct: the wooly mammoth, a giant buffalo, the camel and the first horse—embarrassingly tiny and hardly the noble equine bucking across today's license plates.

At one time, heavy and widespread rains known as the "Great Pluvial" created many vast lakes throughout the northwest. Forests and immense grasslands produced conditions for big game similar to those still found in central Africa. Then the climate became drier, the long Altithermal drought which may have created Wyoming's dune country. The native horse and camel died out sometime between 10,000 and 8,000 years ago. In another 2,000 years, the mammoth was gone.

About 15,000 years ago, the last ice sheet melted enough to open a route through Alaska from the broad land bridge between the hemispheres. Great masses of water withdrawn from the oceans to build the Ice Age (Pleistocene) glaciers had lowered the sea level several hundred feet; when the glaciers melted, the oceans again would rise and cover the land bridge. Across this bridge, sometime within the next thousand years or so, came hunters from Siberia—the first of many emigrants.

They Came in Five Waves

In all, five human migrations made their way across the land bridge and later by water when the ocean closed up: Australoid, Negroid, Algonquian, Eskimo, and finally Mongoloid peoples. They were tall and short, very dark skinned and fair, squat and slim; out of this early human melting pot, only one trait became common to North Americans—straight, black hair.

It was about 4000 years ago that the Algonquian Indians came, bow hunters who created a woodland culture in Canada and the northern U.S. Among these were the Arapahoes and Cheyenne, who were later to make their mark on Wyoming. Then came the Shoshones, Uto-Aztecan-speaking nomads, who would work their harsh northland and survive to become Wyoming's first native people.

Thus a complex and varied peoples hunted Wyoming's plains and mountains. Large game populations shifted, but always there have been the mule deer, the antelope, elk—and mountain sheep. Early people were skillful hunters; they processed game and plant food in the mountains and in the deserts. When the wooly mammoth vanished, the bison was their large game. Through the ages, the buffalo became smaller but no less numerous.

Only when the Europeans worked their way west in the 19th century A.D. was there sudden major displacement. They killed all the buffalo, tried to wipe out all people, and seriously ruptured a balance of nature that was thousands of years old. These emigrants saw this as a new land, and wanted to begin with everything fresh and new.

In digging into the human past, anthropologists base time divisions on weapons and tools which can be dated. Thus earliest culture is known as Clovis, then Folsom, Paleo-Indian, Plains Archaic, and Prehistoric, the most recent.

Mystery of Medicine Wheel

The origin of the Medicine Wheel in the Big Horn Mountains is thought to be Indian, even though people may have tampered with it. Two other such wheels in the Big Horns are "very definitely not authentic"—studies show they were built in the mid-1930s by sheepherders.

This is the opinion of a scientist from the University of Wyoming, Dr. George C. Frison, who points out, "The Medicine Wheel might be the stone representation of the turtle. In age, the structure does not seem to be as old as certain romantics would like to believe."

The great stone arrow northwest of Meeteetse, shown in above photo, is considered authentic. The 65-foot-long arrow points directly to the Medicine Wheel, below, some 75 miles distant.

Pteranodon

Tyrannosaurus

CLOVIS: 11,200 B.C. to 8588 B.C.

Hunters of Clovis times were Wyoming's first big game hunters, successfully killing both the now-extinct giant bison and the wooly mammoth, which grew fourteen feet tall. They hunted in groups.

The best evidence for a systematic bison kill during the Clovis period comes from the Murray Springs site. At the Agate Basin site in eastern Wyoming near the Black Hills, bison were driven into a trap in a coulee in February or late March.

The first documented mammoth kill is at the Colby site in the Bighorn Basin (see story page 85).

FOLSOM: 8900 B.C. to 8425 B.C.

Folsom points were often made of opaque red chert that occurs in the Phosphoria Formation. Finds of the typical channeled points have been found many places in Wyoming, including the Green River Basin, the Mud Springs site about 30 miles south of Rock Springs, a campsite ten miles north of Rawlings, the Hell Gap site in southeastern Wyoming, Davis Draw in the northern Bighorn Basin, and in one level at Carter-Kerr McGee site near Gillette.

Buffalo (bison) were driven off steep jumps throughout the Folsom period, such as atop the Big Horn Mountains, in the Red Desert, and at Bonfire Shelter.

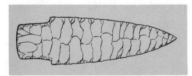

PALEO-INDIAN: 8480 B.C. to 5850 B.C.

Hell Gap bison procurement of the Paleo-Indian period is best documented in the Casper site. Frison excavated this parabolic sand dune and found bones of at least 100 animals. Bison were driven into the horseshoe-shaped dune and trapped there, unable to scale the loose sand with their cloven hooves.

The climax of late Paleo-Indian hunting is represented in the Horner site in northern Bighorn Basin and in the Finley site in the Green River Basin, both scenes of large-scale bison procurement operations and mid-winter kills. A classic arroyo trap illustrates a kill in different terrain south of Sundance on the Hawken ranch.

The camel and horse died out during this period.

PLAINS ARCHAIC: 2470 B.C. to 640 A.D.

A vast drought lasting a thousand years scorched the area during the Alti-thermal period (also Middle Plains Archaic). The radical climate change occurred about

Dr. Frison Shows 10,000-Year-Old Skull

2500 B.C., and curtailed both human and animal populations. Bison continued to flourish only in oasis areas which may have existed near the Black Hills and certain other mountain drainages.

During the Late Plains Archaic period, hunters began to build sophisticated corrals, and to reflect a high stage of understanding of buffalo behavior. Remains of some of these corrals are found in Shirley Basin, in the southeastern Powder River Basin, on a tributary of the North Platte, and at the Ruby site a few miles west of Pumpkin Buttes.

Post holes used for Ruby corrals 1800 years ago are still visible, prototype of the modern cattle corral. Evidence of the first religious ceremony relating to the hunt is found here.

Earliest indication of bow and arrow use on the northwestern plains is at the Wardell site, a bison kill near Big Piney in the Green River Basin. Hunters constructed a corral of juniper and cottonwood which was used for 500 years.

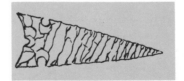

LATE PREHISTORIC: 720 A.D. to 1580 A.D.

Crow Indians are identified as the hunters in buffalo jump kills centered in northern Wyoming during this period. Drive lines up to two miles long lead to jumps on drainages of the Little Bighorn, Rosebud Creek, Tongue River, Big Goose and Piney Creeks. At the Big Goose site, buffalo were jumped off a 50-foot bank in early fall.

A different technique was used at the Vore site near Sundance about 1500 A.D. Frison likens this sinkhole to a rain gauge, and estimates up to 20,000 animals died

Colby Site Gives Up Its Secrets

Wooly Mammoth bones prove man hunted here 11,000 years ago

Among the mammoth bones on Slick Creek at last was found proof that prehistoric people hunted here 11,200 years ago. The long-awaited verification of human and mammoth relationship was established in Wyoming at the Colby site.

Prehistoric animal bones have eroded from western hills for eons. Indian legends tell of Thunder Beasts, Titanothere, raging through stormy skies and plunging to earth, drumming their hooves along the ground. Fossils of sea creatures date back to 200 million years, and mammals to 65 million years.

But perhaps because Europeans persisted in calling this the "New World"—and there was so much of it to explore—it was believed until recently that human occupation in the western hemisphere was not much over 1,000 years old. Some scientists thought otherwise, but they couldn't prove it.

Mammoth remains and Clovis hunting points which would have dated about 11,000 years ago had been reported in Platte County; a dissected mammoth skeleton with charred vertebrae was reported in the Rawhide Buttes area of Niobrara County. Fifteen other mammoth finds were located. However, none—until Colby—could be related irrefutably to Clovis man.

The summer of 1973, Dr. George C. Frison and a team from the University of Wyoming dug carefully into cement-hard gumbo for which Slick Creek is named, five miles east of the Bighorn River. At least 300 feet of an old arroyo contained mammoth bones.

They found two piles of mammoth bones stacked by human hands. Meat had been cut from bones in one pile; the other pile, from which the meat had not been removed, may have been a food cache to which the hunters had never returned. Projectile points of the Clovis era, bone and stone butchering tools were found. Spear points were made of chert from the higher mountains, one found directly beneath stacked bones.

The Colby site had given up its secret, and in such a way that results were scientifically valid.

This site is named for Donald Colby of Worland, who found tooth fragments and a fluted point in the 1960s while operating reservoir building equipment. Several years later, when a mammoth tooth came to the surface, Frison decided to excavate.

Once it could be proven that humans had butchered mammoths there, Frison began to speculate how it had been done. The wooly mammoth could grow 14 feet tall, with sweeping tusks to ten feet in length. The intermontane basin was probably a grassland dominated by taller panicoid grasses when the giant beasts lived there.

"Obviously the chance of observing an elephant in Bighorn Basin gumbo is remote," Frison said ruefully. But he learned what he could of African elephants, nearest living mammoth relatives.

Mammoths, as do elephants, probably moved about in small family units, female-dominated and fiercely vindictive if one is killed. Probably hunters learn to pick off quietly an ocasional animal, spearing one between the ribs before either the speared animal or group knew it was done. The mammoth then could go off and die.

---

there over a 141-year period. He found five levels, four kills in the fall and one in late spring, each time after heavy rains resulted in good calf crops.

Early People Left Clues

Wyoming country must have been full of people and animals thousands of years ago. Early people left so many artifacts behind—and research funds are so scarce—that much of their debris has not been studied. Another handicap is that modern boundaries are arbitrary and do not relate realistically to study of anthropology. Early humans operated by food cycles and climate, as did the animals they hunted . . . along watersheds, up canyons, in the mountain clearings and out on the prairies. Hunters following the bison, or mammoth, or other game, did not stop at the Wyoming state line;

but too often the scholar's funds do.

The Wyoming Archaeology Society has been an instrument for promoting research into the past. Its chapters are Sweetwater, Sheridan, Casper, Cherokee Trail in Saratoga, Cheyenne, and Fremont County. Members work on several levels, from preliminary site surveys to legislative pressure in order to locate, preserve and evaluate sites of early human activity. New laws requiring archaeological surveys of areas to be mined have resulted in identification of many sites and the scientific excavation of others.

Pot hunters, the curious, and even the well-meaning have removed and distorted valuable clues to the world of the past. The medicine wheel in the Big Horn Mountains, for example, may have been altered in many ways by 20th century amateurs trying to reconstruct it into what they thought it should be. It continues to be a source of richly imaginative speculation—one such theory is that it was a primitive observatory, since two cairns line up with the rising sun of the summer solstice, other cairns pointing to sunset and the rising points of three bright stars. Other scholars, however, feel the continual tampering has removed any scientific value it once had.

Bison drivelines are found throughout Wyoming, small piles of stones arranged in lines to help drive a herd to the kill site. Frison suggests some of these were located to provide information on herd control during the drive. Such drivelines also lead into prehistoric mountain sheep traps.

Someone Built the Circles

On a high knoll on the rim of Big Horn Canyon, near Grapevine Creek, a set of rock formations could have been foundations of a long ago community. They are circlets, ovals and semi-circles commanding a view of many miles in all directions; behind to the south is a sheer rock wall which drops 1500 to 2000 feet into the canyon. Lichen-spotted pink sandstone indigenous to the area was used to form the circles, ovals and crescents in fortification-type arrangements. Tiny circlets, no more than 15 inches in diameter stand in the center of the formation. These are about a foot in height. A few flint chips not native to the area were found. Nearest water—today—is a spring miles away on Grapevine Creek. A mile east on a flat above the creek is a concentration of tepee rings.

On Powder River where it crosses the Montana line is another strange, man-made arrangement of rocks near the old Cheyenne-Sioux trail to South Dakota. The main structure is 15 feet by 6 feet, inside diameter, with about a carload of sandstone rubble heaped in a big oval; height is now 18 inches inside and built up to 2 or 3 feet on the lower slope. A backdrop of gumbo and sandstone cliffs too steep for a horse to climb protects the rear.

This is on one of the main east-west Indian trails still used into the 20th century by Sioux and Cheyenne moving from one reservation to another. Many sweat lodges used to stand along Clear Creek and a tepee ring concentration is found along the north side of Powder River. What local ranchers call an Indian water sign, a rock build-up 3 feet high with one arm pointing one mile to water, stands just south of the Big Remington Creek junction. A single log-buttressed unit, which could have been a fortification, sits atop a butte across the river.

Stones Piled for Miles

Bill Jones in cairn

Another mysterious stone feature is the linear arrangement of stone piles and cairns, sometimes miles in length. Neither their age nor purpose is known—or who built them. Frison suspects them to be Prehistoric and Late Archaic in dating.

Of six such lines in the southern Big Horns, four generally run east-west, while two run north-south. One is in a mountain pass, but only extends partially across the

Ancient circles near Big Horn Canyon

pass. Two are located on ridges that slope upward on the mountains. The other three run parallel to the base of slopes, following natural trails. These six lines investigated by Frison each contain from 48 to 136 cairns and/or piles of stone. Other such lines are found in the Upper Owl Creek area in the Bighorn Basin, on the eastern slope of the Laramie Range, as well as in south-central Wyoming.

Six variations of artificial rock placements thus are found:
- Drivelines for herding animals into traps or over precipices.
- Piles of rock in lines too long and in unlikely locations to be drivelines, often associated with cairns;
- Sites at which a single large area is fortified by stacking stones in walls or in the crevices between natural boulders;
- Caves which have stone breastworks across their entrances with additional walls constructed in the cave;
- Tepee ring sites on small buttes and grassy slopes.

Some scholars believe there is an association between fortification sites and areas where buffalo would have been plentiful, possibly built by intrusive peoples who were hunting in other people's territory. The intruders may have built the fortified areas to retreat to if they were caught trespassing; those in the Grapevine Creek area—where the Crows once caught the Piegans trespassing—could support such a theory. Others may be fasting beds, or eagle catching pits.

Evidence of winter camps in Sunlight Basin is found at the Dead Indian Creek site, despite the fact that snowfall is heavier here than in the nearby lower Bighorn Basin. The camp was located so that it could control travel into the Sunlight Basin. Deer and mountain sheep were plentiful.

A 1,200-year-old mummy was found curled in fetal

Sheep corral poles angled inward

position in a mountain cave on the west side of the Bighorn Basin. He still wore the hide garment in which he was prepared for burial. It is speculated that he was a Shoshone. In 38 cultural levels was found evidence that humans had occupied the cave for 9,000 years.

Stories Told in Stone

In the rock art found on canyon walls, in caves and sandstone bluffs, origins of early Wyoming cultures can be traced. Similarities which show up in such widely scattered places as West Virginia and Wyoming, New Mexico and Minnesota, tell of common origins and wide dispersement of similar cultures. The big game animals drawn with "heart-line" from mouth to vital organs is one such example. The "weeping eye"—vertical lines from outer edges of eye—occurs in the southeast U.S., in Wyoming, Utah and on the Columbia River.

Rock drawings in an area centering on Riverton are totally unlike other realistic incised drawings of the northern plains; these designs are pecked in a highly stylized anthropomorph with fantastic headdress and appendages, outlined bodies filled with abstract designs reminiscent of those found in southern California. These are sometimes credited to the Wind River Shoshones who traveled here from southern Nevada; abstract carvings and the mountain sheep motif occur along the Shoshones' migration route into Wind River country.

Designs more typical of plains Indian culture are common east of the Big Horn River: the V-necked man, the lizard, a bisected circle sometimes with a hole in the center and a directional arm, deer and bear, and the turtle symbol brought by the Algonquians. The turtle is credited with creating the earth by raising it from beneath the waters; earthquakes occur when the turtle shifts position. Cheyennes regard the lizard as most sacred of the sundance symbols, which include the V-necked figure.

They Lived Off the Land

Early people in Wyoming could, and did, live off this northern land, with thousands of plants and animals in their pantry. Food, medicine, shelter, clothing, ceremonial objects and utensils were all here for the plucking.

For eons, in the rain shadows of the mountains, people have sat down to gourmet tables, enjoyed perfume, smoking and herbal teas, decorated their persons and homes, medicated themselves. Gum, sugar, tea, flour, fruit, and nutritious tubers grew from the earth. Some plants supplied herbal seasoning for their meat. Others medicated and sedated them.

Sap of the boxelder tree (Acer negundo) was tapped and boiled for sugar. The inner bark of the narrow leaf cottonwood (Populus angustifolia) was another sugar source; so was mountain maple.

They procured gum from sap of the showy milkweed (Asclepias speciosa). Douglas rabbitbrush (Chrysothamnus viscidiflorus) also yielded chewing gum, as did the roots of blue lettuce (Lactuca tatarica). Another source of gum was ponderosa pine, the mucilagimous inner layer of bark.

Dyes for decorating clothing, baskets and home were obtained from several sources. If the bark of red willow was scorched, it could be added to dock dye to produce black. Dock (Rumex spp.) made both yellow and red dye; yellow if boiled alone, red if ash was added and the solution reboiled. Earth dyes were also dug from certain clays or made by crushing rock.

Bags and clothing were fashioned of the bark of big sagebrush (Artemesia tridentata). Baskets were made from slender spikerush (Elocharis acicularis) and longstem spikerush (Elocharis macrostachya); the latter was especially useful in making dish-sized baskets and child's playthings, as well as for larger baskets to carry loads on the back and to hold utensils. Stems of rush (Juncus balticus) also made baskets, the roots used for ornamenting robes. Bull rushes, both roundstem and nevada (Scirpus actus and S. nevadensis) were woven as mats for sleeping, and for blankets. Baskets were woven of split strands of yucca (Yucca glauca).

From sedge tissue (Carex spp.) early humans produced a suggary juice. Wild licorice (Glycyrrhiza lepidota) satisfied cravings for sweets and flavor variety, the rootstocks eaten raw or cooked, or added as flavor to other food. Tender shoots of wild licorice in the spring were cut off close to the ground and eaten raw. Pink jelly was made by boiling bitterroot roots (Lewisia rediviva).

Perfume was made from pineapple weed (Matricaria matricaroides). Its flowers and leaves were mixed with other plants to make a fragrant perfume.

Mint relish came from leaves of the field mint (Mentha arvensis). Plantain (Plantago spp.) young leaves were used as pot-herbs. Milkweed leaves and young shoots were boiled with meat; buds were boiled for soup or with meat. The prairie onion (Allium textile) bulbs were eaten raw or flavored cooking.

Dried leaves of skunkbush sumac (Rhus tilobata) was mixed with tobacco for smoking. Early man smoked

(continued on page 88)

(continued from page 87)
the bark of red willow or mixed it with bearberry leaves and tobacco for a flavorful smoke.

Seeds in Nature's Pantry

Nutritous seeds abounded: Wheat grasses, biennial wormwood, Louisiana sagewort, milkweed, big sagebrush (when other food was scarce), fourwing saltbush, slough grass, sego or mariposa lily, red goosefoot, barn yard grass, spikerush, Canada wildrye, six weeks fescue, sunflower (common and prairie), foxtail barley, prairie junegrass, pepperweed, Indian ricegrass, ponderosa pine, nuttall alkali grass, roundstem bullrush, Canada goldenrod, limber pine, alkali sacaton, sand dropweed, porcupine grass, cattail and yucca.

Seeds of dropseed were parched, ground and mixed with water or milk to make mush and biscuits. Yucca seedpods were boiled. Alkali sacaton seeds were also parched, ground and eaten dry or made into mush. Ponderosa pine seeds were eaten raw or crushed and made into bread. Ground junegrass seeds were made into mush or bread. Pepperweed seeds made mush. Sunflower seeds were eaten raw, or dried, roasted, ground and made into cakes cooked with grease. Barnyard grass seeds were ground into flour and made into bread and mush. Sagebrush seeds were pounded for pinola.

Fresh greens added nutrition and variety to prehistoric tables. Pigweed, dandelion, lambs quarter, goldenrod and wild grape leaves all provided fresh salad.

Berries abounded in prairie coulees, in mountain clearings and underbrush. There were western snowberry, grape, false solomon's seal, wax current, golden current, skunkbush sumac, wild rose hips, service berries, chokecherries, groundcherries, sandcherries, pricklypear cactus, bearberries, ground plum, milkvetch, gooseberries, juneberries, buffalo or bullberries. Berries were a treat fresh or dried for winter use, sometimes pounded and mixed with meat or mush.

Nourishing Root Crops

Tubers of many plants provided bulk and nutrition—the potato, bean, prairie onion, turnip, sedge, stemless spring parsley, horsetail eaten raw or cooked, narrowleaf sunflower, roots of the starlilly and bitterroot (bitter but nutritious, cooking took away the bitterness), leafy musineon roots eaten raw, white prairie clover roots chewed or eaten raw.

Silverleaf scrufpea roots were eaten fresh and cooked, or dried and ground into flour. The common breadroot scruf pea had white farinaceous and wholesome roots; they were eaten fresh and cooked, also dried and ground into flour for cakes. White tubers of the duckpotato arrowhead were nutritious if slightly bitter until roasted; common arrowhead tubers were boiled or roasted. Softstem bullrush root stalks were eaten raw or pounded into flour. Cattail roots were eaten.

Nature Provided Cures

When they felt ill, too, nature's medicine chest provided the cures they often needed.

Common yarrow leaves were mashed and applied to sores, yarrow roots boiled and drunk to cure indigestion. A healing tea was made from leaves of the service berry. A strained back was eased by bearberry leaves and berries boiled together as medicinal tea; wet leaves were rubbed on the painful area.

The whole plant of the ceremonial sagewort was boiled and drunk for fever and colds; small children were bathed in it. Its root juice alleviated eye soreness.

Rabbitbrush healed sores and eruptions on the body. Leaves and stems boiled together were used to wash the affected parts; in severe cases, some of this tea was drunk.

A strong tea of powdered stems and flowers of buckwheat stopped a woman's menses if it ran too long. Tea made from fruit and young shoots of juniper relieved constant coughing and tickling of the throat. Numbness and lumbago were treated by rubbing with a mixture of leaves and stems of gromwell, pulverized and mixed with a little grass. Inner bark of the narrow leaf cottonwood was considered a good antiscorbutic food. Plantain leaves polticed wounds to prevent or cure infection.

Silverleaf scrufpea made a medicine to reduce fever; leaves and stems were ground fine and boiled to make a tea. To bring down fever, the powered leaves and stems mixed with grease were rubbed over the patient's body.

Yellow poltices of boiled stems and leaves of coneflower relieved pain, and were believed to draw out the poison of a rattlesnake bite. It also relieved cases of poison ivy. Dock roots were mashed and applied to swellings and cuts. Abdominal cramps were relieved by a cattail drink made of dried and pulverized roots and the white base of cattail leaves.

And when they got the horse, early man in Wyoming already had remedies for equine ills. An infusion of horsetail (Equisetum arvense) was poured down the horse's throat to rid it of a hard cough. Cuts, sores and infections were treated with the same medications used for humans—all out of nature's drug cabinet.

Fur Traders sought amicable relations with Indians

2. FUR TRADE BLAZED TRAILS FOR FUTURE

The "shining times" of the mountain men in Wyoming lasted less than four decades but their glory days made a permanent imprint on history, geography, and Indian alliances. They also nearly exterminated the beaver.

The trappers who scoured the wilderness for fashion fur were such paradoxes that they became myths in their own time, many of their adventures and discoveries defying credibility. They headed alone into virgin country with only their wits and a "possible sack." Often they never returned. The challenges were addictive, the pristine land a heady wine, and the rewards both material and psychological.

Mountain men also blazed trails for explorers as they mapped the American West, leading them into wonders often considered preposterous in the east. Such was Yellowstone Park, crossed by John Colter in 1807.

No one believed his bizarre tales of 10,000 hot springs, geysers shooting 100 feet in the air, scalding pools in brilliant gem colors, a canyon nearly 2,000 feet deep gushing waterfalls over granite ledges hundreds of feet high. Other trappers—Jim Bridger, Joseph Meek, Osborn Russell—soon verified Colter's "fantasies" at trappers' rendezvous, but such thermal marvels were generally beyond 19th century belief. It wasn't until 20 years later that Daniel T. Potts wrote of it—and not until 1870 that a government survey party finally reached the area; it became the first national park in 1872.

The trapper's lingo reflected the simplicity of his perilous life. Thus, his highs, or "shining times," after the Indian name for the Rockies, Shining Mountains. "Hawkins" was his muzzle-loader, and he put everything possible into his single pack, the "possible sack." "Furfurraws" were anything usable for Indian trade. A "Green River" was his knife, not the Bowie of the southwest but a variation of the kitchen butcher knife; such high quality British knives were stamped GR—for George Rex, so American copiers stamped on the same GR—for which the mountain man supplied his own heteronym.

The trapper's rendevous, a brawling open-air market was one of those shining times—held annually between 1824 and 1840 on the banks of the Green River. Two of those years, 1830 and 1838, this mobile market was moved to the Wind River near the confluence of the Popo Agie and the Little Wind. At this market thousands gathered for business and celebration—Indian tribes to trade hides to the company and garments to the mountain men, trappers to sell hides and stock up on supplies, later tourists and missionaries lured by excitement and souls to save.

Dust clouds of the supply caravan coming from the east signaled the beginning of a rendezvous. A wild band of reckless riders dashed out from the waiting camps, "shooting into the sky as though powder and ball were common as sagebrush." The caravan would leave weeks later, loaded with "plews", bales of beaver pelts for St. Louis warehouses.

The Wyoming rendezvous developed because the upper Green River, adjacent to beaver-rich mountain meadows, became a pivotal area of the fur trade when the Missouri River route was closed in early 1820s. This was on the Great Medicine Trail, historic Indian pathway west along the Platte and Sweetwater Rivers, and to "the Green"—called the Siskadee by mountain men using the Crow word for sage-hens, and Rio Colorado by earlier Spaniards.

Trappers' Riotous Holiday

Besides the Rocky Mountain Fur Company, the American Fur Company, the Bonneville (Astor) Expedition, as well as independents like Nathaniel Wyeth, were all at the 1833 rendezvous. Captain Bonneville described it:

"This, then, is the trapper's holiday, when he is all for fun and frolic, ready for a saturnalie among the mountains . . . leaders of the different companies mingled on terms of perfect good fellowship; interchanging visits and regaling each other in the best style their respective camps afforded.

"Here the free trappers were in all their glory, they considered themselves cocks of the walk. Now and then familiarity was pushed too far, and would effervesce in a brawl and a rough and tumble fight; but it all ended in cordial reconcilliation and maudlin endearment."

In 1837, the artist Alfred Jacob Miller described such tribes at the rendezvous as the Bannocks, Nez Perces, Flatheads, Utes, Crows, Delawares. There were also the painted lodges of Arapaho, and at least 1,500

FUR FORTS TO ARMY

William Sublette built Fort Laramie in 1833 as headquarters for fur caravans and Indian rendezvous. It was Fort William then, later renamed Fort John when taken over by Astor's American Fur Company.

This trading fort was a 130-foot quadrangle of clay, surrounded by walls 15 feet high and topped by a wooden palisade. Bastions in the tower were arranged to allow sweep of the four walls.

Surveyor John Fremont saw it in 1841 and coveted it for the army. In 1849, Maj. W. F. Sanderson arrived with a government check for $4,000, renamed it Fort Laramie, and it became the "guardian of the Trail." Social life took place in Bedlam, a clubhouse. The fort was a wagon train supply post and, for one dollar, wagons were ferried across the Platte River.

Similarly, Fort Bridger on the western end of the trails, built by Jim Bridger and Louis Vasquez also in 1833, was converted to a military fort.

Snakes (Shoshones). Miller was said to be the only painter who ever saw a fur caravan or a summer rendezvous; he made 160 sketches that year in Wyoming, many of which later became an authentic record in watercolor.

Such fun and excitement soon drew tourists. Scottish sportsman William D. Stewart was so entranced he attended six rendezvous; Clark sent his two sons in 1838, and John A. Sutter was there enroute to California gold fields. By 1834, the missionaries had discovered rendezvous. Narcissa Whiteman and Elizabeth Spalding were with their missionary husbands in 1836. Father De Smet, veteran of many, celebrated the "Prairie of the Mass" at the final rendezvous in 1840.

By 1841 the fur trade was over. Mountain men scattered to other work. Thomas ("Broken Hand") Fitzpatrick, for example, was then wagon-master of the 60-member Bidwell-Bartelson party of the "Western Emigration Society." Wed to a Northern Arapaho, "Fitz" was appointed Western Indian Agent in 1846.

They Prized Nature's Values

When the trappers rode into the mountains and onto the prairie, it was not an empty land they embraced. Wyoming's game-rich landscapes were well populated with Indians, friendly and unfriendly. The trappers established a brotherhood with these native Americans, sharing even the enemies of the tribes befriending them. They learned not only the skills and character qualities demanded by the wilderness, but came to view this world through native eyes as they themselves were absorbed in nature's pristine beauty and sternness. They learned Indian methods of survival and communications; they adopted Indian dress, married into tribes, and accepted the values and life-modes.

One account of winter camp on Powder River in 1829 refers to their "tipi literary society," in which trappers spent long evenings reading aloud from the Bible, Shakespeare, Scott, Byron and other authors who never wrote for tepee reading. Some men, tongue-in-cheek, claimed matriculation from "the Rocky Mountain College." Sometimes they gambled at handgame in the adjoining Indian camp. Nights were livened by drums and the shish-shish of rattles; there was dancing, too, either in a large lodge or on open moonlit snow.

So prized were their skills, the mountain men sometimes could combine guiding and trapping, as did John Hoback, Edward Robinson and Jacob Reznor. They guided an Astorian party of 62 men, 82 horses, one woman and two children into Wyoming in 1811; the woman and children were the family of interpreter Pierre Dorion. Near present-day Buffalo, they circled the Big Horn Mountains to the south and followed Wind River.

When the furs were prime, the moutain men took off trapping. In September of 1812, they again joined the Astor party led by Wilson Price Hunt, and began their winter trapping; by January, the three trappers and Dorion were dead, killed by Indians. Hoback's name is carried on by a pass, a basin, and a river in western Wyoming.

He Trapped All Over West

One Wyoming mountain man was Black Beaver, a Delaware Indian who trapped beaver all over the west. He spoke English, French, Spanish, and eight different Indian languages; he was proficient in sign language. Black Beaver had been to the shores of the Pacific Ocean seven different times, and had crossed the Rocky Mountains at numerous points. He was employed by the American Fur Company for ten years, and served America in three wars. He was a brother-in-law of Jesse Chisholm, the mixed-blood Cherokee who laid out the famous Chisholm cattle trail.

Like all mountain men, Black Beaver enjoyed a joke on himself, switching swiftly from understatement to outrageous tall tales. Around the campfires he told how he came to be regarded as a brave warrior: He was at an upper Missouri fort with 20 white men and four other Delawares when Blackfoot Indians attacked. He suggested the Delawares make a sortie to intimidate the fierce Blackfoot warriors; as the Delawares passed through the gate he took care to keep to the rear in case of retreat. A shower of arrows routed the Delawares, and the less fleet Black Beaver was soon in the rear again, hotly pursued by Blackfoot.

He stopped and yelled to his friends, "Come back you cowards, why do you run away and leave a brave man to fight alone?" This made the Delawares so angry they turned and beat off the pursuers. Back at the fort, the commander shook Black Beaver's hand, saying, "You are a very brave man, Black Beaver. You have done this day what no other man in the fort had the courage to do."

A young private soldier in the Lewis and Clark expedition, John Colter, asked for his discharge at Mandan on the way back to St. Louis. The wilderness had hooked him; Colter went on to become one of the most colorful—and durable—of the mountain men.

Colter signed on with the Missouri Fur Company, of which Manuel Lisa was president and the most successful of early traders. Lisa explained his success thus:

"First, I put into my operations great activity; I go a great distance, while some are considering whether they will start today or tomorrow. I impose upon myself great privations; ten months in a year I am buried in the forest, at a vast distance from my own house.

"I appear as the benefactor, and not a pillager, of the Indians. I carried among them the seed of the large pompion (pumpkin) from which I have seen in their possession the fruit weighing 160 pounds. Also the large bean, the potato, the turnip; and these vegetables now make a comfortable part of the subsistence, and this year I have promised to carry the plough.

"Besides, my blacksmiths work incessantly for them, charging nothing. I lend them traps, only demanding preference in their trade. My establishments are the refuge of the weak and of the old men no longer able to follow their lodges; and by these means I have acquired the confidence and friendship of these nations, and the consequent choice of their trade."

When Lisa hired Colter, he was ready to take a group of trappers north and spread them over the country. At the mouth of the Big Horn River, Lisa sent Colter out to inform Indian bands in the Wyoming-Idaho area that he wished to trade.

Colter traveled into Wyoming to the Wind River and Pierre's Hole, crossing the Teton Mountains. After traveling 500 miles, he found the Crows; while he was in their camp, the Crows were attacked by Blackfoot In-

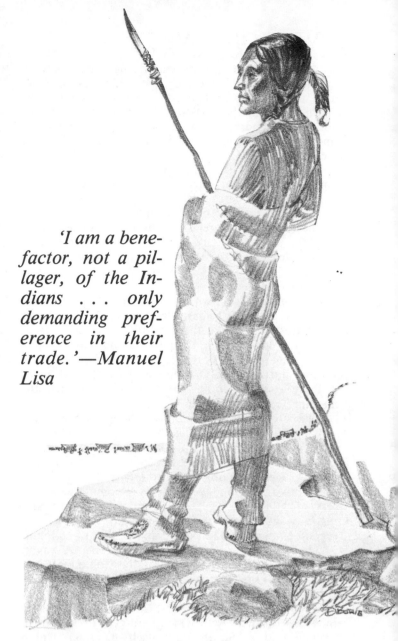

'I am a benefactor, not a pillager, of the Indians . . . only demanding preference in their trade.'—Manuel Lisa

dians; the Blackfoot were repulsed but Colter was wounded in the leg—and worse, was now labeled by the Blackfoot as a Crow ally.

Colter at Last Credited

During this trip, he found an immense tar spring at the forks of the Stinkingwater River, a spot which later bore the name "Colter's Hell." He crossed Yellowstone Park diagonally—but for years no one would believe the wonders he saw there. Clark later named this trail on his maps "Colter's Route in 1807." The historian Chittenden said Colter's trip "deserves to be classed among the most celebrated performances in the history of American exploration":

"Colter was the first explorer of the valley of the Big Horn River, the first to cross the passes at the head of Wind River and see the headwaters of the Colorado of the West, the first to see the Teton Mountains, Jackson Hole, Pierre's Hole, and the sources of the Snake (Green) River, and—most important of all—the first to pass through that singular region . . . the Yellowstone Wonderland."

3. WAGONS WEST

Two main routes funneled the nation's westward migrations through Wyoming mountain passes, from which they fanned out north, west and south. The Oregon Trail was the earliest, the Overland Trail to the south the second; both were known by several other names and routing varied in minor ways on each. Both were as old as time.

Wagon wheels ground deeply into the fragile prairie, as much as 20 feet in places as the wind blew away the pulverized dust. These "highways" grew to be hundreds of yards wide, littered for thousands of miles with camp garbage and debris. Carelessness and filth exacted a high mortality. Tragic accidents were without number, such as falling under moving wagon wheels and freezing to death because of ill timing or lack of trail know-how. Disease was rampant.

The Oregon Trail, which followed the ancient Great Medicine Trail of the Indians, left the North Platte River at Red Buttes to make the easy mountain crossing in South Pass. Just through the pass the road divided, one branch going south of Fort Bridger and Salt Lake Valley, the other northwest to Oregon Territory. This also was the Pony Express Route, the Mormon Trail and the Emigrant Trail.

The Overland Trail, an off-shoot of the Great Medicine Trail, was known as the Cherokee Trail before 1850. The Union Pacific Railroad followed this general route; telegraph lines were relocated here from their original placement along the northerly trail.

The two great highways across Wyoming were vast rivers of humanity by 1841 when 15 California and Oregon wagon trains passed through. Elija White's Oregon company of 112 people and a train of 18 Pennsylvania wagons were among 1842 emigrants. A wagon train of 1,000 pilgrims bound for the Columbia River swelled the 1843 migration. From 1848 through the 1850s the Mormons crossed Wyoming, exacting ferry toll at Green River from later travelers. California gold seekers reined their teams west in 1848, with gold discovered in Montana and in South Pass itself by 1860. Union Pacific's completion of its transcontinental rails in 1869 took some of the pressure off the wagon trails, but traffic continued until about 1890. The first of many homestead acts in 1862 spurred migration even after gold fever subsided.

Many army forts were established along both routes, for the Fort Laramie Treaty of 1851 allowed the U.S. "the right to establish roads, military and other posts." Between Fort Laramie and Fort Bridger were Forts Stambaugh, Washakie, D. A. Russell, Sanders, Halleck and Steele. Most of them were designed to protect the railroad rather than the wagon trains. An earlier fort west of Pinedale, Bonneville, had been dubbed Fort Folly or Fort Nonsense by mountain men in 1833.

The great buffalo herds were a nuisance and the railroad advertised hunting excursions in which a man could shoot all he wished without ever getting off the train. Professional hunters obliterated the buffalo by 1887, but for a few years "sportsmen" displayed shocking lack of sportsmanship. Sir George Gore, guided by Jim Bridger, slaughtered his way across Wyoming with a kill-tally of 2,500. Buffalo Bill Cody, Gen. Phil Sheridan and Col.

Early Wyoming Trails

- **Great Medicine Trail**
- **The Oregon Trail**
- **The Cherokee Trail**
- **The Overland Trail**
- **Pony Express Route**
- **The Mormon Trail**
- **The Bozeman Trail**

George A. Custer helped the Grand Duke Alexis of Russia in an exotic hunt in 1854.

Development of a new tanning process, of the Sharp "Big Fifty" and other high-powered rifles, plus President Grant's pocket veto of a bill restricting buffalo hunting, coincided to exterminate the buffalo at a time when every buffalo killed was regarded as "an Indian gone."

The red-shirted Pony Express riders briefly rode "hell bent for leather" over the Oregon Trail, St. Joseph to Sacramento in ten days. Seven stations between Fort Laramie and South Pass sped the mail onward in this private enterprise that operated 1860 and 1861. Completion of the telegraph and denial of federal funding combined to kill the colorful Pony Express.

Heavy freight wagon trains with their multiple "string teams" comprised a significant portion of traffic on both the Oregon and Overland Trails. The firm of Russell, Majors, and Waddell had 3,500 wagons on the South Pass route. Coaches and freight wagons of Ben Holladay, "king of western transportation," used both routes.

For most of the pilgrims the decision to make this trip to a nebulous land none had ever seen was both

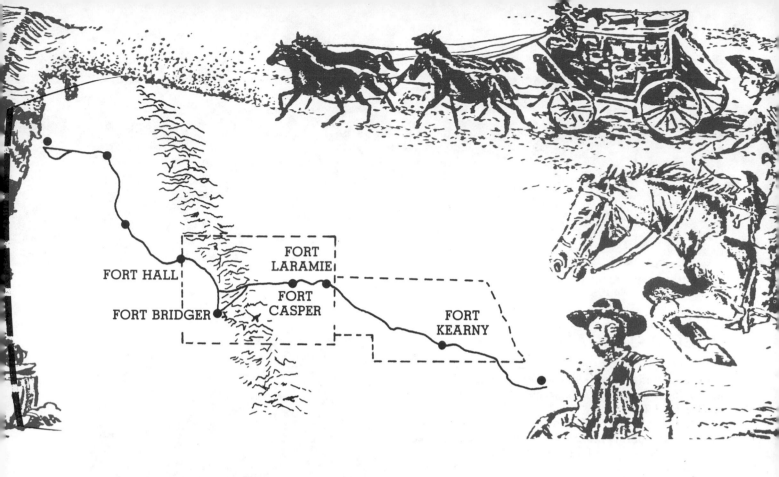

FORT HALL

FORT LARAMIE

FORT CASPER

FORT BRIDGER

FORT KEARNY

heroic and foolhardy. Wyoming was widely publicized as "The Great American Desert," lacking in water, a stark rough country fraught with danger, wild animals and even wilder Indians. They were told the trail ahead was parched and dried up for eight months of the year, locked in by blizzards for the remainder, and "unfit for any but a nomad population."[1]

But the call from Oregon sounded a siren song: "Send us families, mechanics, workmen; send us machinery and plows—for this is the richest land on earth."

As their wagons creaked across this geologic fantasy land, they carved their marks on its wonders—that the western world would remember long this extraordinary exploit.

At dome-shaped Independence Rock 50 miles south of Casper, emigrants engraved names and dates, a "register of the desert." On rock faces of Emigrant Gap, as they passed through on Poison Spider Creek, they also chiseled their names. And exiting from Wyoming, they wrote on Names Hill west of the Green River Crossing.

1. Zebulon Pike and James report on Long's 1819 expedition.

By 1852, wagons cut a wide swath through South Pass. 'Oregon Trail' by W. H. Jackson

13th Battery Field Artillery

BOZEMAN TRAIL FIASCO
AIDED RAILROAD

Three forts along the Bozeman Trail—Fetterman, Reno, and Phil Kearny—decoyed the Sioux and Cheyenne Indians from railroad survey work going on along the Overland Trail.

Clearly in treaty violation, these forts built in 1866 and 1867 did nothing more than draw the fire of enraged Indians. All were closed within two years. Forts Custer and MacKenzie, not established until much later in 1877 and 1899, served little purpose except to guard fort payrolls from rustlers.

Phil Kearny near Story got the worst of it, losing 81 men when Lt. Fetterman disobeyed orders and chased an Indian decoy unit. It also was involved in the quixotic "wagon box fight."

Chief Red Cloud walked out of a treaty council in 1866, on learning the forts were to be built, saying, "My people came to this place to talk peace. You cannot talk peace with so many soldiers . . . there is no reason for more empty words. My people will fight."

And fight they did, until the forts were closed and the troops withdrawn. Only one significant use of the trail had been made: Nelson A. Story slipped a herd of Texas cattle up the Bozeman Trail into Montana the summer of 1866.

Fort Phil Kearny was under heavy fire by Red Cloud's Sioux and Dull Knife's Cheyennes throughout its

Red Cloud won Bozeman Trail war

existence. Supply trains were cut off, game and wood parties harassed, livestock captured. All winter long, the snowbound fort battled blizzards and Indians; snowdrifts grew higher than the line-of-sight from artillery ports. Firewood, food and hay supplies shrunk.

Col. Henry Carrington was an engineer, not a military man, and he built the finest stockade in Wyoming—while tension rose among ill-trained troops. He suspended the post commander for drunkenness and drug addiction. Soldiers hunted deer and elk for food—but even the snow did not fully conceal the mass grave of the men who died with Fetterman. Parade uniforms were chewed by mice. Bacon from Fort Reno turn-

Fort Laramie, Gateway to Wyoming

Ft. Bridger guarded western end

94

ed out to be Civil War surplus. Corn sprouted through sacks because warehouses weren't built; the logs went into the stockade and into Col. Carrington's fine new house.

In July of 1867, woodcutters built an oval corral of 14 wagon boxes 5 miles up the mountain between Little and South Piney Creeks. The 70-by-100-foot corral was to protect their stock. Thirty-two men held off an Indian attack on Aug. 2 until soldiers rescued them during a lull in the fighting—the "wagon box fight."

The soldiers soon pulled down their flag and left the fort; the retreating troops had not gone far when Cheyenne warriors fired Fort Phil Kearny.[2]

The fleeting concession won by the Indians read: "The country north of the North Platte and east of the summits of the Big Horn Mountains shall be held and considered unceded Indian territory. No white person or persons shall without the consent of the Indians, first had and obtained, to pass through the same; that all military posts be left."

The last of the so-called Indian wars centered in Wyoming, but many were virtual massacres—Dull Knife's village in the Hole in the Wall, Two Moon's Cheyenne camp on Little Powder River. Like Sand Creek, Washita, and many other army Indian actions, they were without honor—slaughter of women and children, razing of all possessions in peaceful camps.

To be sure, not all prairie soldiers shared the prevailing view that Indians should be annihilated. "These practices," wrote Gen. Sanborn in 1867, "must sooner or later bring down upon us or our posterity the judgement of heaven . . . for a mighty nation like us to be carrying on a war with a few straggling nomads is a spectacle most humiliating, an injustice unparalleled, a national crime most revolting."

Religion, patriotism, greed, pride and prejudice were all linked in those years under the unholy banner called "Manifest Destiny." The profit potential was neatly joined to patriotic duty in 1842 by John Charles Fremont who mapped the valley of the Platte as the nation's "way west." His wife later wrote in pride, "From the embers of his campfires have sprung cities."

2. Relations couldn't have been all hostile, as a historic display was dedicated a century later by Eddie Ryan of Wheatland, grandson of a Phil Kearny sergeant and Little Flower, a daughter of Red Cloud.

Fort Fetterman had to be closed

They danced instead of fleeing

After the 1876 battle on the Little Big Horn, a few miles north of the Wyoming line, victorious Sioux, Cheyenne and Arapaho fanned out through northern Wyoming and southern Montana canyons and badlands. They knew retribution would be fierce for their annihilation of Col. George A. Custer and his Seventh Cavalry.

Chief Dull Knife took his village of 200 lodges south along the Big Horn Mountains to the headwaters of Powder River, later known as the Hole-in-the-Wall. Here, sheltered by the mountains on the west and an enormous red wall on the east, he hoped to hide his people, through the winter.

A man who had gone to hobble his horses on grass brought the first warning of Gen. Ranald MacKenzie's approaching army. Seated on a hill watching the grazing horses, he felt the ground tremble as of many hooves on the move. He hid just as MacKenzie's Pawnee scouts rode over the hill, watching as they cut loose and drove away the Cheyenne horses.

Familiar by now with army tactics, Dull Knife expected a dawn attack. He ordered women, children and old men to the hills—but to do it unobtrusively to avoid tipping off the watching scouts.

This operation was underway, when a warrior society rode into camp from a successful strike, scalps in hand and demanding a victory dance. The leader discredited the man who had brought the report of army scouts, ordered the horses unsaddled, the celebration to begin. They danced most of the night. At dawn, when the exhausted camp slept soundly, MacKenzie struck.

Philip Rising Sun, age 15, was put on a balky horse, his little brother in front of him, fleeing to the hills amid total confusion in the village. The story of the boy's difficulty when the pony decided to return to camp is passed down in the Rising Sun family—it was all Phillip could do to turn the horse, with bullets kicking up dirt all around him. The village was fired, the Cheyenne horse herd slaughtered.

Snow began to fall and the people fled on foot, without food, clothing or shelter. Rising Sun described a buffalo hunt a few days later—done in silence by men afoot, afraid to use guns because of the noise. They quietly moved among the buffalo, slaughtering with bow and arrow. Thus the band was able to survive. They later made contact with Crazy Horse, but the Sioux, too, were on the run and gave the Cheyennes a cool reception.

Dull Knife

Emigrants carved on Register Cliff   **Independence Rock marked trail**

'I Speak of Many Wrongs We Suffer'

Shoshone Chief Washakie told the governor of Wyoming Territory in 1878:

"I shall speak freely to you of the many wrongs we have suffered at the hands of the white man . . .

"Our fathers were steadily driven out, or killed, and we, their sons, but sorry remnants of tribes once mighty, are cornered in little spots of the earth all ours of right.

"Nor is this all. The white man's government promised that if we, the Shoshones, would be content with the little patch allowed us, it would keep us well supplied with everything necessary to comfortable living and would see that no white man should cross our borders for our game or anything that is ours.

"But it has not kept its word! The white man kills our game, captures our furs, and sometimes feeds his herds upon our meadows.

"And your great and mighty government—oh, sir, I hesitate, for I cannot tell the half! It does not protect us in our rights. It leaves us without the promised seed, without tools for cultivating the land, without implements for harvesting our crops, without breeding animals, without the food we still lack, without the many comforts we cannot produce, without the schools we so much need for our children. I say again, the government does not keep its word.

"Knowing all this, do you wonder, sir, that we have fits of depression and think to be avenged?"

In 1926, Cheyenne veterans of Custer Battle refused to shake hands with enemies 'until we are paid for our Black Hills lands.'

Prairie grave ended struggle

Cherokee blazed Overland Trail

Cherokee expeditions bound for California blazed the Overland Trail through Wyoming and, by 1850, the Pueblo to Fort Bridger segment was known as the Cherokee Trail.

Their own civilization destroyed, the Cherokees sought new land and fresh opportunity.

The Cherokee Trail wound past Pike's Peak down Cherry Creek to the Platte, north across the Cache La Poudre, over the Laramie Plain, around the north end of the Medicine Bow Mountains, across the North Platte and west through Bridger Pass to join the Oregon Trail at Fort Bridger.

It differed from the later Overland Trail only between Elk Mountain and the North Platte. The Cherokees passed between Elk Mountain and the main Medicine Bow range, following Pass Creek to cross the Platte near Lake Creek. Overland travelers took an easier route north of Elk Mountain, crossing the Platte at Sage Creek.

Cherokee trading expeditions long had traveled into Spanish and Mexican territory. One group of Cherokee emigrants left for Texas as early as 1813, their lives made miserable by white men.

Publisher and founder of the San Diego Union, Edward W. (Ned) Bushyhead, was an early Cherokee to make his mark in California. Another distinguished Cherokee writer was John Rollin Ridge, biographer of outlaw Joaquin Murieta.

James Vann, former editor of the Cherokee Advocate, and Martin Schrimsher, grandfather of Will Rogers, led an 1829 party through Wyoming. John Lowery Brown wrote of the 1850 trip up the Cherokee Trail in 1850 in his leather bound "John Brown's Journal."

The Cherokee tried harder than any other tribe to co-exist with the white man, to pass the various "tests" of civilization contrived to deal them out of the American mainstream. Most of their efforts were of no avail.

Chief Little Raven, William Bent

NEZ PERCE SLIP THROUGH ARMY NET

Chief Joseph

At Chief Joseph's Wyoming campfire, a captured white woman saw him as "the noble red man" personified. Grave and dignified he sat, still 400 desperate miles away from his goal.

The Nez Perce humiliated the U.S. army for three and one-half months in 1877, captured October 5th within sight of the Canadian border. By then, Joseph had led 700 people through 1,300 miles of rugged country. They had crossed Lolo Trail with 2,000 ponies, climbed mountains, forded raging torrents, outfought and outwitted army units in 13 battles and skirmishes. Joseph was a hero and a legend, admired by public and military alike.

The Nez Perce slipped through a vast net thrown around Yellowstone Park. Soldiers awaited them on the Shoshone River, the Wind River, and near Crow Agency. Col. Samuel Sturgis took the 7th Cavalry, still stinging from its Custer defeat, to Clark's Fork but didn't wait long enough. Lt. George Bacon left his Targee Pass post just ahead of the Indians, one of his units pinned down until rescued by Gen. O. O. Howard who had pursued the Nez Perce from Idaho.

Army guns enforced 'Manifest Destiny'

Two months before he led Sand Creek massacre, Col. Chivington talked peace with Arapaho and Cheyenne in Denver

Ft. Robinson talks led by Black Coal

4. NORTHERN ARAPAHO LOOKING FOR A HOME

Singing was a form of prayer to the Arapaho, to whom the whole outdoors was a church. When the need for help intensified, the singing turned into crying—and "the Blue Sky People" must have wept many times during the years the tribe was fragmented and pinned on the horns of expediency, looking for a home.

Between 1851 and their final settlement on the Wind River Reservation in 1878, the Northern Arapahoes were given at least six different land bases and tantalized with promises of several more. Gold and "Manifest Destiny" eroded any honor that may have been attached to U.S. treaties or promises. The Pike's Peak gold rush of 1859 chased the Arapaho out of Denver, and Wyoming gold fever at South Pass forced them out of that area; their Chief Black Bear was killed in an unarmed camp in 1870 by the South Pass Militia, a vigilante group.

Manifest Destiny, carried into 19th century west from Pilgrim times, quite simply was an annihilation plan with Christian rationalization.

Arapahoes were at the infamous Sand Creek massacre, where the Methodist minister Col. John M. Chivington led an Army slaughter in 1864 of the peaceful Arapaho camp of Left Hand and the Cheyenne camp of Black Kettle, Nov. 29 along the Big Sandy River in eastern Colorado. The next year, Gen. Conners destroyed Black Bear's camp of 200 lodges on Powder River. Both these incidents followed an 1863 treaty assigning Arapaho to hunting territory in southeastern Wyoming, eastern Colorado, western Kansas, and western Nebraska. It wasn't until 1868, the year of the Washita massacre by the Army, that the U.S. made it "legal" to keep the Arapaho out of all this territory; they were then assigned to Pine Ridge in the Second Council of Fort Laramie.

At Pine Ridge, S.D., however, the Arapaho found Sioux in possession; they requested other land, and were answered the following year, without "benefit" of treaty, by President U. S. Grant: They would move to Indian Territory. It was a continuation of an 1833 policy of President Andrew Jackson—"The Native Americans must necessarily yield to the force of circumstances and ere long disappear."

At the time of the Seventh Cavalry demise on the Little Big Horn, the Army was holding most Northern Arapaho at Fort Robinson for transport to Oklahoma; the Arapaho refused to go, determined to return to Wyoming. The Army had not collected everyone, however, for some were fighting with the Northern Cheyenne and Sioux on the Little Big Horn.

Those Arapaho at Fort Robinson were returned to Wyoming, the military promising them land at all points of the compass. Depressed, some Arapaho left Chief Black Coal's camp to join the Southern Arapaho. Promises at that time had included (1) an assigned area on the Chugwater, (2) land on the Laramie Plains, (3) on the North Platte just south of old Fort Laramie, (4) an area around Fort Caspar to be defined by four Arapaho riders, each supplied with two fine horses, riding "into the directions of the four winds"—at the far edges of their day's ride, rock markers erected by each rider would

Lizzie refused to be 'rescued'

Irony laced a tragedy in Wyoming history for many white people when Lizzie Brokenhorn said "No."

Lizzie was a 39-year-old white woman who spurned attempts to "rescue" her when it was learned she had been captured by Indians at age two. She spoke no English, was happily married to an Arapaho, and had five children.

Her identity was established after Casper citizens noticed her in an Arapaho band that came for supplies in August, 1900. She dressed like an Indian, painted her face, and spoke only Arapaho. Citizens, however, launched an inquiry which was published in the Natrona County Tribune. A woman in Davenport, Iowa, Mrs. A. M. Cook, wrote to the editor seeking further information.

Mrs. Cook told of being in a wagon train attacked by 300 Cheyennes in 1865 near Rock Creek; she hadn't seen her baby sister since, although she herself had been a captive for 16 months. Mrs. Cook's father, Jasper Fletcher, and his family had been enroute to California in a train of 75 wagons; Mrs. Fletcher was killed, three sons escaped, the two girls were captured, and Fletcher himself lay in a ditch for two days, badly wounded.

Convinced Lizzie was her long-lost sister, Mrs. Cook traveled to Casper by train and on by stage to the Arapaho sub-agency where she positively identified Lizzie.

Through an interpreter, Mrs. Cook begged

John and Lizzie Brokenhorn

Lizzie to return to Iowa where she could dress and act like the white woman that she was. Lizzie refused to listen, declaring that she was an Indian and wanted to live as she always had; she could not remember anything about being captured.

Brokenhearted, Mrs. Cook returned to Casper alone. She said this was the hardest blow she had endured since seeing her mother killed, the fact that her sister refused "to give up her wild life and live like a woman civilized." The Tribune editor ever after referred to this as the "sad, sad story of the white Indian woman."

Lizzie's husband, John Brokenhorn, was a proud man who refused a land allotment on the grounds that the U.S. government had no right to portion out to Indians land which was their own. He supported his family as an Indian doctor, a horse trader, and producer of artifacts.

---

define the perimeters.

In early March of 1878, the official word arrived of "temporary" assignment to the reservation of the Shoshones, enemies of long-standing. Under military escort, 913 Arapaho moved their lodges to the junction of the Popo Agie and Little Wind Rivers—it was to be their "camp of a hundred years."

The Arapaho seem to have been closely associated with the Cheyenne for nearly 300 years, since both tribes left Minnesota's Red River area about 1700. Both are Algonquin-speaking and may have come earlier from eastern Canada. Like the Cheyennes, the Arapaho left fields of corn and an agricultural life to become hunters of the plains. Over the next two centuries, the two tribes shared hunting, battles with Indian and white, tribal fractures, U.S. military persecution and massacre, as well as north-south tribal splits.

The Arapaho, however, never duplicated the Cheyennes' warm relations with the Sioux, who were the first to call Arapahoes "The Blue Sky People." Raiding Arapahoes the Sioux said, "came out of the blue sky" upon vigilant Sioux camps, so silent and stealthy were they. And, as noted earlier, they refused to share a reservation at Pine Ridge in 1868.

Division Began After 1789

Tribal division began soon after 1789, when the Atsina Arapaho went on to Manitoba, Canada, as the main tribe moved out onto the plains. As a society where groups, clans, and families operated with great autonomy, it was not unusual that part of the Arapaho drifted south to work the great buffalo and wild horse herds south of the Platte. Another part preferred the northern plains and mountains, eastern spurs of the Rockies in Wyoming and Colorado. The northern group refused to join in the Colorado war of 1864.

A string of military forts also tended to keep them separate, reminiscent of an Arapaho legend explaining the separation:

"It was early morning one day long ago, in the camp of all The People. And the camp, as was our custom, was spread out along the timber by the bank of this river.

"There was this certain Old Lady who went down early to the river bank to draw the morning water. As she was standing there by the river, she saw a strange horn of some monster-animal rising out of the water.

Milestones for Northern Arapaho

Early 1700s — Arapaho left Red River in Minnesota.

1750-1860s — Tribe centered at site of present-day Denver.

1789 — Main tribe crossed onto the plains, Atsina division moved to Manitoba.

1851 — All land between North Platte to Arkansas River, and from Rocky Mountain range to junction of Platte and Cimarron Crossing on Sante Fe Road assigned to Arapaho and Cheyenne. **Peace Council of Ft. Laramie**

1861 — Arapaho tribe rejected Fort Wise Treaty.

1863 — Southeastern Wyoming, western Nebraska, western Kansas and eastern Colorado assigned to Arapaho.

1864 — Col. Chivington holds peace talks in Denver with Arapaho and Cheyenne. Northern Arapaho refused to join Colorado war.
Left Hand's Arapaho camp and Black Kettle's Cheyenne camps massacred at Sand Creek by Col. Chivington's command.

1865 — Black Bear's camp of 200 lodges destroyed on Powder River by Gen. Conners.
Chief Black Bear killed by South Pass Militia.

1867 — Northern Arapaho and Southern Cheyenne given central and western Indian Territory assignment. **Medicine Lodge Treaty.**

1868 — Northern Arapaho relinquished claim to Wyoming and consented to Pine Ridge assignment. **Peace Council of Fort Laramie.**

1869 — Without treaty President Grant ordered Northern Arapaho to Indian Territory.

1876 — Most Northern Arapaho at Fort Robinson, awaiting transport south.
Some Northern Arapaho participate in Battle of Little Big Horn.

1877 — Arapaho at Fort Robinson moved back to Fort Caspar. Several military promises of land came to naught.

1878 — 913 Northern Arapaho placed on Wind River Reservation with Shoshone.

"The Old Lady was frightened. She grasped a heavy branch lying there on the bank; repeatedly she struck with the stick at the protruding horn.

"As she struck, the river course was changed. Now the river went flowing past her feet, right through the middle of the tepees. The new river path grew wider, with all the water flowing through like a new river; and the camp was divided into two sections.

"On that day The People were separated into the Northern and Southern Arapaho."

The U.S. government made the division official in 1867 in the Great Medicine Lodge Treaty, which placed Northern Arapaho and Southern Cheyenne in central and western Indian Territory. Until that time a strong thread of tribal unity had persisted through treaty negotiations and tribal ritual. It is on record that Arapaho leaders acted for the entire tribe at the Inter-Tribal Peace Council of 1840, the Fort Laramie Treaty of 1851, and the rejection of the Fort Wise Treaty of 1861. Even at the close of the 19th century, few Arapaho saw the need of permanent commitment to either geographical group.

What is now the heart of Denver was, for a century, the pivotal campsite of the Arapaho, from about 1750 to 1860. From there, they hunted the plains and moved with freedom, their only boundary the Front Range of the Rockies. The Arapaho campsite was at the junction of Cherry Creek and the South Platte River, an area called "nee-nanee-nea-chee," greasy creek.

'It Happened Like This Before'

Yelling "Pike's Peak or Bust," the gold-crazed '59ers brawled through this quiet Indian village— "strange ones, tense, jumpy, loud, possessed by evil spirits that would not let them be still." Historian Robert L. Perkins described the 1850's camp scene:

"Members of the Arapaho band, silent in damp blankets, stood beside their lodges to watch the wild traffic. Here beside Cherry Creek the '59ers were everywhere underfoot like dogs in a hunting camp . . .

"The soldiers had promised that this country where the Rockies rise from the high plain would remain forever a hunting preserve for the Arapaho and Cheyenne people. There had been a pipe and presents to seal the bargain, and the chiefs had pledged their braves to good behavior. For the most part, the pledge had been kept. Yet now the country swarmed with white men who had come so swiftly and in such great numbers that protest was impossible . . . the Sioux and Pawnee had said that it had happened like this before and now it was happening again."

Many Whips called for the war pipe. Left Hand believed the prospectors had "come to get our gold, eat our grass, burn our timber, kill and drive off our game." Bear Head restrained them by telling of a prophetic vision: In event of war on the white man, a great flood would take place; in his dream, the surging waters engulfed the Arapaho, but left the white intruders on high ground safe from the flood.

Chief Little Raven told the miners he hoped they would find much gold—and "leave this land that, by official treaty, belongs to the Arapaho."

Little Raven, who came to believe that "the road to the white man's peace leads to Indian disaster," witnessed several land-grab treaties—Fort Wise in 1861, Little Arkansas in 1865, the Great Medicine Lodge in 1867, and in 1869 the abandonment of all treaty pretense by President Grant. When Little Raven died in 1889, he passed on to Chief Left Hand the tragic heritage, "We must necessarily yield."

Denver Turns Hostile

It was soon clear that Arapahoes were in the way on Cherry Creek. Formerly cordial white attitudes were changing, and this showed up in print. The visiting apostle of Manifest Destiny, Horace Greely, wrote: "There is a gleam of hope that the Arapaho, who have made the last two or three nights hideous by their infernal war whoops, songs and dances, will at last clear out on the foray against the Utes they have so long threatened." When they returned victorious, the Rocky Mountain News was similarly caustic, "Now, over their mystic circles, fall the shadow of tall buildings."

The rot gut liquor was more damaging than tall buildings. Buffalo Billy and 20 other young Arapahoes died in one night of brawling. And the Rocky Mountain News carried a protest after a group of drunken white "bummers" attacked a camp:

"After dark a lot of drunken devils and 'bummers' went to the lodges and took the Indian women and girls forcibly out, committing acts of violence, which in any other country would condemn the perpetrator to ignominy and shame . . . That same night three mules were stolen from the Indians, taken off some ten miles from Denver and fettered; but the thieves could not steal the trail; the red men found their mules, and on Sunday morning came to me with their complaints . . . I asked the Indians not to make a definite conclusion until I had a talk with the whites, when I am to meet in council and report if the white men of Denver tolerate such inhuman and ungrateful conduct."

The writer was the mulatto mountain man Jim Beckworth, a former slave and an adopted Crow war chief. The people of Denver met and talked. There was no outrage, no punishment. The Arapaho decided to leave Denver.

The grandson of Spotted Calf, Mike Brown (Lone Bear), later described the slow travel of the tribe north from their homeland at Denver. At last at Glendo, the women were making jurky in camp when scouts rushed in to report sighting of a herd of buffalo. The chief made medicine and called the order to ride; Spotted Calf got his horse, which was staked close to the tepees, and led the charge—until his horse stepped in a badger hole, falling on Spotted Calf and killing him; his son, Mike's father, then was adopted by Chief Lone Bear, another famous Arapaho.

Friday was among those electing to go to Wyoming. Widely known as "the Arapaho who speaks good English," Friday was then leader of a large Arapaho camp near upper waters of the Cache la Poudre in Colorado. Found as a lost child near the Cimarron Crossing on the Santa Fe Trail by mountain man Thomas (Broken Hand) Fitzpatrick, he was named Friday because it was on a Friday of late May, 1831. Fitzpatrick had him educated in St. Louis. After rejoining his tribe, he participated in all major negotiations of the critical years of the 19th century.

'If I Wave the Robe . . . It Will Be Safe'

Arapaho settlement on the Shoshone reservation was far more personal than official records show, according to this version taught by historian Pius Moss at St. Stephens School.

Chief Black Coal's people were weary, hungry and ragged after thirty years of harassment. Both the military and the politicians had failed to find them a home. Old enemies, the Shoshones, had been given the Wind River area so prized by the Arapaho, who were now living uncertainly at Ft. Caspar.

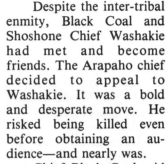

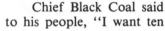

Chief Black Coal

Despite the inter-tribal enmity, Black Coal and Shoshone Chief Washakie had met and become friends. The Arapaho chief decided to appeal to Washakie. It was a bold and desperate move. He risked being killed even before obtaining an audience—and nearly was.

Chief Black Coal said to his people, "I want ten men to come with me, no children or women. We may never come back."

His little band rode west from Caspar, over the hills just south of where Washakie Hot Springs are today. They looked over the grassy clearing below and saw a big camp. It was the camp of the Shoshones. There was a lot of dust, many horses running around; a celebration of some kind was in progress.

Black Coal turned to his men and said, "This is what I came for. I am going down there alone to talk to the Chief, my friend. As I get closer there will be some disturbance. In case I do not come out and wave my buffalo robe within a short time, you must get out of here. They will know I am not alone. If you see me wave the robe, you come down. It will be safe."

He cleaned up, put on good clothes, and used the traditional wrap for his braids. If he was killed, he wished to be dressed properly for burial; if not, his fine dress would show respect for his friend.

As he went down the hill and approached the camp, no one noticed him at first. Then an alarm was given. Angry Shoshones crowded around him, intent on killing him. Black Coal kept asking in sign language to see Chief Washakie, finally convincing them to notify their chief of his presence. Chief Washakie was summoned.

Washakie reconized Black Coal and told his warriors, "Whoever harms this man will have to answer to me." They backed off, and the two chiefs went into Washakie's lodge.

Chief Washakie agreed to put the Arapahoes under his protection, designating the area east of the hot springs for them; Shoshones, he said, would stay west of the spring in the mountain area. They smoked the pipe and Black Coal went out to signal his followers.

5. SHOSHONES LOCATED IN ANCIENT HOME

Granting the Shoshone tribe the "Valley of the Warm Winds" was one of the few strokes of justice conferred on Indians. Shoshone may have been native to Wyoming mountains for several millennia.

This was the eastern range for a tribe of many bands, various stages of development and ways of life, known by several names—Snake, Shoshoko, Comanche, Diggers, Walkers, and Sheepeaters were a few. The Wyoming Shoshone were horse and buffalo Indians, the Wind River band and Comanche; northern bands met by Lewis and Clark in western Montana in 1805 were similarly daring hunters and raiders.

Western bands were more primitive, "gatherers" of seeds and roots; a mummy dated 1,200 years ago, found in a cave west of Cody, is probably a Shoshone "gatherer." Where large game was scarce, they lived on fish, rabbits, roots, nuts, and seeds; they were often called "Diggers," or "Walkers" because they were too poor to own horses. Where mountain sheep abounded they were called "Sheepeaters."

Anthropologists speculate that the Shoshone arrived on this continent about 4,000 years ago, migrating across the Bering Strait.

At least 50 bands of Shoshone, 19,000 people in all, had spread from Idaho to California, Wyoming to Texas, by the early 19th century. The four divisions included 2,500 Wind River Shoshone, 7,000 Comanche, and 10,000 northern and western Shoshone centered in Nevada, Utah, Idaho, and western Montana. By 1950, there were only about 5,000 in all four groups.

The Wind River and Comanche bands acquired horses as early as 1700, when the Comanche, too, were living in Wyoming. The aggressive Comanche rode into west Texas during the next few decades, with less band organization than the Wind River group which stayed together under one chief for about half the year. The northern band also possessed horses and a governmental system, hunting buffalo as far southeast as Wyoming; this band was also skilled in warfare, lived in hide tepees and dressed as did the plains Indians.

Most sedentary of the Shoshone were the western group, which did not acquire the horse until 1847 from the Mormons; their desert environment would not support many horses and they were very poor. They were "gatherers" of wild plants rather than hunters and had no political organization; the largest unit was a family group or small fluid band. They wintered in half-circles of brush without roofs.

Sacagawea

Had Merriwether Lewis and William Clark known the extent of

'I want my people to learn all they can from the white man because . . . they must live with him forever.'

the Shoshone nation when they met Sacagawea, she would not have had to coax them to let her go along to the Pacific. With her newborn baby on her back, she traveled with her interpreter husband, Toussaint Charbonneau. She had been stolen as a child, probably by a Hidatsa war party, and sold to Charbonneau or, as the story goes, won by him in a gambling game. She wanted to see her people again, so convinced the explorers of her usefulness; left home was a second Shoshone wife of Charbonneau, Otter Woman.

Clark soon realized that a woman with a party of men was seen as a sign of peace. Not only that, but she had skills as an intermediary with tribes, and assisted in bartering for Shoshone horses and supplies when they reached the mountains.

According to Wyoming tradition Sacagawea died at Ft. Washakie at the age of 100, April 9, 1884, the woman known as Parivo who spoke English, French, Shoshone and sign. The Episcopal priest, John Roberts, identified her as such and conducted services at the tribal cemetery. Indian agent from 1874 to 1880, James I. Patton, also identified her as Sacagawea. The following year, a man called Baptiste died and was buried in a mountain crevice; he is considered to have been the infant she carried to the Pacific Ocean. And two years later, 1886, Shoogun or Bazil died, a subchief under Washakie thought to be a nephew of Sacagawea. Other evidence places Sacagawea's time and place of death at Ft. Manvel, S.D., in 1812.

'Peace Is an Empty Name'

In the first 40 years of the 19th century, the Shoshone lost their isolation and came into increasingly close contact with the whites. Mostly these were fur trappers, anxious to get along with everybody in order to increase profits, Trapper Alexander Ross told in 1818 of his efforts to obtain peace between the Cayouse and Shoshone:

"The only real object we had in view, or the only result that could in reality be expected by the peace, was that we might be enabled to go in and come out of the Snake (Shoshone) country in safety, sheltered under the influence of its name. Nothing beyond this was ever contemplated on our part.

"All of our maneuvers were governed by the policy of gain. Peace was beyond our power; it was but an empty name."

Under Chief Washakie, the Shoshone were recognized as among the world's best light cavalry. Warriors drilled rigorously in intricate maneuvers which were useful in war and spectacular in peaceful appearances at treaty parleys and Indian gatherings. The tribe's move onto the Wind River Reservation in the spring of 1872 was made easier because the government had ulterior motives: the Shoshone warriors could act as a buffer between "encroaching civilization" and angry Crow,

'This is my country and my people's country. My father lived here and drank water from this river, while our ponies grazed on these bottoms. Our mothers gathered the dry wood from this land. The buffalo and elk came here to drink water and eat grass; but now they have been killed or driven back out of our land.'—Chief Washakie

Blackfoot, Sioux, and Cheyenne.

However, even as the tribe pitched tepees, the Commissioner of Indian Affairs came waving the treaty of 1868, saying it contained an error; the government wanted to withdraw 600,000 acres containing the gold mines at South Pass and the rich Popo Agie valley now wanted by white settlers. An equal number of acres north of the reservation was offered in trade.

"Did the Crow chief tell you to trade their land off?" demanded Washakie, who knew the north land was assigned to the Crows in the Fort Laramie Treaty of 1851.

Washakie refused to trade, but was finally forced to sell— for $25,000 in cattle, 4½ cents an acre. The money ultimately was used to build 15 log and brick buildings for use of white people at Camp Brown (Ft. Washakie).

Shoshones Used as Pawn

The government used the Wind River Shoshone as a pawn in the building of roads and railway west. By defining in 1868 the reservation limit as the crest of the Wind River Mountains, all lands in southern Wyoming defaulted to the government—which played right into the hands of the Union Pacific Railroad. Right-of-way for the transcontinental railroad was now cleared, and vast holdings acquired in Wyoming for future sale and settlement. Railroad and miners also had a friendly Indian buffer against hostile tribes.

Washakie's pacifism sometimes cost him credibility with his tribe. Many left to join war chiefs of northern and western Shoshone bands when Washakie apologized for an angry exchange with Indian Agent Brown. Objecting to building a road connecting South Pass with Bear River via the upper Green River Basin, Washakie said:

"The building of this new road will destroy many of our root grounds and drive off our game . . . we will be much injured by the passage of this new road by emigrants."

So grateful was President Ulysses S. Grant for Washakie's peaceful influence, he sent a fully carved saddle as a gift. The government later collected from the Shoshone tribe the full price, $125, for this saddle.

Washakie: Strategist In War and Peace

As a leader in both war and peace, the Shoshones' shrewd Chief Washakie successfully insulated his people from the worst of the 19th century pillage of Indian tribes.

Certain that it was folly to make war with whites, Washakie consistently refused to fight them—even though he was a valiant warrior. He explained, "I want my people to learn all they can from the white man, because he is here to stay, and they must live with him forever. They must listen carefully . . . if they are to have an equal chance with him in making a living."

A scar on his left cheek was a reminder of a Blackfoot arrow which once glanced off his cheekbone, passing through his nose to his right cheek.

Crowheart Butte is named for one of Washakie's most famous victories. Ending a four-day battle, he met the Crow chief, vanquished him, and cut out his heart.

This battle occurred in the spring of 1866 with Crows camped near the present site of Kinnear. Washakie was in the mountains and his Bannock allies were hunting along the Popo Agie. Washakie sent a Shoshone couple to ask the Crows to leave; they responded by killing the man, while his wife escaped. Bannock Chief Targhee's help was solicited. On the eve of the fourth day of fighting, Washakie and the Crow Chief charged each other on their war horses; both were unhorsed, meeting then with knives drawn. When Washakie at last held high the Crow leader's heart, Crow warriors withdrew in sorrow—never again to face Washakie in combat.

He was a battle strategist, as well as a political strategist. Through his cunning, Shoshone warriors

Chief Washakie

routed a vastly superior Sioux war party in 1868, shortly after moving onto the reservation. The Sioux were spotted approaching along the Owl Creek Mountains, too large a group for Washakie's warriors to meet. Camp was struck.

Women were ordered to pitch the tepees in a valley full of buffalo wallows, each lodge covering a wallow. Horses were hobbled and picketed near the tepees. The men dug into the bottom of the wallows, piling dirt around the inside edges of the tepees. The Sioux attacked what they thought was a sleeping Shoshone village, making three wild charges, riddling tepee walls with bullets and arrows. On the third charge the Shoshone opened fire from under the tepee walls. Many Sioux were killed, the rest fleeing with Shoshones in hot pursuit.

Taller and lighter-skinned than the average Shoshone, Washakie was born of a Shoshone captive in a Flathead camp. His Flathead father was killed by a Blackfoot war party when the boy was five years old. His mother escaped with her five children, eventually joining a band of Lemhi Shoshone on the Salmon River. Later Washakie spent five years with the Bannocks before joining the eastern Shoshone.

In the last treaty he signed, ceding another ten square miles, Washakie secured a lasting memorial. Included in the tract was the present townsite of Thermopolis, and the chief specified in this 1898 treaty that part of the water from the hot spring be forever free to all people and that a campground be reserved for use of Indians. When the land was turned over to Wyoming the next year, the state legislature ratified Washakie's stipulations.

In a major flexing of political strength, Washakie was able to delay for ten years the order replacing the War Department with the Department of the Interior. The order was issued in May, 1899; Washakie protested that the treaty of 1868 promised military protection for as long as he lived. The order was revoked within days. It wasn't until March, 1909, that Interior was able to install its Bureau of Indian Affairs on Wind River.

When he died in his sleep in 1900, Washakie had been head chief in both war and peace for more than 50 years. A military funeral was held, and a granite monument erected by the War Department. His age was listed as 102.

Indian tree burials were usual

Sioux women worked hide, Ft. Laramie

Second treaty of Fort Laramie, 1868, paved way for Bozeman Trail

Coal seam 30 feet thick bands Powder River bluff

6. EONS DEPOSIT
RICHES IN EARTH

Nature was moving mountains to the sea long before the first lunged vertebrates crawled out of the ocean and found it good to dwell on dry land. Silt, clay and mud formed layers at the bottom of the sea that lithified, or changed to rock, and were thrust up by earth forces to form mountains again.

The Rockies in Wyoming were formed in the abolition of a seaway dividing the continent during the past 70 million years; some formations may be 3,350-million years old. The problem is to explain why the young mountain chains occurred inland, 800 miles from the battleground of the western seaboard. The soft continental plate may have broken at the western edge of the Great Plains and the eastern part began to push itself under the western part.

Because the processes of earth formation are especially visible in Wyoming, geologists have conducted student tours from all parts of the nation for nearly a century.

Wyoming's heavily silt-laden rivers have built much of the land mass along the Missouri watershed, as indicated by this report of three days on Muddy Creek in the Wind River Basin. It is by W. G. Sloan, from **Erosion Then and Now.**

"The total discharge of the creek was only 782 acre-feet, but the silt discharge was 145,700 tons . . . in the first eight hours after the creek began to rise there was a silt discharge of 82,000 tons—which is moving dirt at a rate almost equal to the world's record for moving dirt by man and his machines."

Powder River, which flows north to the Yellowstone River, is famous for its silt concentration—"too thin to plow, too thick to drink."

Wind and temperature extremes are influential in the erosion process, and Wyoming has ample of both. Minerals in rocks expand as they are heated and contract in cooling, the rate varying from one mineral to the next. The duration of geologic eras—Paleozoic, Mesozoic, Cenozoic—is found by studying radioactive minerals like uranium which disintegrates into lead and helium at a

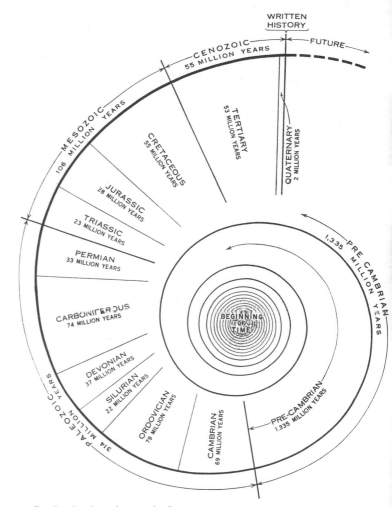

Geologic time is a spiral

uniform rate, thus the amount of lead tells the age of the deposit.

Fossil forms of plants and animals are also indicators of when the land was formed, and what it may contain. In Wyoming, this study of geology has been vital, because the face of the state literally has been her fortune: in mineral development, in tourism, and in agriculture.

105

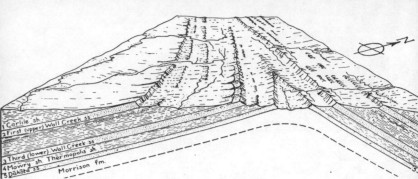

1 Carlile sh. 2 First (upper) Wall Creek ss.

3 Third (lower) Wall Creek ss. 4 Mowry sh. Thermopolis sh. 5 Dakota ss. Morrison fm.

Natrona County's Immense Anticline

Anticline pushed up to permit oil to pool beneath is shown in aerial view, left, in Natrona County. Above, diagram shows the rock formations in relationship to the dome in Oil Mountain anticline.

Control of such immense fields passed quickly from small operators to a few large concerns—Midwest, Ohio, Standard of Indians—which possessed the capital to develop. By 1917, Wyoming had 23 proven fields and five refineries, two at Casper, two at Greybull and one at Cowley. Standard, which took over Midwest operations at Casper, Laramie and Greybull in 1921, built its Casper refinery into the largest in the world. Refineries also were built in Laramie that year.

OIL INDUSTRY FILLS STATE COFFERS

While layered with mineral riches, Wyoming's fortune in the twentieth century was to be in oil and gas. Oil seeped to the surface in springs; it pooled in vast underground storage domes, the broad Salt Creek anticline visible on the surface. Natural gas was so abundant that ranchers found their artesian water wells catching fire. To get the oil, gas was torched in the air by the billions of cubic feet; oil and gas in the shafts hindered coal miners.

Within a single decade, oil became a significant factor in the state's economy; by 1917 it was second only to agriculture and just four percent below in gross income. There were then 23 proven fields, 475 producing wells and five refineries; major fields were Salt Creek, Grass Creek, Elk Basin, and Big Muddy. By 1922, Big Horn Basin counties were reaping two-thirds of their income from oil, production from Hot Springs, Big Horn and Park counties in excess of five million dollars a year. State production in 1923 was 44 million barrels.

Wildcat wells were bored in the 1880's, the first fittingly near Bonanza. But the fount of petroleum was to be no bonanza for independent drillers, however herculean their work or ambitious their dreams. They could not get the enormous financing needed to explore, to build markets, or to expand. This required capitalization of large corporations, development on a scale that multiplied fortunes by the hundreds of millions of dollars.

A market for Wyoming oil largess was slow in materializing, and for 30 years a cat-and-mouse game was played with leases at Salt Creek. The first claim notices were filed in 1883 by Stephen W. Downey of Laramie, who let them lapse while following his dream of gold. Cy Iba was next, four years later; Iba was a veteran of California gold fields, filing many oil claims and doing the required assessment work. The first actually to bring in oil was a Pennsylvanian, Phillip M. Shannon who drilled on the north edge of Salt Creek in 1889, the Shannon Field; he and associates built the first refinery.

As private interests accurately assessed the potential of Wyoming oil, so too did the federal government. It

Teapot Dome—A Scandal

Bribery, perjury, fraud, and stock market windfalls made Teapot Dome forever a symbol of corruption in government. The U.S. Secretary of the Interior himself took bribes for under-table leases on Navy oil worth billions. Wyoming oil men blew the whistle.

The man who took the bribes went to prison. Those who did the bribing went scot-free. Fraudulent oil leases were cancelled. President Warren Harding died before the last courtroom perjury was perpetrated. But friends of U.S. Attorney General Harry Daugherty, who made $30 million on the stock market, kept their profits; Daugherty said he only made $3,000. Sinclair Oil stock rose from 18¼ to 33½, then sagged once the secret lease was extracted from Fall's drawer.

Interior Secretary Albert B. Fall took $100,000 cash from oil man Edward L. Doheny in return for a lease on Wyoming's entire Elk Hills Reserve, plus Navy oil rights in California. Harry F. Sinclair, one-time pharmacist who made it big in oil $380,000,000 worth—also bribed Fall richly, $233,000 in bonds to get the lease on Teapot Dome, the Navy's 9,000-acre deposit.

Harding emerged from the scandal as inept and immoral, his successor Calvin Coolidge as weak for failing to deal decisively with the scandal. So when Herbert Hoover took office, he acted swiftly to erase the onus of Teapot Dome from the Republican Party. He stopped all leasing of government oil lands, and ordered a review of 20,000 leases; 12,000 were cancelled. Oil conservation policies were strengthened.

Teapot Dome thus was also a triumph of conservation over opportunism, as Sen. Gifford Pinchot had wanted Fall's head anyway, for his anti-conservation policies.

withdrew nearly one million acres in Natrona County in 1900 and 1901 from homestead entry. Taxpayers responded with a petition blitz; suits were filed and by 1920, Oil and Gas Leasing Act allowed development by private enterprise for one-eighth royalty; the state could now benefit from both production and royalties on federal oil. It should be noted that the federal government owned 72 percent of Wyoming mineral rights and 48 percent of the surface; the Union Pacific Railroad owned 4,582,420 acres.

New Years Eve in 1901 and 1902 were wild nights in the oil fields, but not with holiday jubilation. Those were grimly serious nights as men defending leases—or trying to jump claims—did it with fists, clubs, and gunfire. Thousands of fires marked the corners of claims. Armed gunmen patrolled for the big firms. Deadlines on developing claims under the Place Mining Law were met.

Violence continued in the oil fields for some 20 years, as wildcat concerns persisted and gushers continued to burst forth. In Elk Basin, some gushers shot 30 feet above the top of the derrick. Whips and clubs met late-comers to the 1915 discovery; one outfit was turned back at gunpoint, the teamsters forced to sneak around the rim in the dark to be in drilling position by morning.

The second Wall Creek sand produced oil at 2,200 feet in 1917, attracting new investors. Salt Creek's production rose to 5.5 million barrels. Lance Creek northwest of Lusk was opened. The discovery well at Grass Creek was brought in by "Uncle Jack" McFadyen for Ohio Oil Company, which had 214 wells producing 19 million barrels by 1924.

Shallow wells in the Byron and Oregon Basin Fields spurred feverish searches for the reservoir sources. Wells at Byron brought in light green petroleum at 700 to 900 feet; when pumped dry, they always refilled. In Oregon Basin Field heavy black asphalt oil flowed scantily—until a gusher at 3,700 feet produced 3,000 barrels a day.

New ability to drill deeper stimulated many oil enterprises. The proved reserve in Big Horn Basin increased to 600 million barrels, as oil was found deep in Tensleep sand of Elk Basin in 1934. Rich finds were made in deeper zones of Oregon, Little Buffalo, Gebo, and Steamboat Butte Fields. Across the state, near Upton, Col. Bob Gose was down to 4,855 feet in 1929—and still drilling.

Murphy oil well at Lander, 1903
Below, Spring Valley, Atlantic & Pacific

Oil: Good for What Ails

Wagon masters stirred up a batch of flour and oil to grease their axles whenever they passed the "great tar spring" near South Pass in the 1830s. This was to become the rich Dallas Oil Field 50 years later.

The earth was so full of oil it oozed to the surface along an oil belt of more than 200 miles.

This crude petroleum seemed to be a balm for nearly everything that ailed man or animal, from a sore toe to rheumatism. You could also burn it in your lamp or lubricate your shoes and machinery with it. It really worked, pioneers said, as a cure for sprains, bruises, cuts, sore throats, and eye trouble. It would remove corns. Furthermore, phials of this magic lubricant from the frontier were requested from far and near.

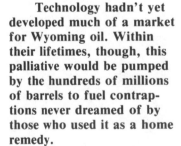

Technology hadn't yet developed much of a market for Wyoming oil. Within their lifetimes, though, this palliative would be pumped by the hundreds of millions of barrels to fuel contraptions never dreamed of by those who used it as a home remedy.

Copper Veins Played Out Soon in Sierra Madres

Copper in Wyoming's Sierra Madre Mountains (Park Range) created a dozen towns and a turn-of-century boom that ranked the state among the leading copper producers. Between 1899 and 1908 when the bubble burst, 23 million pounds of copper were taken from 50 mines. Mine & Smelter Company built the longest aerial tramway in the world, 15 3/4 miles, to move ore from the Pacific slope of the continental divide to the Atlantic slope, where the Godsell custom smelter converted it at Encampment.

Besides dwindling ore, a series of misfortunes caused the demise of the Encampment copper district. Until 1908, there was no railroad and all ore and supplies were freighted, thus costly transportation had taken a toll before copper prices fell in 1907. Accidents, overspeculation, and costly litigation contributed to the copper bust. Stock was oversold, companies went broke, and stockholders sued.

The green-veined or red-crusted ore had been noted long before George Doane and associates began the Doane-Rambler mine near Battle Lake in 1881. Six years later a sheepherder, Ed Haggarty, located the Rudefeha, an acronym of the first two letters in names of three men who grubstaked him—James Rumsey, Robert Deal, George Ferris—and his own name. This rich strike warranted construction of the smelter. The town of Encampment was electrified by power from the water flume system.

Brief interest in the Sunlight Basin spurred filing of claims in 1905. The Winona Gold and Copper Mining

Rudefeha copper camp, Carbon County

and Milling Company laid ambitious plans for a railroad to the mouth of Clark's Fork Canyon, where a reduction plant was to be built. Cost of the 100-mile railroad, however, was estimated at between $5,000 and $6,000 per mile, and the enterprise died.

At its height, the Encampment area mines and smelter employed between 3,000 and 5,000, so the closing was felt in Wyoming economy. Foreclosure proceedings in 1913 in federal district court drew a caustic comment from the Cheyenne Leader that the project "was picked up by crooks who exploited it three different times" for stock sales to Europeans and easterners. Machinery was sold as junk.

Not all the copper boom towns grew from scratch. Copperton existed as a supply station for cattle and sheep companies before the bonanza. And not all of the boom towns died. Encampment became a resort town for dude ranching. Nor were all of them typically brawling mining camps. Developers of Rudefeha decreed there would be

Processing copper ore in 1903 required complex smelter, as at this Grand Encampment plant in Carbon County

no saloons in town, so Dillion was born a mile up the mountainside.

Other copper camps were: Rambler near the diggings of Deane-Rambler mine, Elwood on the edge of the Medicine Bow Reserve, Riverside once a post office called Boggett and site of an 1851 trappers rendezvous, Ute Pass, Anaconda, and Battle near the Portland vein.

Battle began as a frieght stop on the trail to the Pacific slope camps and was the site of perpetual battles between miners and stockmen. The area once had two newspapers, at Battle and at Dillon. Elwood was a busy transfer point for passengers and freight headed deeper into the mountains; all travel in and out of the Sierra Madres for ten months of the year went by sled, because of the deep snow.

A monument to the electric light bulb was erected near Rambler. It was here on the bank of Battle Lake that Thomas A. Edison went fishing one day in 1878 and got his line tangled in a tree; he touched a match to the line to free his rod, setting fire to the platinum tip. It was long-burning, retaining its shape. He later substituted carbon filament and thus invented the incandescent bulb. And Edison was the butt of a miners' joke while there, since even in the 1890s tourists from the east were fair game. Pranksters placed stuffed rabbits around Edison's camp, which Edison and his companion blasted with shotguns the next morning, rejoicing in their hunting skill.

Heroes of the copper camps were the daring teamsters who trail-freighted everything that went in or out of the area, through mud, ice, and snow over perilous canyon roads. Teamster Jack Fulkerson once freighted 17,000 pounds of cable coil for the Rudefeha tramway to the 10,000-foot summit behind his long jerkline teams. All visitors to the copper mines traveled by stagecoach up and down steep canyons, around sharp curves that edged frightening drop-offs.

An Emu and a Coogly Woo

In the tallest treetops on the high mountain craigs dwelled the Screaming Emu, created by the clever editor of the Dillon Doublejack. The Emu was avidly sought by trophy hunters, and could swallow itself when pursuers got too near.

Grant Jones also invented the Bockaboar, a deadly mountain climber with legs short on one side—which could whirl at great heights causing dizzy spells in watchers. The Coogly Woo, a six-legged creature with a sharp tail, could bore holes in the ground with his tail and disappear.

These fanciful tales entertained copper camps as well as people in the east, for one of the Jones' missions was to publicize the mining district; he was hired by a mining company as a public relations man, as well as being the newspaper editor in Dillon. He did the first job well, and Dillon became famous; the second may have suffered but for an employee, Earle R. Clemens, as Jones' solution to being drunk on deadline was to re-run the previous week's issue "because everyone liked it so well."

Not only did Clemens often put Jones to bed and then get out the paper, but he once traveled 15 miles on snowshoes to carry the news to Encampment of the deaths of two linemen in a snow slide. Editor Jones died when a friend, hoping to calm his drunken delrium one night, gave him a fatal shot of morphine. Another writer friend, Willis G. Emerson, tried to make Jones' demise respectable by writing that he died by snow slide "in the savagery of a storm."

The talented, boozing editor, a Northwestern College graduate, had been a reporter for Chicago, St. Louis and Denver papers. He traveled west as a special correspondent, and found his niche in Dillon which was born of prohibition in nearby Rudefeha.

String teams of mules hauled copper from Grand Encampment smelter

Dig into the earth almost anywhere and there was coal, McDonald mine

COAL IN TREASURE CHEST MEANT ECONOMIC STABILITY

The first forty years of coal mining in Wyoming was spearheaded by the railroads, stoking their way across the state in clouds of manipulation and opportunism. State laws, federal regulations, and legal proceedings by the U.S. Justice Department ultimately put a stop to excessive freight rates, labor abuse, lack of mine safety, and fraudulent land acquisitions.

The layer of coal sandwiched into over 40 percent of Wyoming earth was first chipped into in 1868 by the Union Pacific, when it opened mines at Carbon and Rock Springs; mining began the following year at Almy near Evanston. After the whistle was blown on Wyoming Coal and Mining Company, owned by UP president Oliver Ames and five railroad directors, coal was mined in the name of the Union Pacific. Similarly, the only anthracite mining—at Cambria in the Black Hills of Wyoming—was an enterprise of the Burlington Railroad under a dummy corporation arranged by Frank Mondell who became U.S. Representative. Coal at Kirby caused the Burlington to lay tracks from Frannie across the Big Horn Basin.

Wyoming's coal reserve was great enough to supply market demands for 50,000 years to come, estimated the U.S. Bureau of Mines in 1927. This reserve exceeded by more than 70 times all the coal mined in the U.S. in the previous 114 years.

There was so much of it that it would resist early pillage and still provide a stable economic base for the new state. Not fluctuating markets, booms and busts, improper mining practices, nor gigantic land manipulations could undermine the long-term value of coal to Wyoming.

By 1910, there were 42 producing mines employing 8,106 people. Peak production in the first half of the 20th century was reached twice, in 1919 and again in 1945, when it topped nine million tons each year. In between, there were the lean '20s, mine accidents, labor troubles, bad air in the shafts, and even too much oil in one coal

> *'The whole region from the Platte to Pumkin Butte is covered with true lignite beds . . . coal for 50,000 years.'*

mine. But the immense reserves remained as economic insurance for the future.

Mine labor practices imported from the east had several effects in this individualistic commonwealth. First, it was easier, when everything was new, to pass laws monitoring mine safety and to apply labor restrictions. The 1886 territorial legislature did just that. It barred children under the age of 14 and women from working in the mines; it provided for inspectors, and required safety measures such as ventilation and escape openings. Second, the organization of labor, inherent to the mining industry, occurred in Wyoming and inevitably resulted in strikes; the strikes resulted in importation of foreign labor, both Scandinavian and Chinese.

Flexing its political power, the Union Pacific was able to obtain the services of federal troops against not only Indians, but also against striking miners. Most of the forts in Wyoming had been established for the convenience of the railroad; development of Wyoming and of the entire northwest, of course, was dependent on replacing the old wagon trails with steel track. Thus the state was at the mercy of railroads; as they created towns, they also broke them. Many were the early towns that,

Coal abundance built Rock Springs quickly into a brawling boomtown

Cambria coal mine in Weston County typically traced massive pattern in barren valley

like fragile prairie flowers, bloomed briefly and wilted in the frown of a railroad official. The Burlington extension to Buffalo was cancelled because of the "cattleman's war"; townspeople mobilized private capital and ran a spur to Clearmont for 28 years.

Wyoming's worst mine disaster occurred on June 30, 1903, when 171 miners died in an explosion at Hanna. Five years later, two explosions in the same mine killed 58—including the inspector investigating the first explosion. Another inspector sent by Gov. B. B. Brooks determined that the 1908 explosion was caused by the Union Pacific opening up too soon an entry in which a fire was burning. An earlier mine explosion in 1895 had killed 61 men at Red Canyon near Evanston. Men who lost their lives in less conspicuous coal mine accidents over the years are numberless.

Coal was a builder of towns, as well as a destroyer. Even the names of many of these once thriving boom-towns are lost in the past: Carbon, Aderville, Cambria, Cumberland, Dana, Almy, Spring Valley, Gebo, Crosby, and more. North of Sheridan alone there were eight—Carney, Monarch, Kooi, Acme, Model, Dietz, Han'some Town, and Andersonville. Others survived to pulse with the rhythms of demand: Kemmerer, Rock Springs, Gillette, Newcastle, Glenrock, and others.

Cass and steam shovels, Sunrise

111

IF YOU LIVED HERE,
YOU LIVED DANGEROUSLY

Miners at Dana gambled on flaming boxcars tearing across the Laramie Plains. Locomotives in 1889 had no stack nettings on their flues, and embers caught by the wind often ignited coal in the boxcars behind. Rear cars then were cut loose and the engine raced—wide-open throttle and flaming cargo—to the nearest water tower between Laramie and Rawlins . . ."place your bets, boys, will she make it?"

When work was slow in mines north of Thermopolis, the men manufactured homebrew, hidden in an unused shaft with an escape tunnel; false boxcar doors blocked the apparatus from view. At Cambria, miners awaited beer and liquor wagons from Newcastle every Saturday night; but even without saloons, Cambria felt the terror of the Black Hand, and avenged mafia murder with vigilante justice.

Lusty coal mining towns, kin to the mobile track-building towns, were precariously linked to the outside world by the big jerkline freight teams, but somehow they

drew like magnets notorious outlaws of the period, brawling miners from eastern coal fields, and migrants from across the seas, until they were veritable leagues of nations. In Cumberland, migrant Swedes worked from

> *'Splendid arias wafted up the canyons amid grunts and gunfire in the Black Hills of Wyoming at Cambria.'*

tents in a no-man's gap that once had separated Mexico from Oregon Territory; their bandmaster was a veteran of His Britannic Majesty's Coldstream Guard. The first J. C. Penney store was built in Kemmerer, mother store to the vast chain; Penney and Patrick J. Quigley, an Irish coal tycoon, founded the Aderville mine nearby. Finns built bathhouses at Almy and Spring Valley; thousands of Chinese left few graves, their bodies returned to China in urns.

Some women worried about the morals of such communities as Carbon, a "prairie dog town" on the Medicine Bow flats with its stone slab shoddies. When rip-roaring Calamity Jane hit town with her bull team, the women themselves failed to put up a united front—they wavered between condemning her morals and copying her fashion whims. In Carbon, men took Dutch Charlie Burris off a train and hung him for killing two deputy sheriffs in an aborted train robbery with Big Nose George Parrott's gang. Rattlesnake Jack swiped storekeeper Coffee Johnson's international display of Sahara sand, Dead Sea stones, and other oddities from around the world. During Ute Indian scares, women and children were hidden in mine shafts. Fire burned the town once, and women frantically sewed sandbags to control water in one of the seven mines. Carbon died on the turn of the century.

The coal boomtowns north of Sheridan were fifty years in the dying. Han'some Town and Andersonville went first, in the early '20s, Acme not until the '70s. Sheridan boomed and languished with the mines, as this cosmopolitan population of 25,000 camped precariously

Architecture of brewery at Green River clashed with setting

Miner's wives dressed in crackerbox houses to shop in Sunrise, 1902

on veins to be mined. One by one, they vanished—Carney, Monarch, Kooi, Model, and Dietz—only a wisp of white smoke from a deep-burning coal seam remaining to curl over the grinding shovels. The Echeta mine near Arvada boomed twice, in 1909 when horse-drawn ore cars plied its tunnels, and again in 1943 when 165,696 tons were taken by stripping a seam 20 feet thick.

Explosions too often rent the mountain quiet of the Sierra Madres in the jinxed mines of Almy and Spring Valley. Company store practices caused a strike in 1885, demonstrators quelled by Fort Bridger troops; the Union Pacific fired everyone and imported Scandinavians at two dollars a day. Later that fall, the railroad fired all striking miners at Rock Springs and Carbon, replacing them with Chinese. Prices at the company store had not been reduced as promised, to equalize a pay cut taken by the miners.

The earth gave forth too much treasure at Almy, as oil pooled in the shafts and gas formed in the mines. The oil seeped so abundantly that it had to be dipped out before coal could be mined. A San Francisco firm filed oil claims and the Union Pacific had to fight for coal mining privileges in federal court. UP won, but the oil and gas defeated mining efforts, and the mines were shut down in 1905.

Life was as quixotic as the towns—brutal flesh and blood one minute, a phantom the next. Splendid operatic arias wafted up the canyons in Cambria to mingle with the thuds and grunts and gunfire of Black Hand murders. Anthracite coal too hard to mine with a pick required mechanized cutting tools to feed 24 coke ovens in this community of 550 homes. The Burlington & Missouri branch line twisted up this maze of Black Hills canyons, once throwing a boxcar into the pharmacy. Famous freighters of the day found the hidden village, as did camp followers and "hardcase" outlaws: Wild Bill Hickok, Calamity Jane, Buffalo Bill, Wyatt Earp, Poker Alice and many others. The vein pinched out in 1929.

Abundant soda excited financiers in 1903 at Green River

Soda Four Feet Thick
'Cast Sweetness on Desert Air'

Discovery of large soda lakes in Sweetwater County attracted eastern and European capitalists as early as 1880.

Carbonate and sulphate of soda averaged six feet deep over 20,000 acres, according to an 1886 U.S. Geological Survey. Another lake showed solid soda four feet thick 50 feet from shore, and 14 feet thick farther out.

L. DuPont traveled from Pennsylvania to investigate and found Tom Sun holding his claim with a Winchester. DuPont bought out Tom and his partners, Boney Earnest and Frank Harrington who had filed in the early 1870s. DuPont received the first patent for soda from Wyoming.

An Englishman, D. Harvey Attfield, wasn't so persevering. After a cold 60-mile trip to the lakes, he returned to England, saying the trip from Liverpool to Rawlins was easy compared to the trip from Rawlins to the soda lakes.

"To cast sweetness on the desert air," a Chicago syndicate built the town of Johnstown, sunk shafts and timbered. Tons upon tons of soda were hauled by freight team to the rail head. When the railroad raised freight rates, work stopped and the property was abandoned. The property was sold under attachment.

Most stable was John D. McGill's operation. He built a refinery near three small soda lakes he had owned since 1895, hauled the soda to Casper by truck for shipment by rail.

Iron Ore Fed Steel Mills, Bentonite Sealed Oil Wells

Iron ore and bentonite were to be two enduring industries during the 20th century, consistent if not major minerals. Wyoming's low-grade iron ore supplied steel mills in Colorado and Utah; bentonite sealed walls in oil wells, bonded foundry sands, and comprised one-third of the nation's production.

Sunrise iron mine was opened at the turn of the century and by 1917, Colorado Fuel and Iron Company was producing 600,000 tons annually for shipment to its steel mill in Pueblo. Production remained at this level until 1941, when it went over one million tons, then dropped down again. Up to 300 miners were employed.

Iron Mountain in the Laramie Mountains promised rich rewards in 1870, when surveyor Silas Reed shipped ten tons to St. Louis for testing. The results were never published and the ore lay undisturbed for the next century. A small

ore shipment from Hartville began November, 1879.

Bentonite deposits were located in the Big Horn Basin—Cody, Greybull, Lovell—and across the state on the edge of the Black Hills before 1900. The soft-textured clay forms an emulsion which absorbs three times its weight in water, thus its use in many industries.

By 1929, the state was producing about 35 percent of the nation's bentonite, with four plants in the Upton area. Federal Foundry Supply Company built the first plant in 1928 at Jerome. Production in 1935 was 41,000 tons.

Other Wyoming minerals mined in limited quantities included phosphate, gypsum, telenium, vermiculite, limestone, anorthosite clay, jade, trona and silver. Uranium, discovered early in the century, was not to come into its own until 50 years later. Gypsum was used by early settlers to mold building blocks.

DREAMS OF GOLD TURNED OUT TO BE MOSTLY ILLUSION

Dreams of gold glittered enticingly at various times in Wyoming between 1851 and 1930, but all turned into will-o-wisps despite the rich Black Hills strikes just over the South Dakota state line and the enduring production of Homestake mine at Lead. Total gold production from 1867 to 1924 brought one and a quarter million dollars, but enough gold glittered in miners' pans to whip up several frenzies, to lure million-dollar investments and enormous futile effort. With rich strikes in every bordering state, it seemed logical that Wyoming was veined with a "mother lode." This logic too played out, as did every gold strike in the state.

Most promising was South Pass City, where for ten years over 1,500 lodes were worked by shafts, surface pits and placer methods. From 1863 until 1873 when South Pass lost the county seat to Green River, it flourished as a brawling cauldron of notoriety, hope, and dashed dreams.

More than any other Wyoming ghost town, it figured prominently in growth of the west. To thousands of Oregon Trail pioneers it was a significant milestone, and gold fever was at its peak by the time the railroad made the trail obsolete. John Browning, inventor of the automatic rifle, had a gun shop there; Daniel Boone's son, Dan, sold cigars and pipes.

Most costly effort to wrest gold from Wyoming occurred on Bald Mountain at the top of the Big Horns, where four companies in 1891 poured millions into equipment designed to turn flour gold into pay dirt. Up 65 miles of steep canyons, 24 bull teams pulled a Bucyrus amalgamator; five stamp mills once operated in the three-month season at this 9,000-foot site where snow was so deep miners wintering there had to tunnel up to reach daylight. Sheridan Consolidated, Bald Mountain Co., The Sheridan Mining Co., and Fortunatus were the ill-fated investors.

The first man reported to have found Wyoming gold was an old mountain man named LaPondre. He took a bullet pouch full of nuggets to peddle in St. Louis, claiming the gold was from a creek feeding Tongue River. He tried to sell the information but drank himself to death on liquor with which negotiators plied him.

Hope lay for awhile in a mountain known as The Horn, with geologic formations scrambled out of conventional order; rich samples of float rock once promised gold running as high as $3,000 a ton. No profitable mine was ever operated.

Cooke City's promise fizzled out in the 1860s. The

Sluicing for Wyoming gold

celebrated Carissa lode, said to have produced $6,000 a month, failed to pay operating costs in the Wind River Valley, its only legacy Fort Washakie; this military fort to protect the gold miners was first named Auger then Brown, set up at the site of later Lander then moved with the gold. Balloon of the highly-publicized Big Horn Expedition of 1870, to have comprised 2,000 miners escorted by 500 soldiers, was punctured by federal orders to stay out of Indian treaty territory; 116 men finally defied orders, packed in, but found no profitable gold. South Pass City was nearly deserted by then, and only two mines still operated at Alantic City. A gold rush on the Clark's Fork faded in 1889.

A 30-inch chunk of gold-flecked ore from Sunlight Basin won third place for gold ore at the World's Fair in St. Louis in 1895—however, a 1,000-foot tunnel didn't yield enough gold to be worth the effort. The same year, a three-mile ditch was dug by hand to bring water for hydraulic mining into Shoshoni Canyon; it was never used. The next year false hopes were raised on Encampment River, and in the Cloud Peak area in 1897.

The legend of the Lost Cabin Mine fueled hopes of a mother-lode for decades. Two Swedish prospectors brought three small cans of gold to Fort Conner in 1865; five companions had been killed by Indians. They said the gold came from the headwaters of Crazy Woman Creek—but they couldn't find the site again. Rattlesnake Jack, a wolfer, later claimed to have rediscovered their placer but not the gold source.

This stage ran Meteetsee to Thermopolis in heart of outlaw country

7. OUTLAWS LIVED BY TRAIL FRIENDS

Geography aided rustlers in Wyoming, and free-wheeling ranching practices lured many into a life of crime. The "long rope" of the needy or disgruntled cowboy often settled on unbranded calves; one part-time member of the Cassidy gang owned a cow said to have produced 14 calves every spring.

And, honest or not, small cattlemen and settlers sometimes were painted with the same brush as were rustlers, by threatened large-scale operators. Ranchers like the Frewens ran up to 70,000 head of cattle; the Pitchfork sprawled across the Bighorn Basin. Struggling homesteaders had nothing in common with residents of opulent Frewen's Castle except the spectacular scenery—the awesome red wall flanking the lower Big Horns, the infamous Hole in the Wall.

Most stunning view of the red wall is from the roadless tip of the mountains, which the many-mile-long wall parallels. In the sunken valley between the mountains and the vivid rock face, Cheyenne Chief Dull Knife hid his

people after the Custer Battle; the Cheyennes were attacked here along the Red Fork of Powder River in 1876, 200 lodges destroyed by MacKenzie's army. Earlier, the Sioux Chief Red Cloud called this the "last and best buffalo land of my people." It also was a convenient hideout for Civil War deserters.

Rustlers holed up here, or in a similar natural hideout at "Brown's Hole" (or Park) near the Wyoming-Colorado-Utah border—or they moved along the outlaw trail to "Robbers Roost" in southeast Utah, or high-tailed it for the Missouri breaks in Montana. Movements of stolen cattle and horses thus took many directions. Wyoming livestock was driven north for sale; "hot" Montana stock was sold in Wyoming.

"Flat Nose" George Curry is first credited leader of rustlers headquartering in the Hole in the Wall. By 1897, it had become Butch Cassidy's Wild Bunch which, for the next 15 years, robbed banks, post offices, trains, and both coach and freight stage lines. Cassidy was George

Sunken valley of the Hole in Wall was ideal for holding rustled stock.

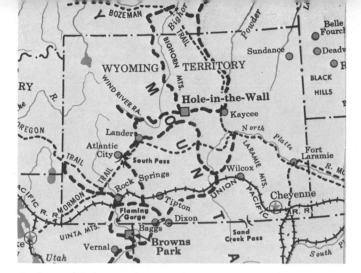

Outlaw trails meshed Wyoming

Parker, the "Butch" from a butcher job he once held in Rock Springs. He was a former Meeteetse homesteader whom neighbors thought was forced onto the outlaw trail by the German cattle baron, Otto Franc; Parker's signature is found on early petitions seeking county improvements. Otto Franc died of a bullet hole while alone on his ranch. Cassidy's equally notorious side-kick was Harry Longabaugh of Sundance, known as the Sundance Kid.

It was in the Hole in the Wall between Buffalo and Kaycee that the Wild Bunch trained their horses, developed their shooting skills—and invented the "altered horseshoe." A detachable clamp on the shoe could be removed, abruptly ending the trail for trackers of the law. Inaccessible canyons carved in the red wall conceal caves and caverns, secret trails which led to escape in all directions. In the sunken valley was ample graze for cattle or horses being held for trailing to "market."

Though both north and south ends open onto the prairie, the Big Horn Mountains bar entrance from the west, and there are only three openings in the long rampart which is crowned by a sheer 200-foot wall. The headwaters of the Middle Fork of Powder River have cut an opening through the wall, and a few miles south, natural erosion makes possible a trail over the top. The southern half of the wall looks impenetrable, but some believe this is the real "hole" in the wall, a hidden trail marked by a triangular white rock distinct against the red wall. A more likely explanation for the name is the western use of the word, a "hole" being a secluded grazing area—thus the sunken valley would be the hole. Wolves with dens in the canyons may have broken this last trail in centuries-old nightly hunting trips to the grasslands east of the wall. Rustlers shared the hole with the wolfers and one of them, Herb Andrus, reported a great gathering of wolf-packs one night totaling over 200 animals. Another wolfer took 600 pelts there in a single season.

Outlaw gangs swung a wide loop over Wyoming. Wherever there were cattle and horses to be rustled, army or mine payrolls to be hijacked, there was outlaw activity in Wyoming Territory and early statehood days. Among gangs criss-crossing the state were the Diamond Mountain Boys, Brush Creek, Rock Springs, Blue Mountain, Robbers Roost, the Red Sash Gang, as well as gangs bossed by Tip Gault, Tom Crowley, Mexican Joe Herrera, and McCarty. (continued on p. 118)

Posse Gave In to Hunger

Difficulties of trailing outlaws are illustrated by the following exerpt from U.S. Marshal Joe LeFors' account of pursuing train robbers. The safe on train No. 3 had been blown up at Tipton. LeFors led one of two posses giving chase. On a hot day in 1900, they tracked three riders and a packhorse across the Red Desert 60 miles to water at Brown's Park. From 'Wyoming Peace Officer'

"I thought Horton's horse about the best and I asked if he (Rawlins deputy sheriff) was willing to ride with me up to the robbers, or at least near enough to shoot their horses. Horton said, "I'll go with you right among them, and if they shoot our horses in surrounding them they will not ride away."

"It was then three o'clock. I told (U.S. marshal) Frank Wheeling, "We must catch them now or we will

Joe LeFors

have a long drawn-out still hunt for them, as in the Wilcox chase, and you know we never did pick up their trail again . . .

"They agreed to try to keep up if I would not run away from them. I took a faster gait, but soon saw the men strung for a mile and a half back, so I had to slow down again. I could hardly keep from calling Horton and riding off from them, but did not want to leave any grounds on which to be accused. We might have the whole chase on our hands, should the others not be able to follow our trail.

"As the sun got nearer the horizon I became nervous. At last I asked the nearest man to send word back that I only had three-quarters of an hour longer to trail in daylight. I pulled out at a fast gait . . . we got to Snake River at sundown and caught sight of the robbers going up a long slope on the other side of the river. They were heading downstream evidently starting out for the night ride, as the next morning we found that they had stopped about a mile down river and had lunch, re-adjusted the pack and, I believe, divided the money as there was a big amount of paper off express packages.

"There were now only twelve of us left out of the forty-two that started. We still had a few sandwiches, so we stayed on Snake River that night and the next morning I picked up the trail again, thoroughly disgusted.

"As the twelve men came up quite near behind me, I caught sight of some horses' legs under the brush . . . the parties had got a fresh mount and had gone on.

"The posse announced: 'We have the robbers' horses and can have them identified. They have fresh horses and we are about afoot. We have decided to go to Big Perkins' ranch for something to eat. We have not eaten anything since yesterday evening.'

"I told them I would run down the second relay of horses if they would follow me. . . . We turned back. I don't think I was ever so hungry in my life."

Bear Brown's rifle contained bear claw marks, testifying to a near escape by the bear hunter. In 1867, he supplied hay for Fort Phil Kearny five miles south of Stoney Creek. Aunt Jennie's Thimble, one of the southern Big Horn mountains, was named for his wife's thimble.

Jennie once entertained Jessie and Frank James—"nice, polite young men" who cleaned their plates with bread and turned them up-sidedown; she found a $5 gold piece under each plate.

Train passengers unmolested by robbers

(continued from p. 117)

One attempt to weld outlaws into the Train Robbers Syndicate was made in 1896, when 200 men from various gangs met in Brown's Hole. A contest ensued to see who would lead the syndicate—Butch Cassidy, then of the Diamond Mountain Boys, or Kid Curry, who was in the Hole in the Wall. Cassidy won, with several successful jobs, including the Castle Gate payroll heist from Pleasant Valley Coal Co. in April of 1897; the victory was clear-cut, as Curry and his gang of 75 were run out of the Hole during the contest year, the law hot on their heels. The syndicate became the Wild Bunch, which re-occupied the Hole, often using Thermopolis as a meeting point.

Justice in early Wyoming was not always exacting. "Law and order" sometimes was maintained without an arrest.

U.S. Marshal Joe LeFors once shared a stagecoach with an old friend, Purk (alias the Merino), whom he believed was one of three train robbers he had unsuccessfully trailed for several days. The two men reminisced . . . of riding the range, of a bulldog and mountain lion fight. At length the man, his neck and hands heavily freckled and filigreed with wrinkles, said he would leave Wyoming—never to turn another trick in the state.

Plans Leaked to Law

The careful planning that had to precede train and bank robberies often tipped off the authorities. Train robbers pre-rode the intended escape route, but Wyoming's population was so sparse and the vistas so wide it was almost impossible to move around anonymously.

When the Billy Nash gang of the Red Desert got ready to rob the Meeteetse bank, the law knew quite a lot about the planned operation. The gang placed one relay of horses north of Laramie, a second relay 20 miles south of Meeteetse on Willow Creek. Only the day of the robbery was unknown, and still the job was not prevented nor the robbers caught.

Said LeFors, late in life, "Those people are all dead now and I am willing that they be left to rest in peace. Some of their folks live right near me here in Buffalo; I will say that they were too much alive then for one man to follow."

This marshal held in respect many of his adversaries: "Those fellows put up something for something. It was always for a big stake. Their motto was, 'If we win we win, if we lose we will not need it' . . . I sometimes think the Curry gang were gentlemen compared with the crooks of today."

Life outside the law required accomplices, and the far-flung ranges of Wyoming and Montana were full of them. Stories abound of gold left under dinner plates, as well as astonishing acts of beneficence and courtesy by unknown riders. Undoubtly some of these strangers actually were well-known outlaws . . . the James brothers, Kid Curry, Butch Cassidy and the Sundance Kid. People on lonely ranches knew them for their humanity in a land where humans were scarce. Also, as LeFors noted, many of the outlaws left descendants who are part of the fabric of Wyoming today.

From the lawman's standpoint, it was nearly an impossible task to track an outlaw through Wyoming's mountain mazes, across the Red Desert or Powder River badlands, and to close in before he vanished into thin air. Besides adverse terrain, the country was settled by people to whom hospitality was a commandment and non-interference in the business of others a cardinal rule.

No rustlers, however, were as bold or successful as "All" McKinnley, who stole an entire trainload of cattle. "All" reached a pinnacle in rustling. As shipping boss for Spear Brothers in 1919, he billed a train load of cattle to Texas from the Northern Cheyenne Indian Reserva-

RUSTLERS IN SKIRTS

Cattle Kate (Ella Watson) who rode astride in skirts, below, was the first woman ever hanged; she built a herd by taking her pay for prostitution in rustled cattle. Belle Starr, a horse thief, was shot. So was "One-Arm" Owens at her Laramie homestead, by the cowman's hit-man Tom Horn. Two other female outlaws met justice from associates' bullets, Polly Bartlett who robbed miners by lacing their buffalo steaks with arsenic, and "Mother" Featherlegs who stashed stolen stock on her hog ranch south of Lusk.

Cattle Kate cast long rope

Horses hidden under sand rocks

Original Spear house on Bitter Creek

tion. Somewhere down the line, he changed its destination, and marketed the cattle where there was no brand inspector. The 25 carloads of cattle vanished without a trace. However, McKinnley later did time in the Montana State Penitentiary for stealing horses from the Sheridan railroad stockyards.

As was the Indian way, early white settlers prized rehabilitated outlaws, and many rustlers later became respectable citizens.

Kinch McKinney, for example, was regarded as a good, trustworthy man after he had served his term in the state penitentiary and went to work on a sheep ranch owned by the U.S. marshal at Rawlins. But Kinch held Cheyenne law at bay for awhile. He didn't think he got a fair trial, and neither did his young attorney. While Kinch was awaiting transport to the pen, someone slipped him a .45 Colt. Failing a break from the Cheyenne jail, for three days he shot at every jailer or deputy in sight. Finally, with all the other prisoners nearly starving, he gave up his six-shooter in return for immunity from prosecution.

Casper Lawman in the Gang

The town marshal of Casper, Phil Watson, was arrested for horse stealing in 1889 by sheriffs from Douglas and Sundance. Three others from Watson's gang were also arrested and convicted; this organized gang operated in Montana, northern and central Wyoming, gathering northern horses and driving them into Sweetwater county, where they were held on a Fish Creek homestead, then brought to Casper where Marshal Watson sold them or shipped them to an eastern market.

Watson had put on quite a show as sheriff, being the officer to cut down the bodies of rustlers James Averell and Ella Watson (no relation but perhaps a partner), who were hung by Sweetwater cattlemen that summer. With the aid of gang members, he was able to impress Casper people with his "courage" in backing down "bad men" on the streets of Casper.

The law was violated both by the haves and the have-nots, outlaw gangs and wealthy ranchers using similar violent methods. Johnson County's "war," for example, was but one episode in the cattlemen's statewide land grab, during which they tried to tar settlers with the same brush as rustlers, and made carnage of the sheep business—the state's leading industry. Both efforts backfired, turned public sentiment against cowmen, and brought federal intervention.

HOW EMPIRES BEGAN

Collins ranch camp early 1900s

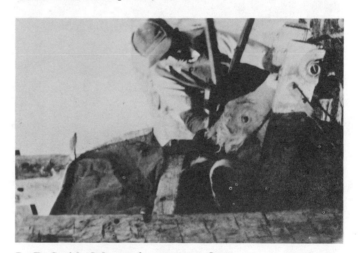

L. B. Smith dehorns in squeeze chute

Harry Fuller, Tom Kendrick, Slim Osburn branding in 1923 at LX-Bar

119

If cattlemen didn't brand their calves, someone else would

Steers on early drives wild and big

Roundup east of Sundance 1887

Supplies packed to line-camps

8. COWMEN FOUND GRASS

Wyoming cattle business attracted men of widely diverse backgrounds: aristocratic and obscure, the wealthly as well as $30-a-month cowhands, painters, plumbers, and steamboat pilots. All were gamblers, for the risks were great but the grass was free. Some of the poor became rich; some of the rich became poor.

Until the Indians were driven out of northern Wyoming, by 1878, the big herds generally stayed in the southern tier. Once the battles were over, the buffalo were dead, and the Indians moved to reservations, the cattle streamed north along the Bozeman Trail.

As always, the scholars were not far behind, and it is interesting that Wyoming cattlemen were studied as early as 1885. Historians interviewed 53 of the state's "typical" cattlemen and found 40 American and 13 foreign born. Six of the latter came from England, two from Ireland, one each from Canada, Scotland, Germany, France, and Russia. The Americans came from 16 states, Maine to Missouri, Ohio to Texas. The historian Hubert Howe Bancroft also recorded occupational backgrounds even more diverse: army men, miners, teachers, freighters, and law enforcement men.

Had the interviewers returned ten years later (after the lessons of brutal winters), they would have found a survivor with different attitudes, tougher in many ways. The hard winter of 1886-7 stimulated changes already underway in ranching techniques. Thus the Wyoming climate forced cattlemen who were to survive to accommodate themselves to abrupt change, a plains Indian trait of which they were unaware.

Astonishing paper profits, visions of a life of ease as cattle multiplied their profits—plus the novelties of the west—attracted many without the know-how to survive. "Virtually every easterner with a few thousand dollars and the consumption wanted to enter ranching," noted Michael Slattery, one livestock man. Richard Trible of New York City visited college friends at the Cheyenne Club in the 1880s and wrote glowingly to "Dear Mommie" of the stimulating companionship and the financial returns he saw on paper. His friends left the comforts of the club once to help with a roundup, and Trimble wrote of the full moon over a roundup scene, coyotes wailing in the distance as night riders circled the herd.

Another less romantically drawn was Joseph M.

Cow ponies filled hitching post at Gillette store in 1907

'The elements never let up on cattlemen who expected to make a fortune by working a couple of roundups a year.'

Carey who came to Wyoming territory in 1869 as U.S. District Attorney. He saw men building quick fortunes in livestock and urged his brother in Philadelphia to enter cattle and sheep raising. He cited a man who, in two years, became wealthy by using borrowed capital —"anyone with capital and a willingness to stick for five years will, with ordinary luck, be worth $100,000." Carey did just that, achieving prosperity, as well as offices of governor and U.S. Senator.

Few of the first wave of cattlemen did survive, however.

One notable exception was John B. Kendrick, a Texas cowpuncher who built 200,000-acre ranch properties and held them to four generations; he also became governor and U.S. Senator. Another exception was Oliver Wallop who, with inherited wealth and aristocratic mein, built the biggest British-owned ranch, became the Earl of Portsmouth, and also left Wyoming property unto four generations; his grandson, Malcolm, became U.S. Senator from Wyoming.

Wallop joined in grandiose ventures with other British cattlemen whose kingdoms eventually crumbled. He and Malcolm Moncrieffe from Scotland supplied horses for the Boer War, shipping 20,000 horses in 1901 and 1902. Sir Moreton Frewen actually built a castle on the Wyoming plains; he married Clara Jerome whose sister Jenny became the mother of Winston Churchill.

The following year Sir Horace Plunkett, an Irish member of the British Parliament, established Union Cattle Company also in southwestern Johnson County. And in 1891 Peters and Alston began the Bar-C holdings; foreman Hank Devoe's wife, May, was the first woman to live in the Hole in the Wall. On the south end of the "hole" along Buffalo Creek, Ed Huck began a large-scale operation from his elaborate ranch home nicknamed Fort Huck. The Fraker family homesteaded off the north end of the red wall.

An End to Free Land

Very few big investors had bothered about the acquisition of the land itself. The Frewens were evicted by homesteaders. The concept of land as "the vast public domain" was no longer realistic. The big operators had failed to learn another lesson taught by this exacting land. Consequences of overstocked ranges, loss of water sources, and the toll of severe winter blizzards were other lessons many learned too late—or not at all.

Cattlemen built and directed the cattle kingdom, even though the myths focused on his hired hand, the cowboy. Historians and popular writers all dug into the pastoral past of the livestock vocation to explain its emergence in the west. What writers failed to take into account were climate and terrain—coping with these two elements required qualities not necessarily needed in more benevolent lands. Qualities essential in Wyoming were independence, and the ability to solve problems alone and on the spot.

The flow of British capital into Wyoming was stimulated by modification in British corporation laws regarding investment trusts. In 1877, James MacDonald, an expert in animal husbandry, was sent to America by an Edinburgh newspaper to analyze production; England then established the Royal Commission on Agriculture, which also sent investigators who took back surprising reports of the "Great American Desert" (an early term for Wyoming's Red Desert) stocked with thousands of cattle.

At first, when Wyoming range was new to everyone, problems such as disease, overgrazing, and predators were dealt with by trial and error. Vast prairie dog towns posed danger to horsemen, as a running horse could easily break a leg in the holes; too, the sly creatures denuded large areas of grass. Wolves were still prevalent, and the shrewd grey killers were blamed for loss of 700 calves in one outfit; cows were found with chunks bitten out of their hips, their tails chewed off.

Heel flies chased cows into waterholes where old or weak animals bogged down. The warble grub of the heel fly grew under the cow's hide, reducing the market value by pitting the hide. Bloating, blackleg, and lump jaw could be devastating. Lump jaw, caused by bacteria, honeycombed the jawbone. Rattlesnakes often bit

Cowboys relax at chuckwagon with trail drive camped on water

feeding cows in the jaw, making it swell to resemble lump jaw.

By 1925, the dreaded scab disease spread by cattle movements throughout the northern Great Plains. Cattlemen were required to dip their cattle in a solution of sulphur, lime or pine tar and oil mixed with water. Some of these dipping vats remain, and old-timers in Wyoming say pushing wild range cows into ten feet of dipping solution was even harder than getting them to swim Powder River. It was a chaotic scene, with cattle run into corrals erected on the prairie, then pushed into a crowding pen, and shoved into the vat. They had to be totally submerged. This was repeated three times, ten days apart in 1925 and again in 1930.

Cattle Denuded Prairies

Ranges were overgrazed critically as stockmen dumped tens of thousands of cattle on the range, contributing to the disaster of 1887. Cattle went into the winter in poor condition. That was the winter cattle staggered into the streets of little towns and froze standing up. As Wyoming's climate held the trump cards, cattlemen prayed for a chinook, the warm "black wind" of the Indians that could bring sudden relief from arching black clouds. The worst storm blew in January 28, a three-day blizzard that froze ice over nostrils and snuffed out the breath.

Still the black wind did not come to rescue cattle fortunes, and when spring came, the stench of decomposing beef wafted out of every coulee in northern Wyoming. Creeks were dammed with carcasses. Rawhide lay over the land for years. Losses had run 30 to 90 percent.

The elements never let up on cattlemen who expected to make a fortune by working a couple of roundups a year.

Drought, grasshopper and cricket scourges were recurrent. Price fluctuations and physical setbacks plagued the cattle and sheep industry. On paper it looked easy: fortunes were made on the three-month trail north —but lost in a hard Wyoming winter. Steers that sold in the south for $12.50 could bring $75 each in Chicago after two years on northern graze; the quality of grasses resulted in both growth and finish. Shipping losses, too, were less when cattle were in better shape than they could be on southern ranges.

Hay, or "stuffing," was found to be a necessity, and ranchers began putting up wild grass. They planted alfalfa. They began rotating their grazing, bringing cattle into protected creek and river bottoms for winter, where the grass grew more lush and it was easier to feed.

The Wrench Ranch just north of Sheridan put up its first alfalfa crop, fortuitously, in 1885; Doc Spear threshed there and took his pay in seed; the following year Spear put up 125 tons of hay at his Big Horn homestead and by spring was able to buy cattle at $10 a head because he had a way to feed them; the Spear Brothers ranch was on its way.

The hoped-for railroad to aid in marketing, connecting Sheridan with Miles City, Montana, never materialized. But in 1924, there was still hope. "This railroad will be a fine thing for Denver as well as for Montana and Wyoming, and people generally do not appreciate how much it will improve conditions here," said the market letter of The American Live Stock and Loan Co. It also deplored the proposed effort to compel liquidations by stockmen with loans on cattle: "It will depopulate the cattle-producing country and destroy the value of ranches for some time to come." Prices in 1923 had risen to $10.28 per hundredweight, from $8.05 in 1921; the bottom fell out that year with a drop from $15.35 the previous year.

W. B. Spear

Ranching Created Towns

Stockyards grew up at rail shipping points, and some towns were born that later died when railroads cut service and stockmen began trucking their cattle to market. Still to-

Child chases bum lamb at early ranch near Fairbanks

Branding, early 1900s

day, in yards like those in Sheridan, Lusk and Casper, on sale day the noise of bawling cattle being hustled through the chutes is the same as 100 years ago.

Largest outfit in the Gillette area at the turn of the century was the 4-J Keeline ranch, running up to 90,000 head on a range that stretched from Spotted Horse, Wyo., to Edgemont, S.D. The Keelines ran as many as seven roundup wagons and shipped from Moorcroft a trainload of cattle every week in the fall. The Keeline outfit came originally from Texas, trailing herds of young steers into the Nebraska sandhill country; these were shipped as grass beef when mature and fat. The outfit gradually worked north and west, making its last stand 18 miles southwest of Gillette.

So vast was the Keeline spread, it was not unusual to find eight and nine-year-old steers which had never been branded. On the twice-yearly roundup, five to ten cowboys worked each area under a roundup boss. A chuck wagon and a bedwagon accompanied each crew; other ranches added their own crews and wagons. Cattle were gathered and sorted into three categories: branded cattle, unbranded, and those ready for market. A beef was killed every few days to feed crews; the cook took the prime cuts, giving the rest of the beef to Sioux Indians who often rode on the fringes of a roundup.

Spear Brothers cattle company, which ran up to 50,000 head of cattle, was run by Doc Spear and his brother. The ranch at Big Horn was purchased in 1885, with other ranches on Powder River below Arvada, near Clearmont, at Clear Creek, and near Lodge Grass, Montana. Much of the Crow Indian reservation was leased by the company, and sealed bids had to be submitted to Washington, D.C. every two years. Spear lived in Sheridan in a 23-room house with four baths.

Routine of a Roundup

The grinding routine of a roundup began with breakfast at 4 a.m.; the cook served dinner at 10 a.m., and supper at 4 p.m. Long days were spent gathering, sorting, counting, and branding, dipping and shipping. A roundup wagon typically had 15 cowboys, each with 10 saddle horses. This horse cavvy was held, along with cook wagon horses, in a rope corral at night, with night hawks riding patrol. Wranglers caught the day's mounts each

A Bronc-Peeler's Tricks

When the horse business was at its height to fill British and U.S. military orders, Bill Briles was one of the wild-riding Powder River bronc-peelers whose ingenuity and skill filled cavalry orders early in this century.

Roundups were held two or three times a year to cut out horses for sale and to shape up the stud bunch, usually started from the river and working one tributary each day. The range, or "cold-blooded" horses were strong, sturdy and smart—"no way we could outrun those horses if a bunch broke and turned back," Briles said.

Usual strategy was to bunch the gathered horses in strange territory until they quieted, then one man rode in the lead, one on each side of the bunch, with a rider or two behind. To gather a bunch of 25 to 100 head, the men ran them out of the draws, posting riders to turn them; later, "we tailed them out with planes and bombed them with flour."

Tricks of the horse business included one Briles used to bring in 12 wild horses by himself from a ranch 25 miles away; he wired the tail of each horse to the foretop of the horse behind. Mares that became bunch-quitters sometimes were "kneed," a knife turned to separate the muscle; this did not damage the hide, and the horse could walk and trot, but the muscle didn't grow back—"unless it was absolutely necessary, I never liked to see it done," Briles explained. One bronc caused so much grief that he finally was taken to the river and ridden on ice—"you couldn't tell which was up and which was down, but that horse never bucked again."

A herd of 60 Angora goats brought up from Texas by Thad Hale was traded back and forth among the bronc peelers of Wyoming's early days. Briles traded a team of broke work horses for the goats, a bobsled and a set of harness, and so ran goats for two years.

Bill Briles

123

One Texas cowboy, bored by miles of driving a wagon, could not resist roping a buffalo. Astonished riders watched the buffalo dragging the buckboard's rear wheels and axle east, while the mules stampeded west with the front wheels and pole.

S Bar T wagon from Lipscomb County, Texas, on Wolf Creek, 1896

morning and turned the rest to graze. Few of these horses were gentled, and bronc riders often worked the cavvy, turning green broncs into passable saddle horses.

Roundup cooks were usually men who had spent years on the range and could not be bullied. The boss' wife visited Bill Smith's camp one day, noticed his bread was ready to work down, and reminded him. Bill kicked the whole pan of dough into a nearby lake. He was said to have shot and killed another cook who came at him with a stove hook. Another notorious Wyoming cook was Crit Biddick, whose puddings—"Son-of-a-bitch-in-a-sack"—are still remembered fondly.

Fall rains added to the cowboy's misery, and for one wrangler the last straw was seeing a sheepherder sitting dry in the sheepwagon, as he sat a wet saddle driving cattle to shipping pens. He was Francis Cowper, bronc rider, government trapper, trick rider—and sheepman: "It rained and rained. We crossed a sheep ranch where the sheep grazed peacefully, the herder in the wagon. I decided the life of a sheepherder was better than that of a cowboy. I drew my time and quit." Cowper had also worked for the Nefsy ranch on Wind River, going for 24 days once in the South Beaver Creek line camp without seeing another person.

Besides breaking horses, Cowper trained his own stunt horse—and was probably the only cowboy in Wyo-

ming fired for changing the oil in his horse. He bought an abused bucker after the horse kicked in the fender on its owner's new car; Cowper trained Scrappy as a stunt horse and rode him for 19 years. During Scrappy's early training, Cowper worked at Osage for Julius Brock and, after the other hands went to work one morning, the boss found Cowper in the corral with his saddle horse standing on four blocks. Cowper's explanation: He was changing the horse's oil. Brock suggested he turn in his time.

With the drought of 1919, the trek from Texas reversed itself. Wyoming cattle had to be shipped to Texas for feed. Many ranchers like the Spear Brothers started dude operations to keep their heads above financially troubled waters.

Wyoming Horses Gain Repute

Horses from northern Wyoming gained repute as a result of careful breeding and specialized marketing. The high calcium content of soil and water was believed responsible for building strong young horses. Horse shows and polo spurred development of horses for these purposes. Dude ranching offered a market for a gentler version of the stockman's cutting and roping horse.

Lively horse sales combined entertainment and business, as unbroken horses were ridden through the sales

---

'I CAN RIDE ARIE ONE WITH A PACKSADDLE'

Packsaddle Jack was an idea man who once rode for Oliver Wallop on Otter Creek range.

He handled a meat delivery one deep-snow winter by tying a bronc to a post, wiring a single-tree to a dry cow hide, and harnessing the horse to this. He then put a quarter of beef on the hide and sat on it, turning the bronc loose.

To stop butchering losses from the herd of the St. Labre Mission he simply shot up the entire landscape with his .30-.30 rifle on moonlit nights.

Packsaddle Jack (Morris) had come up the

Texas trail in 1880, losing contact with his family. He advertised for kin in southern newspapers and was visited soon by a sister with many small children with colds. Packsaddle lined up the children on a long bench with a flour sack. Each time Packsaddle looked their way, they blew their noses in unison.

He acquired his nickname after answering a cowman, when asked if he could ride the outfit's rough string, "Indeed, I can ride arie one with a packsaddle." He did just that.

Wyoming-bred horses gained world reknown for endurance

ring as sellers tried to pass them as saddle horses. Ranch buyers sometimes hired their own riders, and people often passed the hat when volunteers put on spectacular rides. Range horses were rounded up each spring and fall, the colts branded, and horses to be used or sold were cut out of the wild bunches.

A trail of 500 Wyoming horses to Dewey, S.D. for shipping was typical. Three riders from the Sterling ranch moved them the first day to Osage, where they were corraled near the railroad tracks; a train in the night spooked the horses and they hit the corral, knocking it to the ground. The next day was spent gathering them and penning them in the stockyards at Newcastle. On the third day, related one rider, Monte Quest, "We trailed east along the road. Newlyweds in a brand new Ford drove a little too close to one old mare. She kicked out both headlights."

The Beckton Stock Farm on the divide between Goose and Soldier Creeks dates to 1879, when surveyor George T. Beck found the land while buffalo hunting. He built Beckton flour mill with stone burrs brought from Scotland, and raised sheep, thoroughbred horses and cattle.

The Forbes brothers of Boston, grandsons of Ralph Waldo Emerson, bought Beckton by 1890 as a western home. Until the late 1920s it was run by hired managers; then William Cameron Forbes began breeding Rambouillet and Lincoln sheep, Clydesdale horses, Shorthorn and Hereford cattle. A new cattle breed, Red Angus, was started by Waldo E. Forbes and his wife when they took over the ranch in the 1930s. They gathered 18 red heifers and 10 red bull calves culled from leading Black Angus herds. They founded the Red Angus Association of America.

Rope corral held the horse cavvy at night during early roundups

125

'No good stockman ever deliberately overgrazed—and no stockman lived who never did it.'

Kendrick inaugurated as Governor of Wyoming

Senator Kendrick's Long Trail

One of America's Horatio Alger stories was that of Sen. John B. Kendrick, the poor Texas boy who built a cattle empire overlapping the Wyoming-Montana state line. He parleyed disaster into wealth and political power.

His descendants today operate ranches stretching for 200,000 acres through four counties in Montana and two in Wyoming. They comprise an oval on the map 22 miles in one direction and 36 in the other. Both Kendrick Cattle Company and Kendrick Oil Company are family operated.

As a southerner, Sen. Kendrick helped shape the state's Democrat Party along lines later embraced by the Republican Party. He worked energetically in Washington D.C. to curb the power of big meat packers and in 1919 demanded federal supervision of the meat packing industry, obtaining passage of the Kenyon-Kendrick bill in 1920. He opposed the League of Nations in 1919, and secured for Wyoming the $23 million Casper-Alcova reclamation project.

Always a vote-getter, he once told a frantic rally organizer, "I got more votes out there on the manure pile than I will inside," as the rally was to begin and Kendrick still talked at the corrals with cowboys.

A powerful voice in the U.S. Senate, he forced the Teapot Dome oil lease scam out of the closet in 1923, precipitating the nation's biggest political scandal. The shameful affair began with the U.S. Secretary of the Interior, wending its seamy way up to the U.S. Attorney General's office and the President of the United States. Under-table leases of Elk Basin and the Navy's reserve at Teapot Dome—in return for a $333,000 bribe to Interior Secretary Albert Fall—was, Kendrick said, "so disastrous to the national interest and so outrageous in its terms it could never have been negotiated and executed in the open." Fall's excuse that Navy oil was being drained off by nearby leases could not be justified; there weren't any, as Kendrick pointed out. He condemned the fraud as "viciously and criminally wasteful," demanding that the leases be cancelled and the guilty punished.

Eula (left) and John (right) with ranch hands

'Conserve' Was His Law

As a rancher, Kendrick lived by this rule and passed it on to future generations: "No man has the right to use the land as if he was going to be the last to use it."

He grazed carefully, established vast hayfields, husbanded the wildlife, and conserved the precious water. Live beaver were captured and transported in barrels to new locations, where they built new dams to retain water. Hayland at the "K" ranch on Powder River has been under irrigation since 1915.

Born in Cherokee County, Texas, to an impoverished family, Kendrick learned first about livestock from old horses and milk cows. At age 22, he helped drive a herd of Texas longhorns to Running Water Creek in Wyoming Territory; the 1,500-mile trip from Matagorda Bay on the Gulf of Mexico took five months. Two-year-old steers had to be wrestled down for branding by ropers on foot, as horses were scarce. The young cowpuncher began the drive, ill with an intestinal abscess. It was the first of two long cattle drives he made from Texas to Wyoming.

OW roundup wagon carried bedrolls and gear

Chris Grinnell rescues bogged cattle, 1900

He worked for Charles Wulfjen, inspired by Wulfjen's rags-to-riches story—a penniless orphan who acquired substantial Texas and Wyoming ranch properties. Wulfjen's little daughter, Eula, climbed on the young rider's knee when he went to her father's ranch looking for work. At seventeen she married him.

Kendrick's frugality became legendary. He washed and darned his "roundup socks," bought at twelve pair for a dollar. While his cowpunchers were drinking, gambling and shooting up Lusk, he was back at the wagon reading the books he always carried in his saddlebags. Already in 1885, he had started his own herd—with $150 he had saved, five months' salary.

When Wulfjen sold his cattle interests, Kendrick became range foreman for the Converse Cattle Company near Lusk. Those Wyoming ranges were overgrazed by 1884, and Kendrick was sent to scout the north country for new range.

Isolated Land Selected

This was a turning point of Kendrick's career, for the land he carefully selected, land off the settler's path with water and sheltering hills, was to become his own after the winter of 1886-87 bankrupted Converse. Appointed receiver in the bankruptcy, Kendrick actually made money for Converse Company during bankruptcy proceedings. He saw a statement of condition on the Chicago bank in which company funds were held; three days before the bank went broke, he wired an order to transfer all funds to another bank. One more hunch paid off.

Kendrick then bought the OW brand, the machinery, and what Converse cattle had survived the winter. The ranch hands stayed with him. In the five-room log home at the OW, his bride helped with ranch records, and both of them studied. Eula cooked for the roundup crews and heard her children's lessons, for there

was no school. Later, in the governor's mansion and in Washington D.C., she was an able and elegant hostess.

Methods of Adding Land

From Hanging Woman where a complex of corrals made its own geometry in the creek bottom, Kendrick began to put together the pieces of an empire.

Several options were open to a man of his imagination—and he used them all. One was the homesteading route. Ranch hands established claims; Kendrick helped them prove up, then he bought the claims. Desert claims required water works; timber claims required planting of trees; all required a dwelling.

Another means of acquiring key tracts involved script issued to soldiers as a bonus for military service. A rancher surveyed the land he wanted, wrote the broker, Barnes Bros. of Minneapolis; the Barnes's filed a veteran on the property, then sold it to the rancher. Northern Pacific grant lands were added when the federal government granted the NP railroad such lands as it chose from the public domain—thus Kendrick acqquired NP land 200 miles from the railroad route.

Reservoirs, roads and irrigations canals were built on three ranches by 1910, with the "K" and LX-Bar Ranches on Powder River used as winter feedlots for cattle summered on the OW. The stately LX-Bar on the west bank had buildings of pale yellow stone quarried nearby, designed by stone-mason Oscar Husman who trimmed them in red sandstone.

"Happy is the man whose business is his hobby," the rancher often told his children, Manville and Rosa Maye. Kendrick founded the First National Bank in Sheridan with A. S. Burroughs, but sold out when he found banking gave him no pleasure.

Kendrick was elected to the U.S. Senate on a write-in vote; he easily won re-election to two more terms and died in office in 1933.

WAR ON WOLVES

Wolves, gorging on 75 million buffalo carcasses, thrived in the hide hunter's largess. By the time the buffalo were gone, cattle overgrazed Wyoming ranges—and they were tasty, too. Stockmen, however, had the power of Manifest Destiny behind them. They went after the wolves, and by 1900 an estimated one to two million were killed.

When a pelt brought only two dollars, wolves were killed mainly to protect traplines and food caches. Mountain man Jim Bridger told of being jumped by wolves as he set a trap for beaver. Bridger ran for the nearest tree and climbed out of reach. After milling around for awhile, all the wolves departed, leaving one to guard him. A half hour later, said Bridger, the other wolves returned with a beaver, which began chewing down the tree.

Bounties rose as ranges were stocked, until they reached $150 by 1910 and many men earned grubstakes wolfing. A $150 investment for an outfit could be parlayed into three thousand dollars in two or three months. Furthermore, there was always the possibility of "wolf farming", as advocated by The Wolf Hunter's Guide of 1800 by Ben Corbin. Beyond advising raising wolves and leaving females to breed again, this guide had little to say about how to kill wolves—but much about the Bible, free trade, the privilege of living in a democracy, and the foulness of the wolf's ways. It put the sanction of Manifest Destiny on wolfing.

Wolves Were Worthy Foe

Wolf qualities both enraged and earned the respect of those with most at stake—stockmen and wolfers. Sometimes it appeared the wolf was getting revenge, as when it had lost a mate or a foot to traps. Other times, the wolf seemed to tease pursuers, glorying in its skill at eluding and its strength in winning endurance trials. Some of these trials lasted for years, with the wolf laying a methodical pattern of destruction.

One hunter futilely chased a wolf 150 miles during two days, getting fresh horses from ranchers along the way; the wolf backtracked, circled, used ice and snow, mud and sand beds to hide his tracks, and once hid in an old horse carcass. Another hunter trailing a big wolf saw it carry a heavily poisoned chunk of meat, later found where the wolf had eaten it to the bone—and went right on killing livestock.

Some wolfers expressed sorrow when an especially challenging-wolf was run to ground. The dictates of their task revolted many men; "It was awful work, but God, that was terrible big money," said one. Of the killing of pups, another mused, "I have done it many times, but nothing goes more against the grain . . . potential murderers they may be, but at this stage they are just plump, friendly little things that nuzzle you with pleased whines."

Wolves travel counter-clockwise in great circles, 20 to 30 miles in diameter. Their territory may be 250 miles. The timber or grey wolf native to Wyoming weighed 100 pounds or more. They apparently mated for life, becoming loners if the mate was killed. Trappers rated them highly intelligent with keen noses. Litters numbered 10 to 20.

128

Aesop Fable: Crane pulls out bone stuck in Wolf's throat. "Your reward? It's that I didn't bite your head off."

Discouraged after an unsuccessful day of hunting, a hungry Wolf met a well-fed Mastiff. He could see that the Dog was having a better time of it than he was and he inquired what the Dog had to do to stay so well fed. "Very little," said the Dog. "Just drive away beggars, guard the house, show fondness to the master, be submissive to the rest of the family and you are well fed and warmly lodged."

The Wolf thought this over carefully. He risked his own life almost daily, had to stay out in the worst of weather, and was never assured of his meals. He thought he would try another way of living.

As they were going along together the Wolf saw a place around the Dog's neck where the hair had worn thin. He asked what this was and the Dog said it was nothing, "just the place where my collar and chain rub." The Wolf stopped short. "Chain?" he asked. "You mean you are not free to go where you choose?" "No," said the Dog, "but what does that mean?" "Much," answered the Wolf as he trotted off. "Much."

—Aesop

Preference for Horse Meat

Although blamed for astronomical cattle and sheep losses, one Wyoming wolfer said they preferred horses, especially colts and yearlings. Wolves were skilled at cutting out a mare and colt from a horse band, stampeding the rest before they could form a protective ring. They would hamstring the mare as she guarded her colt, then the pack was soon at her throat. Some entire colt crops were lost in this way. Sixteen grey wolves jumped cows off sand rocks to kill them one morning at the mouth of Horse Creek.

In their publicity campaigns to secure state and federal funds for bounties, stockmen began blaming any economic shortfall on the wolf, reporting losses that were mathematical impossibilities. The Wyoming legislature requested help from Congress—and got it in 1915. The worst outrage probably occurred in Montana, which combined a $10 bounty (cattlemen were to get $15) with a program which spread scarcoptic mange; the state veterenarian was required to innoculate wolves with mange and turn them loose. This law was in effect for 11 years,

William Lynde of Sheridan with a wolf at the end of his rope, photographed in 1908

spreading the disease to domestic stock.

Fraud crept into the bounty business. Wolf cubs were captured and raised, the females saved for breeding. Double bounty was collected by taking ears, scalps and pelts from one state or county to another. A bull gopher hide, "messed up with crankcase oil," could be passed as a coyote pup pelt. Bounties and regulations varied so that the ears might turn up in one place, the nose in another—or be taken out the back door and turned in again at the front door. In 1919, the federal government published guidelines. The Ross brothers "broke the (bounty) bank" in Gillette one winter, coming in with 75 pelts; the bounty was paid in .30-.30 rifles and ammunition.

Government hunters were hired under the 1919 law, to exterminate wolves on federal land; this program accounted for 24,132 wolves in Wyoming and adjoining states until it was discontinued in 1942. A trapper could make $200 a month in salary, plus board, plus $50 from the rancher for an adult and $20 for a pup—plus county, state and stock association bounty money. Bill Caywood, one of the best known hunters working for Biological Survey, a forerunner of the Dept. of Interior, made $7,000 the winter of 1912-13; Caywood sent his son down wolf dens for the pups in spring, allowing the she-wolf to live.

Some Famous Wolves

Several notorious wolves were known as "Three Toes," having lost toes in traps and thus easy to identify by trackers. There was even "Three-Legged Scoundrel," killed in 1920 in Tongue River country. Other famous wolves were the Pryor Creek Wolf, the Split Rock Wolf and Cody's Captive. "Old Three Toes" of the Split Rock area was said to have cost ranchers $10,000 and 200 head of cattle. He was trapped by Charles C. Bayer, head of the predatory control program in Wyoming, Nebraska and South Dakota, with headquarters in Lander.

On Sawmill Creek above Lander, Bayer once picked up the trail of what another trapper, Charles Dollard, thought was a large wolf; it had left part of a foot pad in his trap. Bayer trailed it into a hole along a canyon rim.

He unsaddled his horse, wedged the saddle into the opening, then went for help and some large salmon hooks. He tied the hooks to the end of a pole, hoping to pull out the wolf pups. Another ranger was to pull him from the den on signal by the lariat tied around one ankle.

Bayer crawled 30 feet into the den, where it opened into a large room. A clearly non-wolf snarl answered his probe—a mountain lion. His partner pulled him out on frantic signal. Deciding he would get the lion, he made a torch of pitch pine shavings, plugged his ears, and returned dragging his rifle. The concussion of his shot blew out the torch and nearly deafened him; again he was hauled out. The third time in, he found the lion dead of a broken neck and dragged it out, a 150-pound cat responsible for nearby ranch losses blamed on wolves—at least, the stock raids ceased.

Wolves were cleaned out in Wyoming in much the same way as the buffalo, by total extermination. One government trapper, Harry Williams, shot so many wolves within their dens that he grew deaf from gunfire. Another trapper, Shortie Wheelwright, took over 600 wolves in his trapline in the Hole in the Wall one season. "Wild Cat" Sam Abernathy and Herb Andrus were noted wolfers. Rattlesnake Jack "reeked so of wolf scent, he gave off an odor as obnoxious as his bait"; but he caught wolves.

Trapper's Smelly Recipe

Trappers developed creative potions for the wily wolf. One man's recipe was as follows:

Melt cheese together with kidney fat of a freshly killed heifer, stewing it in a china dish and cutting with bone knife to avoid taint of metal. When mixture cools, cut into lumps, making a hole in the side of each. Insert a large dose of strychnine and cyanide in a capsule impermeable to any odor; seal holes with cheese. During the whole process, wear a pair of gloves steeped in the hot blood of the heifer, and even avoid breathing on the baits.

When this was all ready, he put it in a rawhide bag

Charley Flory's pelts cover cabin

When the army sought to destroy the Indian through the buffalo, it perhaps was not understood how much more than meat and hide this animal provided. It truly was the Indians' commissary. For this great gift, thanks was given in all prayers; the buffalo became a part of plains mythology.

The meat itself was handled with precision in one of the most effective methods of food processing ever devised. As dried meat, which required skilled strip-cutting, its weight was reduced by one-sixth and it could keep for three years. As pemmican, or "Indian bread," it might keep up to 30 years. For pemmican, dry meat was pulverized, packed into rawhide sacks, and the heated liquid of the marrow fat poured over; sacks were pressed fairly flat and each weighed about 90 pounds. Pounded dried berries sometimes were mixed with the meat.

The hides had many uses, depending on the age and sex of the animal, as well as the time of year. Heavy-haired winter hides made the best blanket-robes. Toughened rawhide of the old bull's neck made an effec-

rubbed all over with blood, and rode forth on his ten-mile circuit, dragging liver and kidneys of the beef at the end of a rope. Bait was dropped every quarter of a mile.

Bill Briles, a wolfer who retired to Sheridan, preferred to use horse meat for his baits. He would strip out all the fat—"it melts at low temperature, like a hog's fat"—then freeze chunks and put in the poison. In trapping, he made trail sets by chopping a hole the size of a double-spring trap, slipped paper between one jaw, and covered with the same dirt removed from the hole. After a kill, he would remove the animal and skin it elsewhere, cleaning up any magpies.

Briles kept two traplines going, after the wolves were gone, concentrating on coyotes, bobcats and badgers. He counted on catching a coyote in every tenth trap, but one day's haul was five coyotes, a badger and two bobcats. The lines were 12 and 20 miles long, each ridden every other day. He often carried two canvas water bags filled with dry horse manure, lining the trap hole with manure so the trap wouldn't freeze down. Briles pulled his traps by mid-March when the fur started to rub (shed), and hung them in a cedar tree for the summer.

Several types of trap sets were used: On a trail where wolves were likely to step, it was called a blind set; a bait set was made near rotting meat; a scent set was one by a rock or bush on which pungent mix was artfully dripped. Underwater sets had to be checked often, as the pelt could be ruined. A favorite early trap was one designed by Sewell Newhouse, who modified it several times and hoped it would be included in western state seals. A six-foot steel chain and drag hook were attached.

Otto Franc avoided war by withdrawing his detectives

Big Horn Basin nearly had its own cattlemen-homestead war in 1894, precipitated by German cattle baron Otto Franc who owned the vast Pitchfork Ranch. He already had pressured Robert L. Parker into becoming the outlaw, Butch Cassidy, had come down hard on sheepmen, and was in the process of evicting settlers. The situation was ready to explode when, possibly reminded of the Johnson County War 12 years earlier, Franc removed his stock detectives.

Earlier that spring, Franc had Parker arrested for horse theft, convicted and sent to the State Penitentiary—even though Parker presented a bill of sale.

"Franc is the one person most responsible for the criminal life of Cassidy," says Bill Yetter of Meteetsee. "When he was convicted, Parker said that if the world thought him a criminal, by god, that's what he'd be." From his study of Parker's life, Yetter points to a petition for a road in May, 1894—signed by Robert L. Parker. Parker had ridden north into the Green River area from Price, Utah, where he was the son of a poor Mormon family.

Franc apparently ran rough-shod over sheepmen grazing in the Big Horn Basin, writing grimly that "we get their coooperation" in observing a "dead line," across which cattlemen insisted they not move. A problem did exist with tramp sheepherders setting huge forest fires to burn off the timber—but most were not tramps.

The Pitchfork was one of three large ranches which had divided the Big Horn Basin among them; the other two were Col. Torrey's M-Bar, and the Lovell and Mason ranch. Torrey once swam 15,000 head of cattle across the Big Horn River.

Coyote caught in trap about 1910

of the Buffalo Game

tive shield.

Artistic tools, yellow paint, utensils, bags, drum heads and sticks are only a few of the hundreds of uses to which the Indian put the buffalo. No part was wasted—which made the hide hunters' slaughter all the more repugnant to the watching Indians. Tongue River, for example, is said to have gotten its name because thousands of buffalo were killed in its valley and only the tongue was taken.

The buffalo robe hangs on the center pole of the Arapaho sun dance. A special buffalo skull stuffed with sweet sage lies at the foot of the sod altar, which represents creation.

The buffalo slaughter has gone down in history as the single greatest and most wasteful extermination. The hunters moved north into Wyoming, after killing the Kansas herds of three million and the southern herd. Many of the first settlers were bone-pickers, deriving their only cash from wagonloads of bones hauled to rail sidings; this final use was in fertilizer.

'The civilization of the Indian is impossible while the buffalo remains on the plains'—Interior Secretary Delano

The Buffalo, Commissary of the Plains Indian

BONES . . .
Fleshing Tools
Pipes
Knives
Arrowheads
Shovels
Splints
Sleds
Saddle Trees
War Clubs
Scrapers
Quirts
Awls
Paintbrushes
Game Dice
Tableware
Toys
Jewelry

BUCKSKIN . . .
Cradles
Moccasin Tops
Winter Robes
Bedding
Shirts
Belts
Leggings
Dresses
Bags
Quivers
Tipi Covers
Tipi Liners
Bridles
Backrests
Tapestries
Sweatlodge Covers
Dolls
Mittens

HAIR . . .
Headdresses
Pad Fillers
Pillows
Ropes
Ornaments
Hair Pieces
Halters
Bracelets
Medicine Balls
Moccasin Lining
Doll Stuffing

RAWHIDE . . .
Containers
Shields
Buckets
Moccasin Soles
Drums
Splints
Mortars
Cinches
Ropes
Sheaths
Saddles
Saddle Blankets
Stirrups
Bull Boats
Masks
Parfleche, bags
Ornaments
Lariats
Straps
Caps
Quirts
Snowshoes
Shrouds

HORNS . . .
Arrow Points
Cups
Fire Carrier
Powderhorn
Spoons
Ladles
Headdresses
Signals
Toys
Medication

MEAT . . .
Immediate Use
Sausages
Cached Meat
Jerky (Dehydrated)
Pemmican (Processed)

BLOOD . . .
Soups
Puddings
Paints

**STOMACH
CONTENTS . . .**
Medicines
Paints

STOMACH LINER . . .
Water Containers
Cooking Vessels

PAUNCH LINER . . .
Wrappings (Meat)
Buckets
Collapsible Cups
Basins
Canteens

LIVER . . .
Tanning Agents

SCROTUM . . .
Rattles
Containers

GALL . . .
Yellow Paints

HIND LEG SKINS . . .
Preshaped Moccasin

TAIL . . .
Medicine Switch
Fly Brush
Decorations
Whips

**HOOFS, FEET
& DEWCLAWS . . .**
Glue
Rattles
Spoons

SKULL . . .
Sun Dance
Medicine Prayers
Other Rituals

BEARD . . .
Ornamentations

TEETH . . .
Ornamentation

TONGUE . . .
Choice Meat
Comb (Rough Side)

BLADDER . . .
Pouches
Medicine Bags

TENDONS . . .
Sinews—Sewing
Bowstrings

MUSCLES . . .
Glue Preparation
Bows
Thread
Arrow-Ties
Cinches

FAT . . .
Tallow
Soaps
Hair Grease
Cosmetic Aids

CHIPS . . .
Fuel
Diaper Powder

BRAIN . . .
Hide Preparation
Food

9. HOMESTEAD LAWS FLAUNTED NATURE

From the first Wyoming homestead filed in 1870 until the end when 67,315 had been filed, this great debacle caused its own wave of depression to wash across the state long before the so-called Great Depression. Three times as many banks went broke, 101 in the 1920s—27 in the '30s. When all the dust had settled, it was clear that Wyoming would support only 9,000 bonafide farms.

And yet Wyoming did not suffer as much as did neighboring states; Montana recorded 151,600 filings, Colorado drew 107,618. Wyoming ranked twelfth, probably saved much trauma by being off the main lines of major east-west railroads. Homesteaders had to come into the state at Cheyenne, or disembark at Hot Springs, S.D. Even such unrealistic "honyokers" as the brothers who pedaled toward Wyoming on high-wheeled bicycles were forced to give up their bikes at Hot Springs and buy horses.

The statistics tell a curious story: though twelfth in filings, Wyoming was fifth in total acreage—18,225,327 acres acquired via eleven different homestead laws. Yet with this huge homestead acreage, only five percent of Wyoming was ever plowed—95 percent remained virgin land.

What this meant is that the strategy called the "grazing-homestead snare" was widely used in Wyoming, that there was a great deal of tongue-in-cheek homesteading. This perversion of the law was deplored by those unsympathetic to the "cattle barons" of the west. Wrote an editor of Sunset Magazine in 1923: "Here is hoping that the grazing-homestead snare be abolished speedily in favor of a national system of leasing the grazing privileges of public land fit for nothing except stock raising."

This actually was what everyone wanted, but the failure to recognize that most of the Great Plains was uniquely fit for stock raising—this being not at all a condemnation of the land—caused a lot of heartache, futile back-wrenching work, and personal disaster. That homesteading was based on a fiction made its perversions morally defensible to many. "Soft stealing" was another strategy used by Wyoming ranchers to prevent homesteading on their ranges. Homestead land agent I. Hintze complained in Rock Springs in 1905, "It is an undisputed and notorious fact that Crook County is one huge network of illegal fences. As much as six townships are under one fence, and nearly every ranch owner includes land in his pasture to which he has no legal right or title." Cattle country opinion expressed its sentiments differently, "The nester may be alright in his way, but damn his way."

Land Agents Misled Naive

"Come to Wyoming and become an independent man," ballyhooed the land agents, who were often in the employ of railroads. The press agentry and hard-sell reached criminally misleading proportions, however, when it told greenhorns that winter temperatures seldom fell below 10 degrees above zero—that chinook winds blew all winter long, and that livestock did not need winter feed.

The homestead tragedy in Wyoming was more than

crops shriveled by grasshoppers and drought; this resulted from plowing land that shouldn't have been plowed. It was more than naive easterners stumbling into a world that gave no quarter; Wyoming needed men and women to match her glory. And it was more than useless years spent by thousands in hunger, pain, and frustration; most honest homesteaders were unrealistic.

The real tragedy was 60,000 hearts broken by failure to do what couldn't be done, frail human hope ruthlessly shred by winds of the impossible. The bitter lesson: Most of Wyoming just was not farm land. And the wind that had blown for thousands of years over beasts grazing the intermontaine basins and grasslands continued to blow into the decades after the homesteaders' demise.

The heavies in this drama were the eastern lawmakers, men who knew 320 acres in Connecticut or Ohio was ample for any family. In parts of Wyoming, this acreage might not support one cow. The intent of homesteading never should have been applied to the Great Plains.

The wry truth is that where men were able to pervert the law to their own ends, it succeeded—and brought a beleaguered state up by its bootstraps, back to the grasslands economy known by prehistoric men, by the Indians, and by the earliest Texas cattlemen.

Stars Marked Boundaries

Surveying itself employed unique methods. The Colorado-Wyoming border was surveyed by the stars in 1869. And later geological surveying was done by laying a rod on top of a saddle horse; the height from the ground to the top of the saddle was known, so the distance was readily calculated. By 1901 Wyoming was divided into six districts, and the interior of each surveyed.

Though an initial resentment existed between cowman and homesteader, the line of demarkation faded quickly. One man wrote home bitterly:

Your Uncle Sam will give you free, gratis, for nothing, an entire square mile of land. All you have to do is to live on the land for a few years, fence a part of it, run stock or raise crops on it. And when you have received your patent, you can sell the 640 acres to the local cattle baron—for mebbe $2 an acre. He'll tear down your fences and demolish your shack. All he wants is the grazing right.

Subsisting was the tricky part, and within the first year Wyoming taught many of them that this was range country, not farming. Unless one had an outside income or filed near the mountains where greater rainfall held some hope of a crop—if one could beat the short growing season—a farmer could not survive. Therefore, many homesteaders adopted the cowman's methods of accumulating land enough for cattle and sheep operations by filing on abandoned claims, by buying out discouraged settlers—and by importing footloose easterners to

Turn-of-century settler built water wheel to irrigate in Fremont County

file claims nearby, with the sales contract signed before the new homesteader ever came west.

Settlers Tried to Adapt

Even the struggle to meet demands of a ranching operation was a gamble and full of pitfalls, but it held hope of success. Blaine Pleak built his cattle herd to 1,120 head by 1919, wintering west of Spearfish at a cost of $25,000, then selling them in 1921 for $53 a head; the cattle originally cost $70 and $90 a head. He then went to the southwest and bought over 700 head, shipped them back to Wyoming, and the bank at Upton went broke; the bank creditors took both his cattle and land. Pleak then went to work in the Osage oil field, his wife Olive operating a cookshack. Five years later, he leased back his old ranch, bought sheep and cattle, and finally the ranch. He ultimately farmed as much as 500 acres, 360 in alfalfa for winter feed.

Hard work and outside employment was of no avail for John Nolan, however, who was put out of the cattle business by the hard winter of 1911-12. In the fall of 1914, he shipped three carloads of horses, but it took nearly a year to sell them, by which time he was terminally ill.

When Nolans arrived in 1892 at Merino (later Upton), there was no place to eat in town and the children cried themselves to sleep before their carload of household goods arrived. Nolan got a job on the railroad the first summer. Mrs. Nolan did her part with a breathless schedule: She awoke before dawn to milk six to ten cows, feed the calves, take care of the milk, prepare breakfast for up to 60 boarders and her family, put out huge washings, baked 12 to 30 loaves of bread a day, scrubbed, ironed and cared for the children. Nolan became a partner in a sheep venture, later trading for cattle; the children bore their share, riding into blizzards after cattle that drifted as far south as the Cheyenne River. Five of the children died in a scarlet fever epidemic the winter of 1897-98.

The difference between ballyhoo and reality was immediately apparent to many homesteaders. Emil Driskill arrived in an emigrant car at Thornton in 1913. It was snowing lightly as the cattle were unloaded; by morning, it was 24 below zero. Roy Kimsey, his father and three brothers lived in a tent while building log houses on two homesteads; a May blizzard brought four feet of snow, and they took turns sitting up at night to keep the snow from collapsing the tents. Al Brown got lost in a snow-

Homesteader hangs out his wash

storm and had one frozen foot amputated at age 17; he wore a wooden foot the rest of his life. And when homesteader Gus Schutte was buried in March 1936 in temperatures to 40 below zero, the snow was shoveled on either side of the road as high as the bus that came to take the family to the cemetery.

Peak Year Was 1922

Most homesteaders had burned their bridges when they came to Wyoming, betting their all in a game for which they didn't know the rules. The year 1922 was the most active with 5,673 filings; within four years, 1920 through 1923, nearly one-third of all claims were filed (by 1916, it was possible to file a 640-acre grazing claim); this was a decade later than the big rush to states on major east-west rail arteries.

When climate and terrain defeated them, settlers looked for survival alternatives. Recalls Ed Mundell who

---

HOMESTEAD LAWS

PRE-EMPTION (1841-1891)—Before homestead. Purchase of 160 acres for $1.25 per acre.

HOMESTEAD (1862) Claim of 160 acres for home; must live there and make improvements 5 years. Liveable house, cultivate 20 acres, other evidence such as well, fences. Residence 7 months each year, no absence of over 6 months allowed.

COMMUTING Homestead claim could be commuted at $1.25 per acre after 6 months residence with improvements and cultivation. Amended to 14 months residence later.

TREE CLAIM (repealed 1891) Plant 40 acres of trees (later 10 acres) care for 8 years; 160 acres; no residence.

STONE AND TIMBER CLAIM 160 acres purchased at $2.50 per acre; land must be valuable for stone and timber on it.

DESERT LANDS Purchase 640 acres of desert lands impossible of cultivation, irrigate 40 acres within 3 years; $1.25 per acre. Amended in 1891 to reduce size to 320 acres.

FOREST HOMESTEAD (1906) 160 acres at $2.50 per acre; 5 year residence; national forest lands classified nonforested (included Black Hills).

ENLARGED HOMESTEAD (1909) 320 acres; must cultivate 80 acres; no commuting; no mineral rights allowed.

RESIDENCE CHANGE (1912) Change from 5 year to 3 year homesteads. Must live on claim 7 months each year, total 21 months.

GRAZING HOMESTEADS (1916) 640 acres; classified grazing only with no possibility of irrigation; 3 years residence; no mineral rights.

These laws acquired various amendments and revisions; piled upon law until there were 3,500 land laws.

'Come to Wyoming . . . become an independent man.

'The thermometer seldom falls below 10 degrees in mid-winter, and we are visited by the chinook wind all winter long . . . Land (in non-irrigated sections) will yield double that of . . . other states.'

watched hail, grasshoppers and drought take their crops on East Hay Creek, "It became evident that, in order to survive, we would have to have additional income." His dad was a carpenter and moved to the homestead town of Upton, leaving a son to care for the claim. One couple agreed to stay on a homestead near Laramie no more than seven months, if the wife didn't like it. In one month, she said, "There was no question now that we would leave . . . but could we survive until then?" Barbed wire and other improvements required by law gobbled their savings.

The oil fields were booming at the height of the homestead era, and many found employment there. Schools, freighting, and business also offered income possibilities; railroad was still being built. Some left home for weeks and months at a time to work in the mines. There was local coal to be dug and delivered door-to-door by dray. Women made butter, sold eggs and vegetables, and operated cookshacks for miners and rail workers.

There were no more enterprising women than Mary Nolan, a widow with eight young children who filed a preemption claim in 1880, mortgaged it for $375, and paid off the mortgage by carrying mail 17 miles twice a week for four years. Mary also took in washing and sewing, gathering soldiers' clothes in Fort Laramie, and returning the wash to the fort in her big wagon. She went out nursing the ill. She gathered grease from the oil oozing to the surface in the valley, made soap and sold it.

Merino Became Settlers' Upton

Merino in eastern Wyoming became a typical homestead boomtown, a focal point to supply those who flocked to the flatland from rail points. It had a bank, a sawmill, barber shop, saloons, churches and a cemetery. The "City of the Dead," once reached through a boghole across from the coal chutes, is still well kept; bodies were not embalmed, and one was stalled in the bog by a team which pulled the front wheels and tongue off the hearse. County roads leading to the town, its name changed to Upton, were ungraded trails, easily misplaced in a blizzard. But once there was a homestead shack on nearly every 320 acres.

When dapper New Yorker Frank Huff stepped off the train in white spats and fashionable straw derby in 1907, his spit and polish was besmirched before he reached Bill Meeks' barber shop where he was to work; passengers had to cross an alkali bog to get to the depot. One banker hung himself in the lumberyard, another died of the flu in 1918; the bank went broke in 1922, and was resurrected briefly under a board of ranchers and businessmen.

Frank Burdick started the Upton newspaper with an

Stacking hay was slow in 1911

army press packed into the Black Hills during gold rush days. He installed the first telephone from his claim in the timber to the store, and drove the Sundance mail route with a team of white mules. The former Texas cattle trail drover also cashed in on the homestead bonanza by striking a deal with Burlington Railroad and its emigration agent, D. Clem Deaver, to advertise Wyoming.

A homesteader-turned-business man was Charlie Benne, who became the bedbug exterminating marshal of Upton. When Charlie returned from the army after World War I, he filed near Upton, he and his wife Florence building ten miles of new fence one spring. An inventive man, he used a fence post as a reel for the wire spool, placed this in the back of a wagon, then fastened his lariat to the wire and pulled it slowly with Fox, his saddle horse. Florence drove the wagon ahead until the wire was stretched tightly; her team, Cap and Flint, would ease slowly ahead or back as Benne stapled the wire to posts. He sold the homestead to the government and moved to Upton to run the cream station, the elevator, and in 1939 became "city marshal."

Charlie and Florence rented the upstairs above the Pioneer Store. It was full of bedbugs, "so thick you could sweep them up by the basketful." He filled two old tubs with sand, put them in the rooms, added sulphur "and stuff." It was ready to light the next day, a Sunday. The storekeeper, however, told Charlie to go ahead—"man, did I run them out of that store," he chuckled.

Fate Dealt Trump Cards

Homesteading attracted all kinds of people, and some of them were star-crossed.

The Minter brothers, who rode bicycles with high front wheels from Missouri to Hot Springs, S.D. (where they bought horses to ride into Wyoming), brought their possessions in an emigrant car in a year the grass was belly-high on the horses. Charlie was killed in a gunfight which he precipitated. William's son Hike died with rope marks on his neck, in Weston County's most controversial death; the coroner's jury ruled death by natural causes, but when men refused to drive the body with its black, blood-suffused face, Mrs. Minter drove her son's body to town.

Out at the sawmill, a man in the bushes with diarrhea saved Sarah Scudder from the gallows when she killed her husband. Sarah was a bitter woman who menaced customers with her Winchester rifle, and forbade families from attending graveside services for their loved ones; the

By 1916, Newcombs used monster plow

road to the City of the Dead passed through sawmill property.

The abuse she took from her often-drunken husband aggravated Sarah's character flaws. On the evening of December 14, 1913, James Scudder came home drunk again. Arguing, scuffling—and a thump as though he'd hurled her to the floor—were heard by the Cook family who lived in a tent near the Scudder cabin. A. J. Cook, suffering a severe case of diarrhea, spent an hour in the bushes behind the tent, and clearly heard Scudder shout, "Damn you, I ain't afraid of your damn gun . . . I'll kill you before morning and your soul will be in hell." Finally, a shot was fired. Sarah backed out of the cabin, saying, "Glen, go in quick. I have killed him." She had, too, with a bullet behind his ear. No charges were filed and Sarah stayed another year, until a land patent was granted to her.

Rigors of Wyoming often proved more dangerous than the battlefield. Claude A. Thornton wore his new World War I uniform for the first time when he was placed in a cement vault in the City of the Dead. Thornton was the doctor at Upton. He joined the army and made one last call in a winter storm to deliver a baby at Thornton. He left in a railroad handcar pumped by two friends. On the way home in the blizzard, they were struck by an unscheduled freight train.

Miner's consumption took its toll of homesteaders trying to keep afloat with outside employment. John Roach of a shipbuilding family in northern Ireland worked down in the copper mines at Butte in the winter, returning in spring to his Crook County homestake. His wife, Johanna, also from County Cork, traded eggs at the store and wheat for flour. She sold butter, patched patches on her children's clothing, and grew a big garden; Johanna waited five years for a new dress.

Many settlers merged into other ways of life, and

135

stayed in Wyoming. Another Irishman, James Norris Sr., brought his wife and 12 children to the Box R ranch through Canada. A son Bill went to work for True Oil Company and retired as production manager after 25 years. His wife was Anna, daughter of an early cowboy who ran the roundup wagon for the Pool cattle outfit, Charlie Sheldon.

Alex Wegstaff was born in England, and came alone at age 13 to the U.S., where he joined a Conestoga wagon train headed for Iowa. It was 1879, and he sought his fortune in the Idaho gold fields. Before settling on a Black Butte homestead, he worked on the railroad, on ranches, and drove stagecoach from Sheridan to the Bitter Root Valley in Montana. When he carried a payload for Fort Custer, a military escort of six soldiers rode shotgun; even so, he had to outrun two holdup attempts, bullets tearing holes in his coat.

Wildest Tales Often True

It was not unusual to find people of bizarre attainments in tarpaper shacks on the lonely prairie—accomplished musicians with only the wind for a lyre, acute legal minds in a land where justice bulldozed its own raw path, skilled men whose crafts would not be needed here for another fifty years. Many a man who filed a claim had enough high adventure in his past to spin true tall tales through years of snowed-in winter nights.

The bartender at the Red Onion saloon, Jarbo Poulson, could tell as absurd a true story as any of his customers . . . of being shanghaied in Seattle in a sailing ship loaded with wheat, bound around Cape Horn for France. Born in the gold rush days in California, Jarbo and a friend jumped ship in France. At age 17, penniless and unable to speak French, they begged and stole to survive. The boys soon got a purse with enough money to take them across the English Channel; they witnessed a shipboard fight in which a man was stabbed to death, and the British government put them up until the trial. They then hired out on another sailing ship bound for Vancouver, and again had to desert—or sail back to England for their pay. Jarbo was mayor of Upton for several terms.

The life of a settler was pitilessly hard, and not for

Shatzers' sorghum mill, Clear Creek

those who gave way to panic. Lightning on the high plains took its toll. Disease debilitated—they lacked native man's medical skills and usually could not obtain a doctor in emergencies. Robert Rankin's remedy for earache was pipe tobacco smoke, and he gently rocked children for hours, puffing his pipe into their ears. Fire, flood, ticks and rattlesnakes endangered them. They relied on the horse; team runaways occurred, or one could be bucked off a saddle horse and, catching an overshoe in a stirrup, be dragged to death.

Foolish accidents occurred with the advent of autos —John Foltz lit a match to see if his car was out of gas, late one September night in 1926. When the gas tank blew up in his face, he had to walk a mile to the nearest cabin for help.

Comfort Did Not Exist

Makeshift homes on the prairie satisfied legal dwelling requirements, but were miserable in a Wyoming winter. Living conditions shocked many women: "For miles we bumped over jarring ruts," said one Laramie homestead wife, "there was not a tree in sight, no water . . . with my three hats in my lap, I surveyed my domain. Even before I stepped into the little wooden shack where I was to keep house, my foolish dreams died."

Not all women cared to endure. Geographic names

DID HIS FATHER FORSEE TRAGEDY?

A Texas father's dreadful premonition was fulfilled on the Wyoming prairie when George Brock was shot by his father-in-law.

George, 19 and in love, had followed the W. J. McCommis wagon when that family left Texas in 1903. George's father rode several hundred miles alongside trying to persuade his impetuous son to return home. The elder Brock turned back when George promised to go only as far as Amarillo; McCommis, suspected of cattle rustling in Texas, said he personally would take good care of George.

At Amarillo, George asked Ollie McCommis to marry him—and headed for Wyoming.

George filed on a homestead adjacent to McCommis and built his bride a shining cabin. He cut ends from empty tin cans and buckets to shingle the 12-foot-square house of railroad ties; then he covered the ties with red tin . . . to hide the stolen ties, neighbors whispered.

In 1905, George shot and killed Charlie Minter in self-defense. It was so ruled at the inquest, and plenty of people in Upton saw Charlie waiting with a German Luger for George to ride into town that September morning, Charlie held a grudge, was drinking heavily, and vowing to kill Brock.

In 1908, George and his father-in-law were tried for grand larceny in theft of 28 sheep from Metcalf & Neely Co. They were found not guilty.

In 1910, George's wife cradled his head in her lap as he lay dying of three .30-.30 bullets fired by her father. McCommis had "taken care" of George.

When neighbors came to remove the body, they had to pry Ollie's fingers loose, one by one. She had run out carrying their baby, to hold her dying husband. Ollie stayed on their homestead several months, then left for New Mexico. McCommis served one year in state prison for manslaughter and was sent home to die of tuberculosis.

Buckboard hauled supplies many rugged miles to homes on barren prairie.

like Crazy Woman Creek, and Hanging Woman Creek, memorialize such personal tragedies. Gus Chatman's wife of a few weeks packed her things and left; Gus shot himself in the chest and ran, covered with blood, to neighbors who saved his life; he never returned to the homestead shack. Jeff Stout's wife went to town one Saturday and killed herself with a revolver; she lived at the homestead caring for stock while her husband earned money by operating the Burlington coal chutes at Upton.

But Some Saw Beauty

Dispair had its opposite in laughter, joy, and wonder. One woman: "Every evening I would go up on a little hilltop and watch the sun in all its glory tint the clouds." And another: "A mystical beauty, at night the sky splashed with brilliance of stars . . . wailing of coyotes rose hauntingly from the darkness like a primordial symphony of this lonely land." And yet another: "I loved to watch the large herds of deer every morning as they went to water, single file, silhouetted against the sky."

A favorite prank at country socials was to switch the front and back buggy wheels, causing the buggy to tip slightly toward the back. And younger family members sent home early often wired all gates shut, a courting frustration to their elders forbidden to swear in front of women. Recitations, debates, dances, and basket socials spiced rare evenings of fun. Square dances rocked tiny rooms to fiddle and accordion music, "Buffalo Gal," "Turkey in the Straw," and "Arkansas Traveler."

Cow Chips and Featherbeds

Wyoming's first homestead was a one-room cracker-box divided by curtains, the floor of knotty planks—"when a knot fell out, the hole was sheeted with a tin can lid to keep the cold ground air out." In 1870 northwest of Cheyenne, people burned cow chips stored in gunny sacks in the cellar; chips burned hot and left blue ashes.

The featherbed represented security. Bread dough was put inside to rise; the featherbed went along on trips. Cozy featherbeds replaced their original corn husk mattresses, women obtaining the feathers by plucking live, hissing geese, "heads held downward in our laps," recalled Edith Thompson.

A Buffalo area woman had her husband build a screened cage for the children to play in outdoors, so frightened was she of rattlesnakes.

Motorists Risked Disaster

Tractor at Arvada ran pulley

137

CATTLE NUMBERS and VALUES		
Year	Numbers Cattle	Values Per Head
1929	778,000	$59.10
1930	790,000	54.30
1931	837,000	40.30
1932	885,000	24.50
1933	956,000	19.90
1934	1,050,000	16.20
1935	858,000	17.10

SHEEP NUMBERS and VALUES		
Year	Numbers Sheep	Values Per Head
1929	3,471,000	$11.60
1930	3,540,000	9.20
1931	3,894,000	5.80
1932	3,972,000	3.60
1933	3,893,000	3.20
1934	3,873,000	4.10
1935	3,599,000	4.60

'Everybody Dig, Save Meat, Can the Kaiser'

"Say 'I do' to the roadside mailman," became a wry saying that resulted in 22,988 men registering for World War I draft.

Many felt Wyoming was patriotic to a dangerous degree when the state furnished 57 percent of its draft registrants to the U.S. military; the average state furnished 28 percent. And Wyoming with its scant population led all states in number of men ranked Class I, 40 percent. Sheriffs, postmasters and mail carriers helped register men.

Despite complaints that wholesale conscription could endanger output of state products needed in the war effort—cattle, sheep, wheat, coal, oil—many draft appeals were torn up and tossed in the wastebasket without being read. Local board generosity, however, was only one reason for the number who went. There were a larger percent of young men in Wyoming's population than in other states, and they were more physically fit. There were also somewhat more deserters —4.11 percent, in a national average of 3.23 percent.

But the Powder River war cry of the 91st Infantry inspired men on the western front until the Allied victory in 1918. The bucking horse, painted on a drum in France by George Ostrom of Sheridan, became the emblem of the 148th "Bucking Bronc Regiment from Wyoming." It was painted on trucks, helmets and roadsigns, and bucked back into action in World War II around the world. In 1936, a similar bronc silhouette went onto Wyoming license plates.

Wyoming plunged into the war effort, too, by oversubscribing Liberty Bond quotas, giving up candy and white flour, sending hand-knit sweaters to the front. Liquor prohibition was made patriotic, but this was going too far; it wasn't until the war ended that prohibition was voted in for the only "wet state" remaining in the Rocky Mountain region.

It was a time, too, when it was patriotic to hate on the home front.

In Cheyenne, every man was classified in a card index according to the warmth of his patriotism; possibly pro-Germans were threatened with being stripped and painted yellow. The vigilantes rose again, semi-secret and pledged to report any pro-German utterances. In Sheridan, the Loyalty League's business included everything from Red Cross to suppression of sedition. In Lander, the 100 Per Cent American Club burned textbooks and forced schools to quit teaching German. "Filthy lips" of traitorous pro-Germans should not blemish the flag, a Lander woman objected to the common proof of patriotism: Denounce the Kaiser and kiss the American flag. Young Charles Owens was given a medal by the city of Douglas for beating up a transient who destroyed an American flag. And a German baker was suspected of putting crushed glass into bread.

The energetic slogan: "Let Everybody Dig—Save Meat—Save Wheat—Save Sugar—Can the Kaiser," was waved in Cheyenne, where schools proclaimed candyless days. Women were urged by state and county officials to discontinue afternoon teas and midnight feeds. Two families were forbidden to buy wheat because they had allowed previous purchases to rot. Millers were encouraged to use 81 percent wheat kernel in flour; "victory bread" was normally about 60 percent white flour. Two bakeries in Rock Springs were shut down for failure to use the required substitutes, and Laramie baker Nels Bendt lost his license.

Mrs. Larry Brown of Lander, had ten sons serve in France as army officers—and four daughters as overseas Red Cross nurses. She was honored by President Woodrow Wilson. The Wyoming legislature presented a bronze medal to every state veteran.

'I spent half my time changing irons heated on the cook stove.'

'Go West, Young Woman'

Wyoming lured adventurous girls into the homestead trap and courtship wove its spell around their tarpaper shacks. Women were scarce. Each drew, like a droplet of honey, a throng of swains riding out of the sunset.

Unless they were heads of households wives could not file on homesteads, but single women did. They put up cabins, built fence, and fought blizzards in their efforts to secure land titles. Sometimes they did it to increase a relative's holdings, and sometimes with the intent to sell. For others, a homestead became a dowry.

Comely Harriett Newman, a musician, had just completed a five-state concert tour when she and a girl friend received a proposition that was to change Harriett's life. A Wyoming rancher wanted more land and, if the girls would prove up on homesteads, he would buy their tracts.

Harriett and Belle Vickers filed on adjacent homesteads south of Lodgepole Creek in 1909. To satisfy the law, they built separate houses, each on its own side of the common line; the girls lived in one cabin for a few days, then moved to the other, alternating every few days.

Many were the riders who dressed in their finest to go "looking for cattle" near the girls' homesteads. And summer weekends could be spent dancing, picnicking and playing ball at the large Creigh home 40 miles away. The men would ride, while the women drove buckboards loaded with bedrolls and food.

Harriett never returned to Kansas City. She married a wagon boss of the huge Keeline ranch on Dec. 16, 1911, the winter that would reduce the newlyweds' herd from 500 cattle to 86 cows and two calves and leave them with a $6,000 feed bill.

A blinding Wyoming blizzard caught them on their wedding trip to the ranch. At Upton, they had bundled into a buggy among groceries and household goods. Lost in the storm at twenty-below, Boyd Ash let the horses have their heads. The hired man was waiting with a big kettle of stew when the team drew the buggy to the ranch gate. It was their wedding supper.

FINAL HOMESTEAD ENTRIES 1868-1961 (includes commuted)

Montana	151,600
North Dakota	118,472
Colorado	107,618
Nebraska	104,260
Oklahoma	99,557
South Dakota	97,197
Dakota Territory	33,951
Kansas	89,945
New Mexico	87,312
Minnesota	85,072
Arkansas	74,620
Wyoming	**67,315**
California	66,738
Oregon	62,926
Idaho	60,221
Washington	58,156
Alabama	41,819
Missouri	34,633
Wisconsin	29,246
Florida	28,096
Mississippi	24,126
Arizona	20,268
Michigan	19,861
Utah	16,798
Iowa	8,851
Nevada	4,370
Alaska	3,277
Ohio	108
Illinois	74
Indiana	30

FINAL HOMESTEAD ENTRIES IN WYOMING

Year	Entries	Year	Entries
1875	3	1922	5,673
1880	15	1923	4,639
1885	62	1924	3,691
1890	143	1925	3,070
1895	219	1926	2,215
1900	387	1927	1,418
1905	684	1928	1,326
1910	777	1929	1,084
1912	700	1930	811
1913	2,420	1931	724
1914	2,081	1932	810
1915	1,692	1933	367
1916	1,679	1934	754
1917	1,910	1935	935
1918	2,234	1936	335
1919	1,922	1937	254
1920	3,889	1938	213
1921	5,010	1939	172

John Gordon saws ice at ⱻR ranch, 1931

George Hadeshell, Gordon load ice with tongs

THEY EXPECT THE UNEXPECTED

They fished with pitchforks, picnicked in four feet of hail, and rode dirt-moving slips in chariot races—these masters of the unexpected, Wyoming pioneers. And at times they had seen all they owned tumble out of sight in a wall of brown water.

Catfish and sturgeon buried themselves in mudholes when Clear Creek dried up, as happened until 1948 when stock ponds held back water and recharged it. People discovered they could dig out the fish with pitchforks and shovels. "Catfish" Johnson once filled a wagonbox with fish to sell in Arvada. The cattle refused to drink from these fishy-tasting holes.

Hail was four feet deep on the picnic area by the time people could leave a 1926 summer Sunday picnic. A car had been demolished, a team of horses killed, and C. W. Sampson's wheat crop washed away before their eyes.

At the Sampson place near Lieter 150 people had gathered for a beef barbecue. "Uncle Dee" stalled his car crossing Clear Creek. As it began to rain, "eats" were called. The table was quickly covered and the men hitched a team to the car. It began to hail furiously. Just then, high water hit from upstream flooding. Team and car were swept downstream backwards, the car going up a cottonwood tree on a bend in the creek. One horse broke its neck trying to get loose; the other drowned.

The chariot races were held near a ranch dam built on Clear Creek. Dirt-moving slips were turned backward on the bale, the slip driven like a Roman chariot behind a team of horses; it relieved the tedium of seven years of construction, an attempt to keep sand out of the ranch ditches. Ten men and ten teams worked in four crews building the dam and a four-mile-long ditch.

Catalog Brides Ordered

Schoolteachers rarely lasted more than one season, as lonely bachelors wooed them competitively. It was still the day of the mail-order bride and Wyoming was a shock to many. They didn't all stay.

One such bride came to Martin Draw, terrified of the quiet outdoors. When she sat up in bed, startled by sounds in the rafters, a pack rat fell into the front of her gown. The hysterical bride spent the rest of the night in the car, and refused to get out until her husband drove her back to Casper. The marriage was annulled.

Brides could be ordered from a catalog which described each in great detail. A homesteader near Gardner Mountain, Frenchy, put in his order—and built his cabin lovingly around a large flat rock to serve as a table. When the bride arrived, she was shocked by the boulder in the middle of the dirt floor. Frenchy broke the wonderful table apart with a sledge hammer. She soon left anyway, unable to cope with such primitive ways. A part-time trapper and hunter, Frenchy once fell down Dull Knife Pass in the deep snow, bouncing several hundred feet from one ledge to another. His heavy clothing and the snow padded his fall. In faulty English, he described it, "Bum Bum Boom!"

Coping with marital stress was less problem to Wyoming-born girls. Many like Josephine Skiles were full partners; when she married sheepman Leroy Smith, they lived wherever the sheep grazed—on the mountains in the summer, and on winter range the rest of the year.

Mistaken for a Bear

Big Bennett, a successful bear hunter, originally owned the Hat Ranch in the Mayoworth area. He sold about 100 pelts a year, half of which were silvertip grizzly. He once took a man named Fred Pettit under his tutelage. When Bennett returned from hunting, he found Pettit's work so sloppy that he burned a dozen bear hides.

Big Bennett used Packsaddle Canyon to go in and out of Pass Creek to the south. So deep and narrow was the canyon that he carried trees to lean against a series of ledges as ladders. While using this trail, Doctor Blake was shot by another bear hunter; the doctor was wearing a brown sweater and climbing a tree.

Three-fingered Smith lived nearby. A former Texas gunman, he was called back to Texas for an accounting. An old London cab driver, Sam Strickler, drank himself

*As the river takes away,
she also gives . . .
in annual ice harvests
of yesterday and today*

LX-Bar ice harvest 1933, Tom Kendrick in saddle, Tommy Hampton, John Bupp, L. B. Smith

to death below Big Bennett's and hence the name Coachy Creek Ranch. A colorful old Irishman, gardener at the Plunkett EK home ranch in the mid-80s, also homesteaded in the area; Griffin willed his ranch to John Nolan because "he is the most successful thafe on Powder River." Griffin was buried on his place, and the river has washed away his grave.

Settlers were inventive and brought with them skills to solve problems creatively.

Dunkard bonnets were the style on the prairie for Rinker women; a midwife, Mrs. Rinker delivered many babies without a doctor. The Dunkard men were skilled in woodcraft, making cedar churns and buckets, with broadaxes hewing logs true enough to build watertight flumes. The first dentist was Ed Barrett, who learned to make teeth by trial and error; he made Grandmother Brock's first false teeth on the kitchen stove, blowing up his "brew" in the process and festooning walls and ceiling with teeth.

Mayoworth Settled a Feud

Origin of Mayoworth, post office for Hole in the Wall outlaws, is rooted in a bitter trail feud between two men who re-fought the Civil War all the way into central Wyoming. Jones was a Republican and a Union sympathizer. Morgareidge was a Democrat and a staunch Confederate. To make matters worse, Jones' daughter married Morgareidge's son—although it was of this union that a compromise in naming the post office was worked out. May was the girl's first name and Worthington her husband's middle name.

The peacemaker, Mrs. Jones, worked energetically to establish a post office and became the first post mistress; Benjamin Harrison, a Republican, was President. When Democrat Grover Cleveland was elected, the rabid rebel Morgareidges passed a petition to transfer the post office to equally rabid rebels, the Brooks at the EK. But when President William H. Taft was elected, Mrs. Jones regained the post office.

HARRY FULLER'S DICTIONARY

One colorful cowboy who rode "around the world" for the OW, covering numberless miles in the saddle, was Harry Fuller.

During a dance at Kendrick's LX-Bar ranch on the bank of Powder River, it rained hard. There was no bridge, so Fuller hooked up a team to a hayrack and ferried Arvada people across to their cars. On the way back, the river tipped over the wagon. Ernest Kendrick roped Fuller, who couldn't swim, and dragged him upstream to a crossing. Fuller sputtered out of the water, "You damn fool, why did you drag me up the river?"

Following are a few of Fuller's malappropisms.

Molly darlings—dallys (rope turns on saddle horn)
A flip of one ear and a flop out of the other—an earmark
Powder's downpour—afraid
Poder sack—foreman
All wool and a yard wide—OK, good
Cow meat and coffee—a meal
Head of big and little nasty—foreman of a badly scattered cow outfit (originally at the head of Big and Little Nasty Creeks)
Legs came out of the same hole—an ill-built horse
Kid gloves and no socks—a stranger to livestock

"I've been riding him for two years, and the unconscious S.O.B. just found out I was on him," Fuller once said of a saddle horse.

Harry Fuller scrubs cow for lice.

Anglo-Saxon Image
Nurtured in Wyoming

Banjo music in the sagebrush, cafe signs warning "NO DOGS OR INDIANS," and careful nurturing of the Anglo-Saxon image were calculated to diminish ethnic diversity in Wyoming. The state's cultural identity has always been primarily northwest European, people speaking one language, attending the same churches, and possessing a common cultural background.

The Klu Klux Klan flexed powerful muscle in Wyoming in the 1920s. Two Catholic churches and a priest's house in Kleenburn were burned; although no one was arrested, the Klan was believed responsible.

Newspapers often were racially judgmental in their news columns. The Sheridan Press, for example, printed mostly Anglo-Saxon names in its social columns, virtually ignoring Polish, Greeks and Italians. As late as 1980, the Riverton Ranger ran a photograph of two Indian boys being frisked by the police, in unwarranted dimension—eight columns wide by half a page deep. This is the type of publicity typically given to Indians by small town western papers.

Titled Europeans began investing in Wyoming as early as 1880, bringing polo, big game hunts, royal visitors—and their own concepts of serfdom; if they were cattle kings, their ranches were feudal domains. Settlers, in their minds, were peasantry. Some refused to hire any who presumed to run livestock—and the Robin Hoods had their day in Wyoming. Juries, however, had no awe of feudal lords and often ruled that the excesses of one class balanced out the excesses of the other.

Early laborers, coming to Wyoming as railroad builders and miners, were also Anglo-Saxon; they came mostly from the British Isles and Germany, laying track, working as miners, barkeeps and missionaries. They assimilated into the dominant culture and began their upward mobility.

Chinese by the thousands were brought in by the Union Pacific for track work and mining, when the Anglos began striking. The Chinese were docile and willing to work for $32.50 a month; white workers were paid $52. The economic distress this caused resulted in bitter anti-Chinese sentiment—"half-civilized Pagans," these representatives of the world's oldest civilization were called.

Not All Spoke English

Later emigrant laborers, though from Europe, did not blend so easily. They were more visible . . . the Poles at mining towns of Kleenburn, Monarch and Dietz, the German-Russians emigrating to work in sugar beet fields. At the coal mining town of Acme, Japanese and Italians were not welcome in the main part of town; they had to stay in "Japtown" and "Macaroni Flats" at the upper end of Acme. The large Mexican population in Laramie and along the southern part of the state similarly was excluded from dominant society.

Even in a homestead shack there was prejudice against people who did not "spik" English. Frustrated because emigrants did not rubber-stamp school plans, one settler insisted, "They should not be allowed the use of the ballot because they always throw a money-wrench

**Jim Pickett, above
John Lewis, right**

into the machinery that moves our homemade institutions."

Wars are made to order for channeling prejudice into patriotic passion, and both 20th century world wars proved such vehicles for those so inclined. Many aliens living in Wyoming were called back to their native lands to fight—most on the side of the Allies. This included Belgian reservists.

The tragic relocation of 10,872 Japanese into Wyoming's Heart Mountain Center, one of ten in the U.S. during World War II, is a classic in injustice and prejudice fanned by patriotic zeal.

Two-thirds of them were U.S.-born citizens, but "a Jap is a Jap," many Wyoming people insisted mindlessly. When L. L. Newton of the Wyoming State Journal wrote, "Let us demonstrate to them what real Democracy is, that it is the application of the same Christian principles of living and dealing with others which have made America what it is today," the Wyoming Eagle retorted, "Has Mr. Newton gone berserk?"

It was feared Japanese would settle in Wyoming when they were released; Gov. Lester Hunt wrote the War Relocation Director: "We do not want a single one of these evacuees to remain in Wyoming."

Punished for Their Race

"NO INDIANS, NO MEXICANS, NO NEGROES" read signs in Wyoming cafes as late as the 1950s. Indians had been successfully relegated to a pocket in the Wind River Mountains—except for once a year when Sheridan paraded them for tourists during All-American Indian Days. City Hall in Sheridan was built by Indian jail inmate labor.

Negroes apparently were welcome only to work, not to live, in early Sheridan—and banjo music arose from the sagebrush flat at Cat Creek 15 miles west of town.

Rodeo: a moment of danger

HOW TO SADDLE A BRONC

The noose is well aimed, the horse blindfolded. While the horse is upon the ground, the bridle and the blindfold, a black silk handkerchief, are adjusted.

After the horse is allowed to arise, he is held by the head; stirrups and cinches are in the seat of the saddle and the man who holds him by the head takes the saddle by the horn, after having laid the saddle blanket on his back—sometimes it has to be laid there a good many times before it sticks—and with a deftness that comes only after long practice, he lands that 45-pound cow-saddle on top of the blanket.

He looks out for strokes from the flying feet and, as in the case of the blanket, after many trials he must with one hand insert the latigo into the cinch ring and with firm hold, cinch the saddle with one pull.

The first pull is a critical moment. The horse goes high into the air.—from photographer L. A. Huffman's brochure, 1878.

10. DUDES GO WEST

"When the last bit of range is fenced up and gone
And Progress has had her say
When the last ol' moss horn is put on the cars
The honyok at last gets his way . . ."
　　　　　　　　　　　　　—*Bruce Brockett*

This nostalgic lament was good for the dude ranching business, built as it was on the mystic of the old west. In reality, "fencing-up" did not mean disappearance of the range. In terms of climate and topography, "the honyok" (homesteader) could never "get his way" in Wyoming. And even though ranchers began to ride the range in four-wheel-drive pickups, snowmobiles, airplanes and helicopters, "the day of the horse" would never be over. Climate and terrain made a lie of the lament. But it was a convenient cover to prevent the unmasking of the mythical cowboy, who never was the Virginian.

In truth, when there were cowpunchers of heroic stature, they did not long remain in that position. A cowboy/wrangler/cowpuncher was quite simply a hired hand. Mechanical inventions and rising costs would unhorse him, anyway—even if settling of the "free" land question did not.

"Don't mistake the nice young men who amble around wire fences for the old riders of the plains," artist Frederic Remington advised Owen Wister, author of **The Virginian** which was set in Medicine Bow. Wister, who didn't know much about working cowboys, went to Remington when he was asked in 1903 to write an article on cowboys. Wister ignored the advice and wrote instead of "wild men" who "sprang from the loins of the West," a Sir Lancelot, an American Robin Hood. More truthfully, the cowboy lived a life that was dirty, dismal, and tedious.

But the myth never died. And dudes, in a sense, have been playacting that myth for a hundred years.

Dudes, however, brought their own customs, shaping the lifestyle and economy of northern Wyoming. Dude ranches became a training ground for rodeo—and the western moon over the corrals was often a catalyst for alliances that would inject new capital into the state. Many ranch hands married their fortunes.

Nature Created Drama

Influence of the dudes on the development of Wyoming has been called "a form of controlled species development"—a transplant of people with the potential for success as well as the means to attain that success. Those who decided to put down roots in Wyoming were hardy, rejoicing in the awesome weather changes and its startling impact on a harsh land. Thus, nature itself continually fed the excitement sought by these easterners. Dude ranching capitalized on an intangible spirit—"dude ranches are the resorts that make red-blooded people happy," rhapsodized railroad brochures of the '30s.

An economic stabilizer during hard times, dude ranching increased the need for horses, grain, hay, machinery, and "urban cowboy" clothing. It was the weather vane for growth of industries frankly catering to good times for the wealthy from out of state: hunters,

143

While chasing a throwback cow in 1907, Spear rider Fred Givens and another rider urged their horses up a scoria pinnacle, noticing the higher they climbed the more rattlesnakes. Soon there was one under every sagebrush. Picking their way through, near the top they saw a sinkhole with rattlers tangled two feet deep and hundreds more under a red ledge.

Fifty years later, he returned to the spot and found the ground roaring with the sound of an underground rattlesnake den. He and friends set off a case of dynamite; the roaring stopped, the stench of snakes spewing forth.

Rodeo excitement could be staged

fishermen, investors, the rich and famous whose activities were attended by national publicity. It was all good business for the state of Wyoming. Guides, outfitters, taxidermists and meat packers specializing in wild game set up their private businesses catering to guests—"never call them customers," ruled Howard Eaton, father of dude ranching.

As many dudes put down permanent roots in Wyoming, the state benefited mightily. Those who became influential in politics helped stop the wanton destruction of wild game which, too, had been part of the state's history: "sportsman" Sir George Gore shooting 2,500 buffalo in a single day, the slaughter of magnificent bull elk for two ivory teeth, the killing of buffalo for their tongues.

Concern for the state's esthetic treasures created alliances between a broad spectrum of outside investors —dudes, foreign royalty, easterners—with local cattlemen, sheep ranchers, homesteaders, merchants. Their common goals: To promote and enjoy Wyoming. If they could make money in the process, this too was desirable.

Dudes became ranchers, businessmen, politicians—and dude wranglers. The political and financial intermingling of owners of large working ranches and investors who came to Wyoming as dudes enriched the state in many ways. Dude ranchers Alden Eaton, Willis M. Spear, Frank Horton and Leonard Graham all served in the state legislature. Conservation, they knew, was good business. Their paying guests wanted to see wildlife, to ride among it, to photograph, to hunt and fish. Many, like Spear, had stocked lakes with trout, cleared winter-killed trees, and planted new forest seedlings. They worked to restock the Big Horns with elk, and one, Allen Fordyce, started his own private elk herd.

A battery of sophisticated state bureaus emerged, some so innovative they set the pace for conservation policies nationally. Yellowstone Park, as the first national park, became the proving ground for management policies. The Wyoming State Game & Fish Commission became a reputable bastion of conservation, working constructively within a political format that demanded natural resource development.

Father of Dude Ranching

The father of dude ranching, Howard Eaton, headed west from Pittsburgh in 1879. On the way to Wolf Creek near Sheridan, he started the first dude ranch in America in the Dakota badlands, made friends with Teddy Roosevelt and the Marquis de Mores, and forged firm links with early free-wheeling cowmen as a founder of the Montana Stockgrowers Association.

But trailing dudes 200 miles to Yellowstone Park, Indian reservations, and the Custer Battlefield became too arduous from the Little Missouri badlands. Eaton and his brothers Ellis and Alden bought a ranch on Wolf Creek in 1903. The town of Sheridan was 18 miles away, steeped in Indian history, and boasting 30 saloons, six churches, two opera houses and the luxury Sheridan Inn. English landed gentry had settled south of Buffalo where Moreton and Richard Frewen from England built Frewen's Castle.

Here, with the backdrop of a glorious western sky over the Big Horn Mountains, corrals, trails, and the smell of saddle leather, the Eatons set a mood where easterners could re-live the adventure of pioneering America. This was Eaton's cocktail-time toast:

> "If you've breathed the air of her hills and plains,
> If you've watched her peaks in the gloaming,
> If you've felt her pride when her horsemen ride,
> Then you'll join in this toast: 'To Wyoming'."

Maintaining the mystic of western ranch life required the cowboy, "dude wranglers" they were called. These men were a glamorized version of working ranch hands, personification of the cowboy myth. The business developed its own language. Female guests were happily called fillies; on a working ranch this would have been an insult to womanhood.

Other fundamental differences between the two types of ranches generated ill feeling between the working ranch hand and the dude wrangler. Early dude ranchers tried to mitigate this by hiring capable riders and organizing open rodeos to show off their skills. Bill Eaton could rope up to five mounted riders in one loop. Rodeo greats like Paddy Ryan were lured into dude wrangling. Other dude wranglers like Curley Weitzel and Fred Larsen were also top rodeo hands. Dude connections took Weitzel to Hollywood where he became a movie double for Hoot Gibson and Wally Wales, Wales being the stage name of Floyd Alderson, cousin of Big and Little Bones who ran the Bones Brothers' dude ranch across the Montana state line at Birney; Weitzel later joined the "101 Wild West Show," learned flying from Oliver Wallop, and started Big Horn Airways. Wrangler Larsen bulldogged a buf-

144

Dudes helped build rodeo

falo in the movie, "Buffalo Bill and the Indians" and had a part in "Endangered Species."

Wranglers Wed Fortunes

Another fringe benefit of dude wrangling, marrying the dudes, had a decided impact on northern Wyoming lifestyle and economy. Men who possessed ranching skills often married eastern women who had the capital necessary for building large stable ranches.

Weitzel, for example, successively married two Eaton dudes; Paddy Ryan married a TAT dude; Eddy Reisch married a Tepee dude; Kelly Howie married an Eaton dude, bought the Hat Ranch near Kaycee, learned to fly his own plane, and began to play polo. Harry Fulmer, who gave Sheridan $300,000 to build a library and left a trust fund to run it when he died, married a dude while a wrangler at Eaton's and bought the E. R. Dinwiddie ranch on Tongue River near Dayton. His father had arrived in Wyoming to work on the railroad. Artist Hans Kleiber tried his hand at wrangling dudes. Bruce Brocket was also a poet. Jim Niner sang to them with his guitar. One dude liked it so well he became a dude wrangler, Michael Morton who eventually married another Tepee dude and became manager of the King Brothers cattle and horse operation.

Former dudes like Howie's wife, Elizabeth Blanchard Merriman, carved their own niches in northern Wyoming. Colleges, hospitals, civic theater, the arts and agriculture . . . all these benefited from dude talent and largess. English equine competition was brought by Brinton, Wrights and King, as the Mountain States Combined Training Association. Cattle and horse breeding have been upgraded by former dudes with the financial resources to underwrite expensive ventures: Jack and Ginny Chase have done much for the Red Angus breed, Mary Bourdon worked to improve beef cattle at her Rapid Canyon Ranch, the polo horse market developed to meet needs of a dude enterprise.

By 1929, early dude ranching had peaked at 31 such ranches in the Big Horn National Forest, with guests still making the final leg of their trip west by stagecoach. The IXL ranch began in 1912, the HF Bar of Frank Horton was 35 miles south of Sheridan, the Quarter Circle U in Tongue River Canyon, the Tepee Lodge 22 miles south of Sheridan, and the Spear-O-Wigwam named for the Indian-spear brand used since 1882 by Willis M. Spear was in the forest west of Big Horn.

Lander Hosted First Rodeo

As long as there have been horses to be broken, there has been some form of wild horse riding—at first on the range, at scattered ranches, and at horse sales throughout Wyoming. As a commercial public spectacle, rodeo began in the 1890s and was encouraged by dude ranches, later as town and tourist promotions.

Lander is credited with the first in 1893, Laramie next in 1895 when two were staged—"broncho bucking" at the Labor Day program and wild horse riding at the stockyards. Cheyenne in 1897 was visited by Buffalo Bill (William F.) Cody's "wild west" exhibition at the fairgrounds; Frontier Days began the following year and, except for World War I, it has been annual ever since.

To basic bronc riding, roping and bulldogging were added such novelty extras as wild cow milking contests and wild horse races, in which the bronc was first eared down by biting its ear. Tricky cowboys, who may have wrangled thousands of cows and never milked one, figured a way to beat the odds by going into the contest with milk in their bottles—thus one team actually won with a steer, mistakenly driven in with the cows.

Cheyenne's first Frontier Days included a half-mile gymkhana race; contestants rode halfway, dismounted, turned their coats inside out, remounted and rode one-eighth mile, dismounted again, lighted cigars and rode in with umbrellas furled and cigars still lighted.

Designation of Wyoming as the Cowboy State and adoption of the bucking horse logo were signs of the commercial importance of rodeo. License plates have carried the bronc since 1943. Over 70 annual rodeos developed throughout the state.

The word rodeo did not come into general use until the 1920s.

In 1936, the Cowboy's Turtle Association was organized, which turned into the Rodeo Cowboy's Association (RCA) and drew a line between amateur and professional rodeos.

EAST AND WEST HAD TO MELD FOR DUDE RANCH TO THRIVE

Successful dude ranching required the combined skills of east and west—often in a partnership with one contributing eastern contacts and the ability to view the west as exotic, the other skilled in ranching, hunting and western lore. Some easterners quickly acquired western skills and thus became independent operators.

The IXL was one such dude enterprise, converted in 1912 by an Englishman, J. B. Milward, from Captain Grissel's working ranch near Dayton; it was named after Grissel's crack British cavalry, the Ninth (IX) Lancers (L). Trapper Lodge in Shell Canyon, on the other hand, was started in 1906 by farwesterners, Gay and Watson Wyman; it grew, as had Eatons, from an excess of visitors who became paying guests.

In Jackson Hole, ranchers guiding hunters eventually built cabins for their customers. The first identifiable dude ranch there was opened in 1908 by Struthers Burt of Baltimore; guests had to come 104 miles by wagon from St. Anthony, Idaho.

11. SHEEP THRIVED IN WYOMING HILLS

The longest furrow in the west, Gillette to Buffalo, is a striking symbol of greed and brutality. This furrow plowed in 1901 was the only "dead line" visible of many drawn all over Wyoming to prevent sheep from feeding on free grass desired by cattlemen.

During the first decade of the 20th century, 16 sheepmen were killed in cold blood, saddle horses, sheep dogs and property were destroyed, many thousands of sheep were shot, clubbed, or run over cutbanks by cattlemen and their hired hands. Hundreds of incidents were reported, rewards vainly offered—but only two such massacres resulted in convictions. Documented sheep killings add up to 17,000 and this figure probably was much higher; thousands more were killed in rimrocking incidents, and by range horses driven through bands of sheep.

All this happened during a period when Wyoming led the nation in wool production, when many prominent Wyoming men ran sheep and, curiously, many cattlemen did, too. Ironically, most of the attacks were planned by men who had made fortunes on free public grass, men who often discreetly left the state before the attack occurred.

Such arrogance and violence could not last. Popular sentiment turned against the savage cattlemen, and the upshot of it was that they "cut off their noses to spite their faces": A halt was called to free grass. The malignancy on the Wyoming plains caused President Theodore Roosevelt to appoint a Public Lands Commission which set the stage for leased and regulated grazing —establishment of the U.S. Forest Service, and later the Taylor Grazing Act.

The war was declared in 1897 when Jackson Hole cattlemen organized a "committee of safety" and issued public notice that no sheep could pass through the hole under any circumstances. That same spring, Otto Franc who established the Pitchfork Ranch in 1878 visited sheepmen in the Big Horn Basin to obtain their agreement on a demarkation of cattle range; he wrote, "We succeed in getting them to agree." Dead lines were set up in the upper Shoshone Valley in 1901 and sheepmen were threatened with violence by the Stockman Protection Assn.

The 60-mile-long furrow was plowed as a visible boundary by northeastern Wyoming cattlemen. They hired men with teams and a camp outfit to plow until they reached Buffalo; from the head of Deer Creek they plowed down the divide between Deer and Bull Creeks, crossed Powder River, plowed up Crazy Woman to Dry Creek, and on to Buffalo. It was late fall when the plow reached its destination.

The Waisner brothers crossed the furrow in 1902 with two bands of sheep. The first night raid came as a surprise, raiders burning the sheepwagon and shooting sheep which were bedded down for the night; the sheep stampeded, piling up as they ran. An estimated 500 were killed. The second raid occurred in late fall. The wagon burned and 1,500 sheep were killed by gunfire or run over a cutbank on Black Bill draw which empties into

'I built a monument so you will know where I have been.'

Sheepherder monuments cap hills

Herder's original mobile home

Wild Horse Creek. One herder was shot through the shoulder.

As in most such cases, though their identity was known, the criminals were never arrested. No compensation was made; these two raids, plus a wet spring during lambing, broke the Waisners. One man, Bill Briles, said he was on circle with another rider when his partner filled lamps with gas. Who did it? "Interested parties found a way," he said evasively, then described in detail two incidents. Sheep were charged into cuts, stacked up, run

Trailing to range, sheep herd fans out on rich Wyoming grass

over with horses, and shot. The stock detective? "He just as well stayed home. Nearly everybody in that country was on his list."

Among other such massacres that occurred during this ten-year harassment:

•3,000 sheep clubbed to death on the northwest bank of Bear Creek, Dec. 28, 1900, belonging to Robert R. Selway of Sheridan. Shorty Caddel, one of the raiders, named the others in 1955: Barney Hall, Charles Thex, Tug Wilson, William Boal, Frank McKinney, Frank "Booker" Lacy, Walt Snyder, Bill Munson and George W. Brewster. Two were Brewster riders on the Quarter Circle U; Boal ranched on Hanging Woman and was a son-in-law of Buffalo Bill Cody; the remaining six worked for John B. Kendrick at his OW Ranch which sprawled down Hanging Woman across the Montana state line.

•Shot to death in July, 1901, 13-year-old Willie Nickell by Tom Horn, hit man for the cattlemen, Willie's father Nels shot in the arm and hip, and many sheep killed. Horn was hanged in Laramie in 1903.

•2,000 or more sheep killed, 15 Rock Springs bands scattered, herders driven out of country July, 1902, in New Fork country of Green River Valley. By 150 masked men.

•3,000 sheep killed, herders murdered in 1902 in Big Horn Basin.

•H. P. Rothwell, owner of the Padlock Ranch on Owl Creek accosted by 13 riders while moving a band to summer feed above the Wood River divide; two bands of wethers ahead of Rothwell rimrocked for two days.

•3,000 sheep of Jesse D. Lynn run over rimrocks on Trapper Creek, the two herders made to wade at gunpoint in the icy creek.

•E. D. Metcalf of Buffalo sent his herder and 6,000 sheep across the "dead line" furrow; his wagons burned, the sheep all shot.

•4,000 sheep belonging to L. L. and Louis A. Grantz killed Aug. 24, 1905, by ten masked men, team of horses killed, 3 sheepwagons, harnesses and provisions valued at $8,000 burned; sheep dogs were tied to the burning wagons. Louis Gantz died a month later.

•400 sheep of George Crosby killed when Montana cowmen rimrocked a band which had grazed over the state line in the Pryor Mountain area.

•3 men killed, 2 wagons burned, a band (up to 3,000) of sheep killed, telephone wires to Basin cut, in Big Horn Basin April 2, 1909; killed were owners Joseph Allemand and Joe Emge, and Jules Lazier, hired men on leave from the French army. Herbert L. Brink, sentenced to hang, outlived the four given prison terms: Thomas Dixon, Edward Eaton, Milton Alexander and George Saban; Albert Keyes and Charles Farris gave state evidence and left Wyoming.

Stockmen Overtaxed Ranges

This bloody decade spawned an enduring fiction that sheep ruin range, a subterfuge used to spur cowboys into the frenzy needed to commit murder. Overgrazing by both cattle and sheep was widespread in Wyoming's early get-rich-quick days. Quite simply, there were too many of

147

Basques have been prominent in Wyoming's sheep industry since its beginning. Many settled around Buffalo, where nearby summer range at the top of the Big Horn Mountains recalls mountain meadows of their native Pyrenees.

Basque herders in Big Horns

both on the range. Sheep, however, could utilize herbage ignored by cattle, and were able to graze areas uninhabitable to cattle. They also could meet their water needs by eating snow in the winter.

Wool was Wyoming's leading industry from 1908 to 1910, when sheep numbers rose to over six million. Sen. Francis Warren was president of the National Wool Growers Association from 1901 to 1907; Dr. J. M. Wilson of Douglas was national vice president in 1906. Gov. John E. Osborne raised sheep, as did Jim Bridger and early Mormons. George T. Beck, prominent in state and national politics, was the largest woolgrower in Johnson County in 1884. Sheepman J. B. Okie spent $100,000 in 1898 to build a palace at Lost Cabin.

Though earlier flocks had been trailed in, sheep did not come in large numbers until 1877, when trail drives from California and Oregon began to reach Wyoming. Two brothers, Thomas and James Howell were reported to have trailed some 200,000 from California in the '70s and '80s. Many woolgrowers came from Scotland, like David and James Dickie who ran 20,000 high quality Rambouillet sheep and 1,000 cattle in the Meeteetse area; the brothers were buried in their $30,000 mausoleum built for two.

Robert Taylor, who began near Rawlins and later moved his operations to Poison Spider Creek near Casper, ran 100,000 head at his peak. In Big Horn Basin, Sayles Sheep Company ran 30,000, and Jesse D. Lynn ran 40,000 on Shell Creek and Black Butte. H. P. Rothwell ran nine bands on Owl Creek, summering in the mountains above the Wood River divide. Considered one of the best managed in the Basin was W. T. Hogg, Inc., which in 1917 sold 20,000 sheep and 1,000 cattle to Eychner and Winning of Johnson County; Hogg ran fine-wooled Rambouillets, using Shropshires, Hampshires and Lincolns for cross-breeding.

Tramp sheepmen were almost universally disliked. Usually owner-herded, these bands moved about the country scrounging as they could, often around homesteads on grass settlers hoped to keep for themselves. The tramps also were accused of indiscriminate burning of forest timber so their sheep could graze easier. This in-

spired artist-rancher A. A. Anderson to initiate the plan for the first significant national forest, 9,500 square miles in which limited use was enforced—a bitter blow to all sheepmen.

The state of Wyoming began paying bounties on predators in 1897, $5,613 that year, accelerating to $25,177 by 1904. In 1905, the legislature appealed to Congress for help; government trappers were employed. Conservationists finally obtained a federal ban of poison on federal land, and later totally, which frustrated the sheepmen. Thallimide sulfate, strychnine, 1080, and cyanide all were banned at one time or another; cyanide was restored to use in 1975.

Storms Sear Industry

Because sheep can be fragile creatures which, in adversity, quickly lose their will to live, a little wet weather at the wrong time can cause devastating losses. This is particularly true at lambing time and after shearing. George H. Saban in Big Horn Basin tried to trail 10,000 freshly sheared sheep in a late spring storm; he lost 3,600 of them, sold the rest and went into cattle. Winters of 1888-89, 1911-12, and 1919-20 were savage, Wyoming sheep loss estimated at 236,663 in 1912 by the U.S. Dept. of Agriculture.

Drought, winter, and plummeting prices nearly destroyed the industry several times. Drought the summer of 1919 caused one-third of Wyoming's sheep to be shipped out of state. Winter set in six weeks earlier than usual and stayed, ending with an April storm said to be the most severe since 1878. One-third of the state's remaining sheep were lost. Then prices fell—in one week from 80 cents to 25 cents a pound for wool, sheep dropped from $18 to $6, lambs from $12 to $3. Said Laramie Plains sheepman Frank S. King, "Of credit there was none and the stockmen were up against a wall."

Tariffs Tied to Party Politics

Party politics were played with tariffs at the turn of the century, accounting for most woolgrowers voting Republican. The Democrats believed in free trade, while Republicans favored import tariffs. The price of wool

Jean P. Harriet unloads on mountain top

Coyotes Meet Challenge Of Hunter by Adapting

Echoes of staccato coyote barking criss-cross the night horizon, sounds of the west's most durable varmint. He has adapted with humor and skill to all control measures tried over the past century.

"They'll dig out your trap, push it out of the hole with their nose, turn it over without tripping it—and leave it there for you to feel like a damn fool," said one trapper. Poison baits, too, were quickly psyched out by coyotes; they began using the cyanide pellet gun as a city dog uses a fireplug.

Coyotes adapt both their way of life and feeding habits, in response to man's behavior. Hunted by plane, they changed their own hunting hours; they learned, too, to dive into a hole at the sound of an airplane, though not their nature to hole up from danger. When hunters start intensive control in an area, litter size increases; up to 80 percent of the yearlings begin breeding, too, though this is not customary. Dens are moved to gumbo hardpan areas where tracks can't be seen.

Some lambers try to fool coyotes by setting up flagpoles tied with flapping material. Others burn pots of sulphur, or erect tepees in the hills so coyotes will think humans are near. But you never fool a coyote twice, they all lament.

Frustration has guided researchers into trickery, too. A chemical that tastes like tabasco sauce was developed at the University of Wyoming in 1977. Sprayed on lambs turned into a pen with hungry coyotes, it repelled the coyotes. "They'll try to take a bite and then immediately back off," said Robert McCulloch, graduate school dean. "If they get enough, they'll run to water or try to rub their muzzles in the dust." Coyotes for the UW work were supplied by a scarred rancher who ran them down with a snowmobile and wrestled them to the ground.

And sheep perfume sold in Montana gave off a sulpher-like odor unpalatable to coyotes. Sheep were dyed pink and blue in a South Dakota experiment.

swung like a pendulum, according to which party was in power—going abruptly from 6 cents to 20 cents a pound, and back down again just as abruptly. An indicator of political mood was Pat Sullivan's ad for two-year-old rams in a 1902 Stockgrower & Farmer: "Would just as leave sell to a democrat as a republican."

Price ceilings on lamb, mutton and wool during World War II put many woolgrowers out of business, as labor and feed prices soared. Huge stockpiles of domestic and foreign wool threatened the market for years to come. In order to rebuild the damaged industry, a federal incentive price was set in 1955; growers were paid the difference between this and actual market price for wool. Six Wyoming sheepmen got checks for over $100,000, and about 100 received between $20,000 and $100,000. A total of 339 woolgrowers quit the business between 1968

and 1974, 72 percent shifting to cattle.

The freighting required to pull great trains of wool wagons from shearing pens to railhead added much to Wyoming's early economy. The crews needed to shear millions of sheep annually provided jobs for many; one such itinerant shearer, Jake Houghton of Upton, estimated he sheared 490,000 head in his lifetime, first with hand blades and later with shearing machines.

A herder usually cared for a band of two to three thousand sheep, sometimes using black sheep as counters on a ratio of one to 100. With his well trained dogs, reading material, and his monument-building hobby, the herder normally lived a quiet life. However, he had to be ready to respond instantly to emergency—sudden storm or maurading coyotes, bobcats, eagles, and wolves before they were exterminated.

Wind River girls, Nanny Simpson and 100 candles.

Gambling was something to do

12. ON THE RESERVATION, OUT OF SIGHT

The Shoshone came from the far west, the Arapaho from the far east—and the incompatible twain did meet in war and in peace, forced at last to share a reservation homeland, to resolve all issues in a ponderous dual tribal council with double committee membership and under the aegis of concern for two very different nations of people, whom history had made basically inharmonious.

Life in Wyoming's slum, the Wind River Indian Reservation, is reported vividly by Grace Wetherbee Coolidge during the first decades of the 20th century—the "lost period" in Indian history when every soprano who could find a buckskin dress was singing "The Land of Sky Blue Waters," when churchmen hurried to baptize Indians in the name of the BIA, and sociologists were so busy collecting exotic stories that all failed to note that the Indian race was too tough to vanish. Disease and federal neglect, however, took their toll during these transition years. Old tribal enmity—plus their opposite roles in the white occupation—kept Shoshone and Arapaho politics simmering.

The affluent lady from Boston who married the full-blood Arapaho Episcopal priest was an anomaly herself. It was not uncommon for white men to marry Indian women, and these unions were tolerated but never really accepted. The children of such marriages were discriminated against by whites and Indians alike. In fact, the Episcopal pioneer, the Rev. Roberts tried unsuccessfully to stop the marriage of Grace Wetherbee and Sherman Coolidge; failing that, he performed the ceremony in 1902. Grace was a writer of professional caliber and her simple, factual stories of daily life on the Wind River were published in Collier's Weekly and The Outlook. Humor, heartbreak, dissolution, and dispair were her themes—the themes that dominated reservation life of the times. A collection of these stories was published in 1917 as **Teepee Neighbors**, reprinted in 1984 by the University of Oklahoma Press.

Two Kinds of Neighbors

Of "teepee neighbors," she cited two varieties, "The first is the man who hates the Indian. He lives generally across the boundary line . . . his mind is full of the old evil stories of the past told always from the side of the Indian's enemy. And he broods and he draws conclusions and he condemns . . .

"Then there is the far larger class whose attitude is one of absolute indifference and uninterest. Familiarity has bred in them a kind of comfortable contempt . . . (the reservation) offers a field wherein many indifferent and incompetent individuals may safely work a little and worry not at all . . . for once in, it is almost impossible to be ousted."

"By far the most harrowing fact of reservation life," she wrote in 1910, "is death—the great, omnipresent, overwhelming and constant nearness of death." The death rate for Indians was 32 per 1,000, contrasted with 15 per 1,000 for whites. It was not uncommon for mothers who had born up to 14 children to have lost them all.

The Rev. Coolidge himself described the reservation situation thus:

"Indians receive food every week from the government, but their rations for the week can only last, at the most, three days, so what provisions are given are sufficient to keep them alive for only half a week . . . here are a noble people endowed with every capacity and capability, under circumstances beyond their control, starving to death inch by inch, in sight of the American flag—a people who have every claim, by every principle of patriotism, of policy, of Christian love, mercy and justice, to be cared for until self-supporting, by the government of these United States. It is not only a mistaken policy but also a cruel and wicked treatment."

Coolidge, as the boy Runs-on-Top, was captured in 1870 during an Arapaho battle with Shoshones and Bannocks near Lander; he and his brother were given to U.S. troops, renamed and raised by military families. The Northern Arapahoes had continued their war with whites, in alliance with Cheyennes, until they negotiated a portion of the Wind River Reservation, under threat of being sent to Oklahoma.

Much of this warfare was still fresh in the minds of reservation Indians, such as the 1874 attack of an Arapaho-Cheyenne village in a gorge at the head of No Wood Creek, when U.S. troops and 166 Shoshones surprised the village; known as Bates Battle, this resulted in retreat when troops failed to take the cliffs above, a vantage seized by the Cheyenne and Arapaho. In reservation memories, too, were many of the outright massacres and sackings of villages: the 24 Cheyennes pursued 60 miles by Gen. Patrick E. Connor, all killed and scalped; Connor's destruction of the 500-lodge Arapaho village of Black Bear and Old David on Tongue River.

Thus much of early relations was hardly conducted by men of good will. In fact, the famous Jesuit negotiator, Jean-Pierre De Smet, said, "Nine times out of ten, the provocations come from whites—that is to say, from the scum of civilization, who bring to the Indians the lowest and grossest vices, and none of the virtues of civilized men . . ." A congressional inquiry concurred in 1865: "A large majority of the cause of Indian wars are to be traced to the aggression of lawless white men, always to be found on the frontier . . . many agents, teachers and employees of the government are inefficient, faithless, and guilty of peculations and fraudulent practices upon the government and upon the Indians."

However, there were people exercising Christian love on the early reservation, and some were influential.

One was Margaret Louise Simpson, whose father became an agricultural advisor there. As a teenager, the Episcopal girl volunteered her services to teach at Catholic St. Stephens School. This remarkable woman, who was to be the mother of Governor Milward Simpson and "Nanny" to her tall grandsons Alan and Peter, spent much of her life teaching and working with Shoshone and Arapaho children. She taught the daughters of Arapaho Chief Black Coal, and the Shoshone Chief Washakie was often a guest in her home. She was honored on her 100th birthday when reservation children traveled to Cody to light candles on her cake.

Fire destroyed agency records about 1905, and this loss became an excuse for changing Indian names to white names; "Strikes Again," for example, became William Shakespeare who later as "White Wing," with putty to re-contour his nose into an "Indian nose," appeared before the King and Queen of England with Tim McCoy's Hollywood troupe.

Important to self esteem was an invitation to St. Stephens basketball team by Chicago tournament officials, the escort of young dancers to Washington—and the granting of citizenship in 1924. In World War I, Indians had not been considered for military service; in World War II, their volunteer record was outstanding.

There was little work, and the depression of the Thirties was simply an extension of what had always been (some Indians said they fared better during the Great Depression than ever before, since they were included in general work and welfare programs). For them, however, depression lasted into the 1940s. Indians "were compelled to sell their last pony at a great deal below the real value," Coolidge reported, and even to "sell their own daughters to wicked men for a mouthful of something to eat."

Lands Steadily Whittled

The granting of reservations often appeared to be stop-gap appeasements of Indians until further whittling could be achieved. This was the case even with the Shoshones, whose Chief Washakie had carefully nurtured good relations with the whites in the hope of saving his people.

A scheme to throw half the remaining reservation open to white settlement was perpetrated in 1910. The tribe was asked to buy water rights granted by treaty. Pretext was that the federal government had turned over control of water to the state of Wyoming; only properly filled water claims were recognized and, as non-citizens, Indians could not file. Since the tribes had no money, they were pressed to sell land in order to buy these rights.

Scene of the meeting in which Indian Bureau men intended to convince Indians of this logic was reported by Grace Coolidge. Young men and mixed-bloods already had been swayed, and they rose in spurs and bright neckerchiefs to espouse the BIA line: "It is a question of water rights. We must have money to buy those rights and how else can we obtain it? It's an obligation to our children."

Patriarchs stubbornly refused to budge from the treaty position. Said one, "Let the white man from Washington go but a mile yonder, and he will see the river that flows down our valley and waters our land. It is there. It is ours. It is born in these mountains above us."

The BIA spokesman replied that "having water does not necessarily mean having rights to that water . . . times and conditions have changed. Although the question of priority has still not been decided, the Indian Bureau says that you as a tribe may buy your water rights. This thing is intricate and impossible to elucidate to the older people, your leaders. They must just hear my statements and . . . believe."

One of the elders condensed what they had been saying in the following speech laced with sarcasm:

"The strangers came like a flood, like our rivers in the spring; they surged over us and they left

Shoshone Sister Mary, right, and Catholic country church—a work of art

us—as we are. Perhaps this was the will of the Stranger-on-High, we cannot tell . . . but these strangers on earth were not altogether unkind to us. For what they took, they gave a sort of compensation. It was as though they carried away from us fat buffaloes and handed to each of us in exchange a little slice of their meat. They deprived us of our valley and our mountains but gave us each 80 acres of the land. They sent more strangers with chains and three-legged toys to measure off correctly for us. They gave us wire for our fences, but only enough so that we must spend much money for more. They gave us seed, but also so little that we were driven to buy more. We worked—some of us with the chains and three-legged toys—some at the ditches, every way we could . . . now, in his kindness, the Great Father in Washington sends to us this man. But what has he said to us? 'Give up the 80 acres, for your children to be born, give up the money you earned, give up your homes, as you gave up this valley and these mountains. The white men need them.' "

An intrusion during the 1930's federal reclamation effort resulted in loss of hundreds of thousands of acres to the Riverton-Boysen irrigation project, some of it later restored. Indian irrigation in the west began long before the advent of the white man but as soon as the federal government supplied impetus, Indian projects were almost instantly mired in BIA bureaucracy. The first Indian irrigation projects authorized in the U.S. were on the Wind River Reservation and on Fort Belknap Reservation in Montana, both in 1884. By 1963, Wind River had 38,994 acres under irrigation, with an additional 16,418 authorized for development.

School Children Suffered

Education under early assimilation policies of the BIA was a source of antagonism among Indians and knowledgeable whites, alike. "Why does the government place our children in schools where they must remain until 18, yet take them no further in their studies than the fourth grade . . . then send them out into the world to compete with whites from the universities?" Wind River critics asked. Many non-government-educated Indians were college graduates. Sherman Coolidge was a visible and vocal example—"they (BIA-educated) come back to their people only half educated . . . to meet overwhelm-

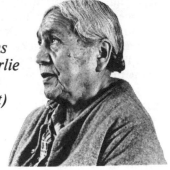

Chief Washaki's sons Dick and Charlie (above), Mary Boutone (right)

ing influences." His wife Grace spoke vigorously against the "Carlisle system" of Indian education established in 1879, the same year Indians were legally declared "persons" by U.S. Courts; some of her most heartbreaking stories focus on children removed from their homes. BIA manual-labor training schools modeled after the Carlisle "experiment" also were severely criticized in 1928 by Lewis Merriam and other educators in "The Problem of Indian Administration, Report of a Survey."

School problems in 1903 led to the arrest of Jim Tosah, a full-blood Shoshone, over the issue of correcting school children. Tosah led an assault on the Episcopal mission, "liberating" all Indian children. The agent, Captain Nickerson, ordered a 51-man Indian police force to arrest Tosah; all turned in their badges and resigned.

Miss Indian America XI, Michelle Portwood

Hollywood Star Tim McCoy

Nickerson abandoned the reservation, telling U.S. Marshal Joe LeFors, "There are about 300 Indians on a high ridge four miles west of here and a congregation of tepees in the valley with perhaps more men than that . . . do your business through Frank Smith, the acting agent."

LeFors arrested Tosah single-handed, obtained help from the opposing Washakie faction of the Shoshones to escort the prisoner to Lander. In Lander, he invited the prisoner's father, old Chief Tosah, to a feast. The son was convicted of assault-to-kill and incarcerated in Rawlins.

In a foul-up of the common federal practice of allotting reservation education to churches, Wind River received both Episcopal and Catholic ministrations. (The Indian Act of 1884, still in effect, gave the BIA charge of "civilizing and Christianizing" Indians; thus many early Indian agents also were churchmen, adamantly opposed to—and destructive of—Indian religion.)

The Catholic Bishop of Omaha, whose diocese included what would soon be the new state of Wyoming, heard that the government planned a school at Fort Washakie, and offered $5,000 to furnish it if the government would allow his church to operate it. The Rev. Jutz arrived at Lander in April, 1884—only to find the agency had assigned the school on the Shoshone side of the reservation to a Welsh Episcopal minister, the Rev. John Roberts. Learning that the Arapaho had no school, Jutz pitched his tent at Black Coal's camp near the juncture of Little and Big Wind Rivers.

Cinema's Wild West

Wind River Indians went to Hollywood in 1922, an event which turned a Wyoming adjutant general into one of the most celebrated movie stars of the time.

The bright lights of Hollywood hadn't even been turned on when Tim McCoy followed his dreams of cowboys and Indians westward. The Chicago youth got off a train in Lander in 1909 and soon was both; the "blue-eyed Arapaho" became a cowboy, learned Indian sign language, was given the name High Eagle, and participated in Arapaho ceremonies such as sweat lodge and tribal dances.

He went to World War I as a cavalry officer and, when he got home, was appointed adjutant general to develop the early Wyoming version of the National Guard. Known for his Indian connections, he was approached by a Hollywood scout who needed 500 Indians for the epic silent movie, "The Covered Wagon."

The studio would pay five dollars a day, 50 cents for each child, and one dollar a day for each horse and tepee—a lot of money for his impoverished Indian friends. McCoy quit his job, hired on as technical advisor, and launched a recruiting campaign. He signed all Arapahoes and Shoshones who would go, then completed his quota with Bannocks from Fort Hall, Idaho.

The Wind River Indians boarded a train at Rawlins bound for Milford, Utah, where most of the filming would take place; an Arapaho horse herd of 300, trailed across country, also was loaded on the train.

13. HARD TIMES OF '30s

One of the cyclic droughts natural to Wyoming struck during the late 1920s and caused national depression effects and policies to burrow deeply into the state's economy.

Had it not been for the drought, it is unlikely that the depression would have had such effect. Until 1932, Wyoming cared for its own—plus hordes of migrating poor. Only ten banks closed in the '30s, dropping the total to 73 which may have been a reasonable number; during the '20s homestead boom, 101 banks went broke. The homestead dilemma had been resolved, either people adapted or departed—what was left, 8,000 farms of 67,000, could be maintained.

Wyoming winter winds blew dry in 1930—lack of snow and rainfall in 1933 dropped average percipitation by 3.3 inches in three months. Ominous dust storms, red from out-of-state fields, blotted the sun. When this cleared, the sun swarmed with high-flying grasshoppers zeroing in on any vegetation left alive. Armies of crickets moved relentlessly, impossible to turn aside or fight. Livestock diseases never known before, jackrabbits breeding with celerity—and perplexing federal schemes—disoriented the political heart of Wyoming.

People were hungry, but in Wyoming they had been hungry before—cowboys and sheepherders alone for months in isolated camps, weather-stranded folk fighting both hunger and cold, settlers trying to farm land that shouldn't be farmed. It was a condition that went with the land.

By the end of 1933, the governor was telling the Legislature, "As public servants we have failed to measure up to our responsibilities" in dealing with ravages of drought and hunger. Wyoming was the only state which had not borrowed from the federal emergency relief loan program. The Legislature decided to cooperate with the New Deal, after listening to Gov. Leslie A. Miller chastize them for false pride:

"I wonder whether we are entitled to indulge in pride . . . we have thousands of cases of undernourished children, both children and adults lack proper clothing."

As the drought continued, lawmakers found property taxes could not bear their usual burden. The 1935 Legislature imposed a two percent sales tax. It repealed liquor prohibition and put the state in the liquor wholesaling business. It also repealed the "gin marriage" law requiring a five-day waiting period, hoping to attract more out-of-state wedding business.

The agricultural extension agents perhaps were closest to the disaster gripping the state. They had already staged jackrabbit and magpie drives; 2,090 of each were killed in Star Valley. They kept close watch on the falling markets, tried debt adjustments, and knew ahead of time what federal remedies were likely. And some of them questioned these publicly. The proposed purchase program drew this statement from A. W. Willis, extension economist, in 1933:

"Is it possible to have over-production in a country, when a great number of its citizens are ragged and hungry, a great number of its buildings un-

Black dust 'blizzards' buried farms and towns

painted and run-down, the citizens walking instead of riding in an expensive car?"

By September of 1934, the livestock purchase (and slaughter) program was ready to proceed in Wyoming. Willis then made a wry prediction: "The general outlook is good. Things could not get much worse without ending in some kind of revolution." No one could imagine a lower point; optimism seemed a safe bet.

But things could get worse, and they did.

Livestock Shot, Let Rot

In 1934, 285,227 cattle were bought, 17 percent condemned, bringing 4.2 million dollars to Wyoming growers and lienholders. Campbell County sold 32,966, the highest number but with the lowest percentages of condemned; most were range cattle. Big Horn County, with the highest percentage of condemned cattle, sold only 2,847, mostly dairy cattle. In Washakie County, sale of 2,013 was largely a culling program; it was not a critical drought area. The rancher received $3.00 to $6.00 a head; his creditors received from $1.00 to $15.00 per head. The large numbers of condemned cattle caused bitter controversy.

The government was buying Wyoming sheep at the rate of 5,000 daily, then the quota was raised to 15,000 per day. Over half a million sheep were bought from 1,626 growers, the grower receiving $1.00 per head, his creditors slightly more. Hogs were bought, $275,000 worth of mostly sows and little pigs, shot and buried in pits. Wyoming hog farmers lost so much money "it will be difficult for them to convince themselves that hog prices will ever come back," said Willis.

Killing animals and letting the meat rot was a shocking concept to many. In Casper it was feared an epidemic

Condemned sheep were shot on parched ranges, 1934, Dana sheep

of disease would result from rotting carcasses, many in watersheds. Both cattle and sheep were destroyed on the range, some of them skinned. Indians were given some of the slaughtered cattle, which they dried for winter food.

"It was just the wrong thing to do," extensionist Dr. R. A. Wilson, said. "Trying to balance supply and demand by cutting the supply. They should have increased the demand by circulating some money . . . instead of killing livestock and not letting people who are hungry have it."

Said one rancher, "They looked over my livestock, and shot the calves. We were allowed to butcher one and eat it." Such wanton destruction of food before the eyes of hungry people became one more resentment toward New Deal policies.

Some ranchers looked for alternatives. One stockman shipped two carloads of his top yearling steers to Omaha in late July (1934)—and received a freight bill for $1.59; the steers didn't pay the freight to market. Railroads cut rates for feed brought in and livestock shipped out of drought counties; the drought rate certificate, obtainable from the county agent, was attached to the bill of lading. They issued 52 such certificates for 765.8 tons of feed, and 11 certificates for 11 carloads of livestock relocated in non-drought areas.

Feed Scarce and Costly

Little feed was raised and prices were high. All ranchers were urged to cull their herds through the emergency buying program. Hay was bought and stockpiled in various counties by the Rehabilitation Corporation. County agents decided who could buy this cut-rate feed, issuing 724 disbursing orders. A total of 1,153 tons of hay, 33 tons of purina, and 16 tons of tomahawk

feed were re-sold for $20,136.76. The Red Cross sent a carload of cottonseed cake and corn to Niobrara County, a total of 5,000 tons of grain to the entire state.

Drought caused more range poisoning than normal. With grasses decimated, cattle and sheep were eating unfamiliar plants—which filled the void left by receding grass.

One strange new "disease" in cattle turned out to be poisoning from a small moss-like lichen suddenly plentiful all over Converse County. One sheepman lost 50 head overnight, while the band was on the move; it was discovered they had trailed over woody aster. Another area had larkspur poisoning. A waterhole came to be known as Poison Lake; a chemist from the University of Wyoming finally determined that the water was not poisoned at all —the culprit was selenium poison draining into streams from plants in the area.

Locusts Dropped from Sun

During these years, each disaster seemed to beget a new disaster until there was truly a pestilance upon the land.

Migratory grasshoppers dropped by the billions out of the sun on Crook, Campbell, Weston and Niobrara counties, winged armies of destruction. Mormon crickets flooded the country, marching inexorably over every barrier. Dry conditions stimulated jackrabbits and cottontails to record breeding achievements. As the rabbits multiplied, so did the coyotes.

War was declared on anything that threatened the food supply. Prairie dog and ground squirrel campaigns were undertaken. Magpies, eagles and buzzards were poisoned, trapped and shot. One shotgun shell was given out for each pair of jackrabbit ears, a box of .22 rifle shells for 15 to 20 pairs of ears. One year's harvest included 3,417 coyotes, 140 bobcats and 55 bear.

And just when all else was going wrong, it seemed the earth itself would blow away. Orville Ashment, Crook County agent, said Goshen County nearly did blow away in 1939—"they had a heck of a time nailing it down," with soil conservation measures like mulching and strip farming. The dust storms began in 1930 and continued for nine years.

Chickens and gardens helped support many families; eggs, broilers and produce were marketed to pay the grocery bill. This practice put a gleam in the eyes of bureaucrats and, in 1934, relief organizations began county and state gardens, setting up canning projects. As was too often true, they proceeded without knowledge. Seed arrived so late there was not enough moisture for germination. Heavy hail battered many gardens to a pulp. Relief supervisors had to be taught how to operate a tin can sealer installed in the Methodist church basement in Cheyenne and, counting their yields before the seed was planted, figured how many tomatoes, beans and corn would fill a one-quart jar. Supervision was inept; produce arrived at canneries in poor condition.

Six recreation camps were set up for rural mothers, strategies to build skills and morale. Here, 542 Wyoming women were trained in recreation work, social hygiene, canning meat in tins, and handicraft; they wrote essays on thrift and worked on personal development, guided by the home extension service.

Social Ailments Grew

Rugs of overalls and rubber-tired rustlers were other signs of the times. Shoplifting, suicide and library use rose. Marriage, birth, and divorce rates swung with the pendulum of depression economics. A few people toyed with the communist party, but a relief workers' strike failed in Cheyenne; snow and cold prevented a demonstration in Torrington.

A mattress project produced one-dollar mattresses and 25-cent comforters for low-income families. A mattress took 10 yards of ticking and 50 pounds of cotton; comforters took five to ten yards of percale, five pounds cotton batting. Rugs woven of worn-out overalls insulated cold cabin floors. Butter and coffee went down to 22 cents a pound, pork roast to four cents. By March 1935, there were 10,760 people on relief in Wyoming.

A common crime was theft of coal from railroads and coal yards. The "rubber-tired rustler," a mutant of mechanization, wasn't the only one stealing livestock; many were rustling in order to survive. Two miners unemployed for more than a year, slaughtered a horse for meat for their families; charges were dropped when they agreed to pay the owner for loss. A group of 70 hungry hobos killed a steer near Sheridan; when law officers went to their jungle to find the criminal, all claimed guilt and were loaded onto a flat car headed out of town.

Librarians found their work doubling, as people did more reading. Book check-outs at the Cheyenne Carnegie Library rose to 208,809 in 1932, up from 124,163 checkouts in 1929; classics and old favorites were being read, with light and humorous fiction spurned. As the bottom dropped out of the economy, divorces also dropped—from 704 in 1929 to 598 in 1932. Divorces rose in 1936, 1937 and 1939—as tempers flared under long-standing

Auctioneer Jim Mader sold remains of homestead dreams

financial pressure. Births and marriages climbed when hope did, following a year of prosperity; between 1935 and 1940, the birth rate nearly doubled the annual death rate, 4,698 births, 2,386 deaths. Curiously, Wyoming did not lose population during the depression as did neighboring states—population rose by 25,000, to a total of 250,742 by 1940.

Education both suffered and benefited during depression years. High school attendance grew, older students going to school because there was no work. One-fifth of Wyoming teachers earned less than $600 a year, five percent made less than $299 and the state lost 228 teachers. In one instance, the teacher received $45 a month; the district held out $5 to guarantee her contract, and she was charged $30 for room and board. Wyoming Stock Growers, meeting in Cheyenne in 1933, considered suspending schools for a year. Federal funding became available in 1934, Sheridan receiving $13,000 because 25 percent of students came from rural areas. By May, schools in 18 counties had applied for federal funding.

Economics Manipulated

Credit and debt adjustment efforts were predicated upon the depression, not upon the drought. That the bottom dropped out of the livestock market was a depression phenomenum; glutting of the market, however, was caused by the drought. And drought occurred eight of the ten years between 1929 and 1939. Creditors in Laramie County began by taking a 36.1 percent discount, going as high as 50 percent; a loan then was arranged to cover all debts and assure a "new start"—this, in 1934, with five more years of drought ahead.

Production was curtailed by applying constant pressure for acreage cuts. Wheat growers in 1933 were paid $400,000 for acreage idled. It was hoped this would increase prices. The state economist, however, said, "When the consumer has no money . . . a reduction of 90 percent in production will not have much influence on price." A pre-war parity base was used in trying to manipulate the economy, but it was concluded that either prices had to go up 40 percent—or commodities bought by growers had to come down 40 percent. Farmers were demoralized by the very record books they were urged to keep.

Early in the depression, Wyoming appeared to take an isolationist view—"The gloom and depression . . . of the east has been met with courage and optimism in Wyoming" and "This state has felt the effects least of all the states" and "Wyoming is in comparatively good condition." This was all true, as both Wyoming's unemployment rate and the percent of population on relief remained well below the U.S. average throughout the depression.

Westerners, whatever their party, distrusted federal bureaucrats. They believed in the virtues of self help and did not want to admit a need for generous, long-term state spending for relief and welfare. Sometimes these high-sounding statements contained a grain of hypocrisy; for example, the Wyoming Stock Growers' 1936 attacks on federal encroachment on the livestock industry—after availing themselves of three years of federal drought livestock buying, expensive rodent and predator control programs, free dams built on their ranges, and payment for unplanted acres.

Criticism of New Deal policies, however, crossed party lines and much of it was valid. "It was like putting a workhorse harness on a Shetland pony," snapped Scotty Jack, speaker of the House in 1933. Too much confusion, complexity and experimentation, it was charged; federal supervisors were too numerous and too well paid, employees engaged in overlapping activity.

Gov. Miller, a Democrat criticized by his own party for not throwing all Republicans out of office, insisted on projects of permanent value. "This is tax money," he said, "and must be spent impartially in accordance with need, regardless of political considerations." His greatest complaint about New Deal officials was that they tried to establish in Wyoming programs not appropriate for a sparsely settled state. His administration resisted federal policies. Most labor reforms thus were rejected.

Predators Were Hunted

Predator drives proceeded out of need, but federal involvement received reluctant state approval. An already semi-arid climate became a catalyst, in drought, for many disastrous impacts. Insect and animal eradication efforts were only a few.

Epidemics razed the rabbit population every few

CCC: 'Forgotten Flotsom'

The Depression "made men," western style, of easterners in Wyoming, where they flowed by the thousands into CCC camps and WPA work crews. The Civilian Conservation Corps, which took young men from 18 to 25, worked in the forests, built sidewalks, community buildings, roads, flood control projects and water mains.

Most CCC boys were "the forgotten flotsam on the backwash of an economic system which had broken down," and their camps—32 in Wyoming—were "like a movie prison scene" to one writer. Of one million men enrolled the first two years, many were products of steel and concrete jungles who "suddenly became men" in the west where they found the stillness of the night more terrifying than the rumble of elevated trains or the blast of foghorns.

Some were tough, embittered and anti-social, taking the CCC as an alternative presented by the police. Most were from impoverished families caught in a depression like Wyoming weathered at its fiercest during the height of the ill-conceived homestead days.

In one Wyoming camp, a food riot was put down by men armed with pickaxes. Table scenes were often rowdy, with men beating on tables with mess gear. Word of a plot to throw cold potatoes reached the captain in one camp; he stepped on a stump and warned, "I have taken all I can stand from you. The first man who throws a potato in that mess hall tonight will get a bullet right between his eyes." He stood by the mess door with a holstered revolver on his hip.

If undisciplined, they were disciplined. If they came west in poor physical condition, they soon perked up in both body and spirit.

Within a month the men had bared their backs to the sun and were bragging about the daily production of their crews. At first, they took a ten minute break every hour; as they toughened, the breaks lessened. Those not routed from bed by the 5 a.m. whistle were dumped from their cots. If they didn't willingly shower, they were forced under; the rebellious were handed axes and crosscut saws and put on wood details. There were wholesale discharges from some camps, but few accidents—one man sliced his foot lengthwise with an axe; his foot was saved after an 18-mile ride back to camp and a 130-mile truck trip to a hospital.

By the end of a summer, these young men were described as "tougher, browner, heavier, more self-assured, confident and cooperative." They began to take pride in their work, and for ten years the U.S. Park Service enjoyed the best fire protection in its history.

The Needy Streamed Into Wyoming

The westward migration that reached Wyoming in 1931 was unwelcome and strained an already poverty-burdened state. The first wave of "Okies" from the dust bowls of the midwest, desperate people from the south, and from the east, reached Cheyenne in that year. They wandered into the southeast corner of the state afoot and in jalopies with no brakes and bare tires; they brought beloved possessions and children in various stages of ragged dress and hunger.

"Go west, where there is plenty of work," they had been told—and for three years Wyoming officials vainly tried to pass the word east that there was no work here. There was no federal relief, either. Until Christmas 1934, the state operated its own transient relief facilities, closed finally on federal orders to induce people to return home and stay if they wanted relief.

By 1933 when federal aid arrived, one of every five Wyoming citizens was receiving relief of some kind. It was proposed that schools be closed. Seven thousand farm families not on relief needed help to avoid losing their property.

But by October 1932, the city of Cheyenne had aided 20,000 transients, first through a relief committee, then the American Legion, and later through the Salvation Army. The Red Cross was so overburdened in Cheyenne by this time that it withdrew relief, keeping only clothing and sewing projects open. That spring and summer, the Veteran's Bonus Army, one platoon after another, passed through enroute to Washington, D.C. Each group of 200 to 300 stopped and was fed—until July, when it was discovered that many were in the 17 to 20 age bracket, too young to be veterans.

Despite its own problems, Wyoming opened its heart with generosity for the impoverished migrations.

As this grew from a trickle to a flood, drives were conducted throughout the state by the Boy Scouts and the Legion. Benefit shows and dances raised money for aid. Kiwanis, the American Auxiliary, Help-One-Another Club and many other civic organizations chipped in.

---

years—in 1926, 1932, 1936, 1939. Tuleremia was suspected. Rabbits thus were not considered safe for human consumption, to be handled with care by hunters. During localized epidemics, both jackrabbits and cottontails died in large numbers in winter and spring.

Shotgun drives in Goshen and Niobrara counties accounted for 5,000 jackrabbits; the governor and county commissioners bought the ammunition. WPA crews were sent on night rabbit missions throughout the state. When local rainfall in east central Platte County in 1934 produced 10,000 acres of crops, jackrabbits moved in by the thousands from drier areas. A relief crew encircled fields with salt and strychnine baits, destroying 1,400 black-tailed jacks. A rabbit and magpie drive was credited with saving 150 tons of hay and preventing much loss of poultry; over 2,000 of each were killed.

Ground squirrels and prairie dogs were poisoned. Ranchers donated horses, boarded relief workers, and often furnished labor for these eradication efforts. The war on predators went into high gear in 1929, aimed at coyotes, bobcats and bear. Taking one coyote in four sections only harvests the crop, but does nothing to reduce the numbers, finally pointed out Adolph Hamm, district game management agent.

Coyotes are survivors. Sheepmen were fond of the aphorism: "When the last man on earth has died, a coyote will be there cleaning his bones." Indeed, coyotes chewed off feet caught in traps, lived, and bred mightily. A Natrona County hunter, C. D. Lee tracked to her den one female coyote with three peg-legs, one so short she had no use of it. Lee killed her with a shovel as she stood to fight. Eight pups were found in the shallow washout den. And Lloyd Smethurst came upon a peg-legged coyote while hunting his saddle horse, bridle in hand. The startled coyote blundered into a bush and Smethurst knocked it unconscious with his riding bridle.

Voracious Insect Hords

Besides the local grasshoppers which seemed to multiply in direct ratio to the drought, the '30s brought visitations of the dreaded migratory grasshoppers, or locusts. These came in awesome swarms, hit and run invasions against which there was little defense; an international conference on them was held in London in 1932.

Grasshoppers threatened in 1936 to destroy crops in six northeastern counties; Sheridan, Crook and Weston counties were hardest hit. The WPA employed 700 men through spring and summer to spread thousands of tons of arsenic dust. Rain in June, 1937, brought relief. By 1938 the grasshoppers were under control—and the migratory locusts struck without warning. Hardest hit were Crook, Campbell, Weston and Niobrara counties.

Deadly arsenic was the only defense against hordes of crickets that infested many Wyoming counties.

"Crickets would just sit in the rutted tracks of dirt roads. When you drove into them your wheels would spin," recalled Orville Ashment. "They didn't hop or fly. Just walked . . . marched all together through the whole county at the same rate, in the same direction."

Cricket fences detoured them into pits where they could be burned. The fences, often two or three rows deep, were rolls of tin about a foot high erected in front of advancing armies. When some got caught, crickets behind walked over fallen comrades until they had made a bridge. Thus arsenic on the egg beds was the only effective strategy.

Jack Lytton, who lived east of Powder River, said the river stopped the crickets swarming across fields and ranges from the northwest. He first saw them in the summer of 1937 while working for Kendrick Cattle Co.

Mormon crickets swarm over building

Wheat fields along the Wyoming border were black with Mormon crickets. "We sprayed poison every day, but with little success. The road to Sheridan was slick with those run over."

Crickets laid 50 to 200 eggs per square foot in beds over 35,000 acres in Converse County. Tons of arsenic dust, 33,250 pounds, were spread on the southern third of the county to protect 250,000 acres. Relief workers were tested for susceptibility to arsenic poisoning, and a first aid station was hauled to the field each morning.

Drought Dangled Hope

The people who built Wyoming were fighters. They didn't give up easily, and rarely excused their failures.

The path traced by the drought through the decade of the '30s was so erratic that it built false hope; time after time, those hardest hit thought they had "got a handle on it," but just as predators were controlled, overproduction curtailed, creditors and banks coaxed into refinancing . . . the dry years again were upon them. From 1929-30, when scant winter snowfall dried up irrigation ditches—through 1939, the final dry year—there was a constant "building back" process underway; banks began rebuilding in 1935.

Farm valuations reflected the desperate times: In 1930, the value of Wyoming farms was $206,852,171; by 1935, value had dropped to $166,773,698—despite a slight increase in number of farms. Irrigation projects were launched, such as Big Thunder in Campbell, Weston and Niobrara counties; seed loans to $50 were extended. In late 1936, the federal government bought 300,000 acres of Wyoming land on the theory that it would not support human subsistence, returning it to grazing, forest and recreational use. The depression ended with 8,000 total farms, 6,000 of them under irrigation.

Dam Powder River?
The Threat Lingers On

The specter of Moorhead Dam still haunts industrialists and ranchers, alike. Tattered curtains droop in a broken window; dry wind weathers the logs of saloon and general store, abandoned for half a century. Cement foundations gape vacantly on a high plateau. A sidewalk leads to more such foundations on the Powder River valley floor.

These are skeletons from bureaucratic closets, superimposed on signs of old Indian trails. And new generations of ranchers wait in the shadows to combat each new assault on Powder River water.

The ghost town of Moorhead on the Wyoming-Montana line is a relic of the homestead era imposed on wild, arid badlands by eastern politicans who thought anyone ought to be able to make a living on 160 acres. As the homesteaders dried out or blew away, cattle and sheepmen bought their holdings and adapted to this old buffalo range—knowing what easterners didn't, that the land would never adapt to them.

Up-river, site of abortive Moorhead dam four miles north of the Wyoming line lie remains of a newer federal project, which also didn't pan out. Not before $3 million went the way of Powder River's topsoil precipitate was the project stopped.

But Moorhead keeps right on rearing out of the political quicksand.

Old 1940 plans for Moorhead dam were dusted off in 1970. Industry again applied to states of both Wyoming and Montana for water from the silty Powder. The site lies near the south end of a string of coal gasification plants planned between Gillette and Colstrip.

Intake Water Co., a subsidiary of Tenneco, Inc. of Houston asked Montana and Wyoming approval of a new proposal to build the dam; specifications were the same as in the 1940 plan with one exception—paper allocation of water was shifted to replace "flood and silt control" with "industrial" usage.

More than a dozen other proposals for Powder River development were filed with the Wyoming state engineer. Under a 1950 pact, Montana and Wyoming must concur on Powder River development.

Feisty Clark (Speck) Ritchie of Buffalo dusted off files of his 35-year-old anti-dam fight. Other ranchers along the Powder braced for another round; biologist Dr. John Watt dug out his old siltation records which prove a dam would clog with slit within two years.

Draining 350 miles of some of Wyoming's and Montana's roughest country, the Powder is unique among rivers. "Mile wide, inch deep . . . too thin to plow, too thick to drink," went the jingle.

It flows true north out of the Big Horn mountains onto the flatlands. Warming first its southern upstream regions, spring often forces runoff into its still-frozen, downstream (up on the map) northern reaches—causing horrendous ice jams. At flood stage, the river channel slices back and forth across a mile-wide bottom, grabbing enormous chunks of land and depositing it elsewhere.

(continued on page 160)

Bill Lynde's outfit on Powder River ice, big sleds hooked together in winter

(continued from page 159)

Treacherous quicksand bars figure in many a western cattle-drive tale—and still pose danger. Its capricious channel continues to amaze those who know it best, as it undulates across the alluvial flat between ramparts of shale and gumbo. With each channel change, the quicksand deposits also shift. Much of the year it can be waded.

But there are times when, swollen with flash floods, it rips out its bank to deposit silt many feet thick—and swirl tons more into the Yellowstone, hence to the Missouri and, finally, to the Mississippi. A 1923 flood completely buried eight-foot fence posts in the silt.

Three types of erosion saturate the water with fine, light soil that becomes quicksand; it's a mixture of sand, pulverized red shale, gravel and gumbo clay. There is wind erosion, bank erosion, and raindrop erosion. All of this is not rich topsoil. An almost-sterile "blue type of soil" runs from the river's south prong. Other tributaries bring in alkali dust able to grow nothing, and poisonous in concentrations.

It Became an Albatross

The politically hot potato that was Moorhead dam began half a century ago when Bureau of Reclamation and Army Corps of Engineers reached into their files and chose 25 previously surveyed damsites. Calling politicians together, they offered, in effect, "Build 15 of these. Choose what's most politically advantageous to you." Wyoming Sen. Joseph C. O'Mahoney opted for the Moorhead site four miles into Montana, thinking it was in his territory; it was to hang lake an albatross around his neck.

Bureaucrats began sowing tax dollars over the sterile badlands. They drew up pounds of plans, built two towns, carved roads—and spent $3 million.

A town was built below the damsite—with sewers, streets and sidewalks. It later was found to be unwisely located. Engineers swarmed over the ridges, drilling holes. Workers resurfaced the Bitter Creek road to bring in supplies and construction material 75 miles from the railroad at Gillette.

A second townsite was established high on a windy plateau. Most foundations were poured, houses built, appliances trucked in through the rough country. A road was carved out of the sagebrush on another ridge, passage to what would be the spillway excavation.

Ranchers Stopped Dam

Meanwhile Wyoming ranchers were amassing facts and forces. An amendment to an appropriations bill by the dam's sponsor, Sen. O'Mahoney, finally put a stop to it in 1944.

Work on the town stopped, a ghost town created of a town that never knew life. Buildings were boarded and padlocked. A few years later still-crated appliances were declared surplus, claimed by the Forest Service, and moved to the west coast.

Now, wind whispers in juniper and pine over what was to have been a roaring dam boomtown. Concrete foundations lie in the grass like house-shaped cookie cutters. A sidewalk goes nowhere . . . young cottonwood trees not indigenous to the high plateau shake golden leaves into excavations where another intruder, cheat grass, indicates an old roadbed; sagebrush has not yet grown back.

Hearings in Montana, Wyoming and Washington, D.C. had mustered formidable foes to the dam.

Sheepmen, the Farm Bureau, the Izaak Walton League, western newspapers—even garden clubs as far east as Maine—rallied to the anti-dam crusade. A report by nearly 100 non-governmental engineers to President Harry Truman called planning and execution of the Missouri River Basin program "almost entirely backward," lacking in over-all national policy on land and water; they charged the program was authorized in haste and lacked an inventory of basin resources.

Co-author of the Pick-Sloan plan, W. G. Sloan, yelled foul play. Protesters had caught the bureau unawares, complained Sloan who chaired the Missouri Basin Inter-agency Committee.

14. GREAT JERK TEAMS SUPPLIED THE STATE

To say that the jerkline teamster was the key to Wyoming's early growth would not be an exaggeration. Mine shafts could not have been dug, oil wells drilled, towns built, or wool hauled to market . . . had it not been for the bull-whacker, the mule-skinner, and drivers of the multi-horse teams.

The lords of the jerklines, who paired as many as 12 teams to pull tons of freight, linked the isolated camps, mining towns and homesteads to the outside world. They were hardy, flamboyant men, dragging the Red Desert sand, fording Power River quicksand, their big string teams careening up mountain canyons, and across the miles of prairie. To those who listened long weeks for the jangling harnesses, the cracking whips and bellowing freighter, he was larger than life.

The sleek mule teams of Munkres and Mather were the pride of the trail north from Cheyenne, in handsome harness, fine wagons and skillful drivers; an outfit usually consisted of 24 mules and eight wagons, or two teams of ten mules each. Government freighting also was done with mules, usually from Camp Carlin.

The bull-whackers drove oxen, four to eight yoke pulling a big double-box Studebaker, lounge, and two trail wagons. The rear wagon had a built-in kitchen, with a door that swung down as a table. The trip from Cheyenne to Buffalo could take two months.

The big string teams that supplied southwest Wyoming had to drag through desert sand from one waterhole to the next. The freighter had to arrange to stop on water each night, and distances between water varied. In the fine sand, the horses sank to their fetlocks with each step. Wide wagon wheels, six to eight inches, were used by desert freighters to keep from sinking too deeply. Even so, the pace was slow and arduous, the driver sometimes getting off the wagon to lead his outfit across the parched land. Rock Springs to Jackson was over 100 miles; Eden Valley could be reached in three days.

Harnessing such a team took know-how. The harness was fastened only at the hames and at the belly band. To unharness, it was opened both places and laid over the lead chain. A nosebag of grain was put on each horse when it was in position for harnessing, making it possible for one man to harness many horses. The jerkline was hooked to the lead team and to the halter of every horse down the line. The entire "string team" was turned by jerks on this single line.

Bill Lynde who freighted northeastern Wyoming for many years, in winter hauled sleds on Powder River's sinuous ribbon of ice—"you'd meet yourself a-comin' back." A sled loaded with 13,000 pounds of oats and 100 bales of hay once broke through the ice during a snowstorm. Lynde had to wade in icy water to unload the sled as the wide box rested on the ice. He then linked his teams together to pull out the empty sled—and reloaded.

Six to eight-horse teams pulled sleds hooked together, hauling freight from the railroad at Arvada into northeastern Wyoming. Freighters learned to stop their outfits in a semi-circle at night, in order to get moving in the morning—after runners were loosened with a crowbar. River ranchers remember the sound: "You could hear them long before they came around the bend in the river, yelling and whips cracking."

During the hard winter of 1919-1920, the freighters returned to the railroad loaded with cowhides. They reported cows so weak they were hung in slings, calves with frozen feet chewed off by starving hogs, wolves in the breaks preying on outlying stock. Some ranches worked three skinning crews at once. These freighters included Dave Campbell, Matt Thoet, Less Lish and Fletcher (Denver) Williams. Most freight outfits kept a stove going in a tent set up on the back sled, where the driver could thaw himself as his teams plodded up the frozen river.

Jerkline team loaded with wool hauled into Gillette from northeast corner of state

Early power plants were prototypes, like Tramway No. 2 at Carbon, above

Electric Generation Swings on Pendulum of Market Demand

Natural gas had replaced coal for heating in the 1930s, making early power plants obsolete. Forty years later, the economic tide had turned; coal gasification plants by the dozens went on the drawing boards.

Coal-burning electric utilities at Glenrock and Kemmerer expanded in the 1960s. By 1977, there were five large electric utilities plants across the state, and two experimental gasification plants in operation in Carbon and Campbell counties. The Jim Bridger plant in Sweetwater County generated 2,000 megawatts. Glenrock and Platte County each had 1,500 megawatt plants, Lincoln County a 750 megawatt, and Gillette a 330 megawatt experimental air-cooled plant.

The industrial rush to build would soon create excess generating capacity, as it became clear that a miscalculation was made in the amount of energy that could be marketed. Conservationists were to seize upon this and demand a shift of the energy mix from nonrenewable to renewable sources—and more efficient consumption.

Sugar beets were a crop leader for 50 years, until rising costs caused factory shutdowns. Architectural ingenuity converted this one at Sheridan into an office building in 1978.

15. A SOLVENT STATE

Men at the reins of early government had the painstaking task of pulling Wyoming up by her bootstraps. Serialized dreams of riches vaporized in hard winters that bankrupt millionaire stockmen, in demise of army payrolls, mining boom-busts, and the non-taxable status of nearly half the state's land and 72 percent of the minerals federally owned.

Railroads were both a blessing and a curse. Westbound hordes that had re-supplied their caravans in Wyoming now sped through with hardly a purchase. Further, the railroads claimed their properties weren't taxable, since they were chartered to perform duties of a public character. For the Union Pacific, this was 4,582,520 acres. Without this, the state had only 394,789 taxable acres. Fortunately, the railroad lost this issue in the U.S. Supreme Court, so that one-third of early Wyoming property tax came from the UP; on the minus side were UP's import of cheap Chinese labor, failure to improve shops and passenger stations, its town-lot policies, excessive freight rates, and inflated coal prices.

Somehow, the grit to defy adversity—plus an enduring faith in Wyoming's destiny—sustained early builders. Often it seemed nothing lived up to their expectations. The first state budget was $168,000, $250,000 in 1897; there wasn't enough money to finish building the state penitentiary, and appropriations to the new university had to be cut back to $5,000. Fifteen banks closed the year Wyoming became a state, the state itself losing $44,000 in one closure. Laramie, the hope of industrialization, lost its glassworks, flour mill and cigar factory in quick succession; its rolling mill, employer of

180, was on the skids. Negotiations for new businesses fell on deaf ears, for the 1890s were bad everywhere.

Thirty years would seem a long time to bear patiently the 1873 words of Joseph M. Carey—"be not discouraged, much toil and perseverence must be endured . . ." Political careers rose and fell in that time. Patience, however, would be rewarded. By 1917, Wyoming was prospering and the worst economic agonies were over.

The huge Swan Land and Cattle Company went broke in 1887, as did Converse Cattle Company; Union Cattle Company was bankrupt by 1888. Warren Livestock Company went into receivership in 1894. The largest mercantile in the state, also a Warren enterprise, stayed afloat but with a struggle. In Rawlins, there was a boycott against soldiers and U.S. marshals enforcing a federal court order against a Union Pacific strike in sympathy for striking out-of-state workers. More than 800 Wyoming men lost their jobs and five Rawlins men were arrested, including the newspaper editor, the city marshal and a court clerk.

The Nation Had a Stake

Often criticized for reliance on federal funds and projects, politicians nevertheless took a long and pragmatic view of state finances. Geography and geology had determined that the state would play a vital role in national progress, first as a highway to developing the entire northwest and second in the wealth of critical minerals—coal, uranium, oil and gas. Further, federal interests had been served in drastic reduction of the volume of taxable land. Even in 1975, the federal government spent $1.41 in Wyoming for every dollar of federal taxation collected; the turning point came the following year.

Wyoming's fortune was to be in oil. In 1921, the state's share of federal royalty on oil extracted from her bosom was $748,445. This income rose swiftly with market surges, wildcat frenzy and new technology. By 1924, income on federal oil was $4,223,298; this declined, then rose after World War II until mineral severance tax revenues reached $45,576,641 in 1977, and Wyoming received $59 million as its share of federal royalties.

By then, there were 14 refineries in the state and 12,100 people were employed in oil and gas extraction, with 12,300 working in other mining. A school section in the Salt Creek Field brought many millions to the state. The state and counties had collected property tax on all crude oil production since 1913; other oil revenue came in from leases on state lands. Indeed, expanding oil production helped cushion economic difficulties in the 1920s and 1930s.

Geography: The Final Word

Distance from market and lack of a large labor pool were two drawbacks to industrialization of Wyoming. Because of its remoteness from the nation's large population centers, transportation would always be a high-cost factor. This, too, would determine population levels, with imported labor numbers fluctuating with the raw materials market. The arid state didn't have enough water for many industries—this would be the main reason coal slurry pipelines were found not feasible in the 1970s. The climate, too, with its wide-ranging temperatures and bitter winters, was another drawback. None of the foregoing elements could be changed; geography would have the final say in many matters.

Regular infusions of federal money continued to be necessary to keep the economy viable. During World War II, the federal government spent over $130 million in the state for war facilities and supply contracts; World War I had also brought prosperity. Warren Air Force Base helped keep Cheyenne's economy healthy. Wyoming became a major intercontinental missile center, with Minuteman and Atlas installations helping stabilize finances.

Pipeline to Encampment snaked across hills in 1903

Ice plant at Evanston provided jobs at turn-of-century

Gold-feverish South Pass City, key to westward trails, also gave Wyoming women the vote

Women's Militia stands at attention for statehood ceremony

WYOMING WOMEN ALWAYS
- **Had Voting Rights**
- **Asserted themselves as**
  - **—Public Officials**
  - **—Business Women**
  - **—Outlaws**
  - **—Ranchers and Farmers**

Nellie Scott

Esther Morris

WOMEN USED VOTE, AND HELD OFFICE

Though it took women nearly a century to wrest the vote from a male dominated world, Wyoming women were quietly voting, holding public office, operating businesses, ramrodding both ranches and rustling schemes, 62 years before women in the rest of the United States.

Women were given the right to vote, property rights, and protected from school wage discrimination by the first territorial legislature in 1869. The suffrage bill was introduced by William H. Bright, supported by territorial secretary Edward M. Lee who had vainly introduced a similar bill two years earlier in the Connecticut Legislature.

A tea party in boistrous South Pass City is often cited as the peg with which to credit Esther McQuigg Hobart Morris, a woman "heroic in size and masculine in mind"— but Wyoming historian T. A. Larson doubts this. Morris is said to have elicited pre-election promises from both Bright and his opponent that each would introduce such a bill. Struggling U.S. suffragettes, at any rate, selected Esther Morris as their heroine and she did serve in 1870 as the first female

justice of the peace. The next year she charged her husband with assault and battery and left him to live with a son.

Known now as "the equality state," Wyoming followed into statehood with enfranchisement and other rights for women. The legislature had wired Sen. Joseph Carey: "Wyoming bids me say to you she will stay out of the Union 100 years if she cannot come in with woman suffrage in her Constitution."

The first woman in the world to cast a vote was white-haired Louisa Ann Gardner Swain, who stopped at the Laramie polls on her way to buy yeast. Like Swain, most of the one thousand women in Wyoming did cast votes that September day in 1870— and most of them Republican; this led to a futile 1871 attempt by the Democrats to disenfranchise women.

The first woman in history to be called for jury duty was Eliza Stewart, a Laramie teacher, who was sworn in with five other women in March 1870 by Judge John Howe in an effort to obtain justice on the frontier.

*'Build roads,'
said voters*

*'Develop our resources
but with care'*

Wind River Canyon road scores granite

Early oil well polluted stream

WYOMING POLITICS
HAD A SOUND RING

Wyoming has reaped the political benefits of continuity in public office—her ship of state steered by long-tenured people of power and talent. They created a diversified economy which also prevented any single industry from seizing a monopolistic grip, despite forays by railroad, cattle and oil interests.

Grassroots attitudes united early behind several principles which have always furnished philosophical guidelines for politicians: (1) Develop resources, with environmental concern; (2) Be conservative, neither radical to the right nor to the left; (3) Seek federal spending but not intervention; (4) Verbalize pride of state, promote and protect; (5) Adhere to frontier values, independence and self-reliance.

The first of Wyoming's great politicians was Francis E. Warren, R., twice territorial governor, first state governor, and U.S. Senator for 37 years. Though called a "pork barrel artist," he nevertheless realized the new state could not become solvent without vast infusions of federal funding—and he kept the umbilical cord to Washington, D.C. throbbing with life. Warren fulfilled early needs to increase migration, to build industry, to strengthen agriculture, and to develop resources.

Paralleling Warren's career was Joseph M. Carey, R., for 46 years a public servant—U.S. attorney for Wyoming, associate justice of the Wyoming Territorial Supreme Court, territorial delegate to Congress, governor and U.S. Senator. He led the statehood movement, promoted reclamation, founded the Wheatland Colony, and lost control of the Republican Party to Warren.

A third early strong-man was John B. Kendrick, a cattleman as were Carrey and Warren, and a Democrat who tried to avoid partisan politics. Unbeatable at the polls, Kendrick was governor from 1915 to 1917, then served in the Senate until his death in 1933. Called the "craftiest politican the state has ever produced," Kendrick concentrated on furthering Wyoming's economic interests, with special attention to livestock, sugar beets, and reclamation. He also bared the Teapot Dome oil scandal to the nation.

Party alliances of the significant Wyoming politi-

Francis E. Warren

Joseph M. Carey

Milward Simpson

For related stories on Sen. John B. Kendrick, see page 126; for Sen. Malcolm Wallop, page 54; and for the political Simpsons, page 53.

cians have been evenly divided between Democrat and Republican, with the record showing the Democrats as more conservative than the national norm and the Republicans perhaps less so. In fact, it is often hard to tell the party by the players. Kendrick was as conservative in economic philosophy as either Warren or Carey, who was once a Bull Moose Progressive. Faced with the desire to develop resources and to achieve solvency, all assiduously courted federal funds and projects.

Successively a part of six U.S. territories and four foreign nations, Wyoming not surprisingly drew into politics cosmopolitan men and women of exceptional talents and diverse backgrounds. One such man was the grandson of a U.S. President and the great-great-grandson of another, Benjamin Harrison and William Henry Harrison. Bill Harrison, R., Sheridan attorney and rancher, served five years in the state house of representatives and ten years as Wyoming's lone U.S. Representative.

1861-1863

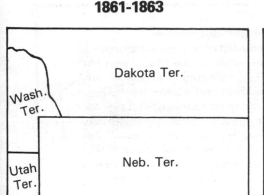

Wash. Ter.

Dakota Ter.

Utah Ter.

Neb. Ter.

1869

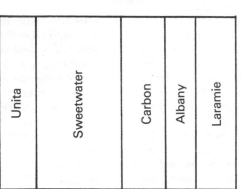

| Unita | Sweetwater | Carbon | Albany | Laramie |

Today

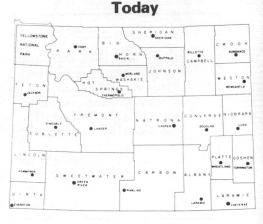

Joseph and Robert Carey were a father-son political team whose influence stretched over six decades. The Simpson "dynasty" went into its seventh decade in the 1980s. The political influence of the two families overlapped in the 1920s and '30s, as the Carey power wanned after Robert followed his father in the governor's chair, and the Simpson power ascended. Milward Simpson, R., served as governor, 1955-1959, following years as a state legislator and two decades at the reins of the University of Wyoming board of trustees. Milward's son, Alan, was elected U.S. Senator in 1979; another son, Peter, was elected to the state house of representatives.

Some Died With Their Boots On

Many men and women devoted entire working lifetimes to elective public service. And, in frontier tradition, some literally died with their boots on—Keith Thomson, R., one month after election to the U.S. Senate following three terms as a U.S. Representative; Sen. John B. Kendrick, D., at age 76; Gov. William B. Ross, D., of appendicitis complications in 1924; and Lester C. Hunt, D., who shot himself in his Senate office after six years as governor and eight in the U.S. Senate.

Demonstrating the most staying power in the U.S. Senate was Joseph O'Mahoney, who looked after Wyoming business, agriculture and mineral industries there for 25 years, then was drafted to finish out Hunt's term. A Democrat, O'Mahoney was the Irish protege from Boston of Sen. Kendrick, and filled out the latter's last term. His independence earned quick approval back home, when he bolted his party to oppose a Supreme Court reform plan; he introduced the Synthetic Fuels Act of 1944 that laid groundwork for broadening coal uses, brought the alumina plant to Laramie, and presented to Congress the over-all Missouri River Basin plan.

Wyoming's U.S. House of Representatives seat was held for 26 years by Frank W. Mondell, R. Teno Roncalio, D., Cheyenne lawyer and banker, son of a Rock Springs coal miner, was elected to this post five terms. Gale W. McGee, D., served 18 years in the U.S. Senate. Clifford P. Hansen, R., Jackson Hole cattleman, won the governorship in 1962, then was sent to the U.S. Senate for 12 years. Gov. Frank. A. Barrett, R., went on to serve four terms in the U.S. House and then took away O'Mahoney's Senate seat.

Stanley K. Hathaway, R., served as governor for

GOVERNORS OF WYOMING
1890-1985

NAME	TERM OF OFFICE
Francis E. Warren—R	Oct. 11 to Nov. 24, 1890
Amos W. Barber—R (Acting)	1890 to 1893
John E. Osborne—D	1893 to 1895
William A. Richards—R	1895 to 1899
DeForest Richards—R	1899 to 1903
Fenimore Chatterton—R (Acting)	1903 to 1905
Bryant B. Brooks—R	1905 to 1911
Joseph M. Carey—D	1911 to 1915
John B. Kendrick—D	1915 to 1917
Frank Houx—D (Acting)	1917 to 1919
Robert D. Carey—R	1919 to 1923
William B. Ross—D	1923 to 1924
Frank Lucas—R (Acting)	1924 to 1925
Nellie Tayloe Ross—D	1925 to 1927
Frank C. Emerson—R	1927 to 1931
Alonzo M. Clark—R (Acting)	1931 to 1933
Leslie A. Miller—D	1933 to 1939
Nels H. Smith—R	1939 to 1943
Lester C. Hunt—D	1943 to 1949
Arthur G. Crane—R (Acting)	1949 to 1951
Frank A. Barrett—R	1951 to 1953
C. J. Rogers—R (Acting)	1953 to 1955
Milward L. Simpson—R	1955 to 1959
J. J. Hickey—D	1959 to 1961
Jack R. Gage—D (Acting)	1961 to 1963
Stanley K. Hathaway—R	1967 to 1975
Ed Herschler—D	1975——

'Hold fast to frontier values,' voters required

Mob Destroys Mobile Newspaper

As the Union Pacific spiked its rails across southern Wyoming, everything had to be mobile, at the rate of six miles a day—and so was the newspaper which chronicled its progress from Nebraska and Colorado. The Frontier Index met a violent end in Wyoming at Bear River City, which also soon met its end.

The tabloid newspaper, mounted on a railroad flatcar, had reached 15,000 circulation when it got to Laramie City. Fred Freeman decided to put down roots in Laramie, and his brother Legh continued with their portable presses.

Legh viewed Bear River as a winter camp, set up his type and tent south of the tracks near the slaughterhouse. He editorially attacked the rowdies, the mail robbers and murderers.

Vigilantes strung up three young outlaws one night, and Freeman was accused of inciting the activity. A mob formed, shot the marshal, and headed for the Frontier Index. A friend rushed to the back door, thrust his mule reins into Freeman's hand, and yelled, "Go!" The mob ransacked the newspaper office and set it afire.

---

eight years, a record until Ed Herschler, D., took office in 1975—he was still governor in 1985. Others with longevity included Scotty Jack, D., ten years as state auditor and two as secretary of state; Jack Gage, D., superintendent of public instruction, secretary of state and acting governor for a full term when Joseph D. Hickey, D., resigned a month after his election to be appointed to the Senate vacancy left by Thomson's death; and Arthur G. Crane, R., acting governor when Hunt went to the Senate—elected secretary of state after 19 years as president of the University of Wyoming.

Women Used Their Rights

Three women have demonstrated staying power with the electorate, starting with Velma Linford, D., state superintendent of public instruction until her liberalism took its toll after eight years; she then received a federal appointment in Washington, D.C. Minnie Mitchell's, R., long political career began in 1952 when she was elected treasurer; she completed 19 years as an elected official with three terms as state auditor. Thyra Thomson, R., popular widow of Keith, bested that record with her long service as secretary of state; she was first elected in 1963 and proved to be unbeaten for 20 years thereafter. And, of course, the nation's first woman governor was Nellie Tayloe Ross, D., (taking office 20 days before Miriam "Ma" Ferguson of Texas); Ross later served for 20 years as director of the U.S. Mint.

Two Wyoming men have been appointed U.S. Secretary of Interior, neither with happy results. Former governor Stanley K. Hathaway served five weeks before turning in his resignation. James Watt served three years before forced to resign in 1984. Both returned to law practices that specialized in representing energy companies.

Caution Tempered Development

Development rarely has meant uncontrolled exploitation of natural resources. Beginning with early mine safety codes on the cutting edge of statehood, elected officials generally favored restraints as industry simultaneously was encouraged.

Hathaway's administration passed the Wyoming Air Quality Act in 1967 to create an Air Resources Council, and a one percent mineral severance tax in 1969; the severance tax was a milestone for state financing, as it had been sought by both parties since 1923. An open-cut mining reclamation act, a land-use act, creation of DEPAD (Dept. of Economic Planning and Development) and DEQ (Dept. of Environmental Quality) all demonstrated Hathaway's concern for the environment —despite the hostility later of environmentalists in the Department of Interior.

Disaster funding, military spending, livestock supports, development of royalty-bearing federal oil pools, and uranium production were generally approved. More ambivalance existed toward depression programs, prohibition, wartime price ceilings, federal assistance in highways and schools; "The Yellow Stripe Blues" sung as Gov. Joseph D. Hickey closed the 1959 session dramatized Hickey's losing battle for yellow highway stripes, favored for visibility in snowstorms. And Wyoming became the only state unable to accept federal matching funds for public schools, after the legislature repealed the enabling act allowing it.

TRAIN DERAILED FOR COWS

The engineer on the Clearmont-to-Buffalo run had to open 21 gates, and neighborliness was his motto. Passing a car stuck in a mudhole, he might back up and throw out a tow rope. The train often stopped to pick up mail or for a visit with farmers along the way—and if it hit a cow, it almost always derailed.

The Wyoming Railroad, Buffalo's answer to the Burlington which had passed it up, was a privately capitalized 29-mile spur line. It operated for 28 years, although even its boosters conceded it could cost as much to ship stock from Buffalo to Clearmont as it did from Clearmont to Omaha.

It was variously nicknamed "Sagebrush Annie," "Sagebrush Special," "B.C.-B.M." (Buffalo-Clearmont and Back, Maybe), as well as "Duffy's Bluff" after general manager Charles B. Duffy.

Mishap was its middle name. Its run sometimes took days in the winter. Once it was stuck in the Redman cut for a week. When it backed up to take a run at a snowbank, put on full steam—the wheels might be frozen to the tracks.

16. READIN', WRITIN', COWS, TYPESETTIN'

Wyoming educators and legislators spent years sorting out 19th century contradictions in order to build a viable educational system.

One governor told students, "You done good" . . . thus the education budget could be cut. Another reminded teachers, "$25,000 worth of cattle is respected more than $25,000 worth of brains." The state's top educator advocated emphasis on manual training. A prominent writer ranked culinary skills above poetry in curriculum priorities. A teacher called for more rambles among the beetles and butterflies, less teaching of "dry rules." And settlers just wanted a school up every coulee.

The only thing everyone agreed upon was the need for public schools, as had the first territorial legislature in writing it into law in 1867.

The system grew prudently, brick by brick—it would be 76 years before community colleges were allowed to open. Only the one-room schools multiplied without restraint; brass recess bells rang in 1,226 coulees by 1926. There were 400 school districts in 1920, ultimately reduced to 53. The University of Wyoming, started in 1886, soon began to teach more poetry than typesetting; it stopped offering college preparatory work—and Laramie was forced to build a high school.

Higher education was a dream shared by many across Wyoming just after statehood, and one of the earliest attempts was at Big Horn when the Wyoming College and Normal School opened in 1892. Residents sold $100 scholarships, land was donated, and everyone danced in the light of the kiln fire when the brick was burned for a building. Only four students were graduated from this short-lived institution which closed in 1898 for lack of money.

From private schools in the military posts, Wyoming schools worked through primitive—and cold—country classrooms into an integrated system that included high school career options, and culminated in a soundly-structured state university. Until the University of Wyoming was on firm footing and increased population demanded them, junior colleges were not permitted to detract. The first legislature provided for separate schools in districts with 15 or more Negroes, but none was ever established.

Practical Courses Demanded

Curriculum, money, and teacher training were uppermost in minds of early educators. Traditionalists lost many arguments, as frontiersmen opted for the practical. The fight for manual training was led by J. H. Hayford, the Laramie editor who became first superintendent of public instruction; he favored such courses as watchmaking, telegraphy and typesetting, over classical education.

Popular writer Bill Nye supported Hayford, commenting that "a cook makes $125 a month, while a bilious poet would be bothered like sin to get a job for $5." Former governor John W. Hoyt, who favored classical education, sympathized with teachers over the frontier value system; he was named first president of the

First University of Wyoming building

university, to the dismay of territorial governor Thomas Moonlight who condemned Hoyt as a theorist.

First Schools Multiplied Districts

School districts grew like mushrooms in a sheep shed, until there were more than 400 in 1929; Supt. Velma Linford was given the job of eliminating half, which she did by 1962. Ten years later districts had been whittled to 42, and the school boards in Big Horn and Fremont counties brought suit against the reorganization committee. Offices of county school superintendent were abolished in 1969 and most of the one-room schools were closed in the resulting consolidation.

By sled, afoot or horseback through the snapping cold came Sheridan County's first pupils, to the stone house at Big Horn. Some students brought their rifles, as the area teemed with wildlife. Sheridan's first school opened in 1879 under a dirt roof in the town then called Mandell. Empty granaries were sometimes used as schools, like the one where Katherine B. Houston taught from a banana crate; a packrat baby dropped from the ceiling down her neck one day.

School terms were flexible to accommodate the rural economy and the weather. Some schools were held only in the summers, others three months in the spring and three in the fall. Water often had to be hauled from a nearby creek. Schools in the Sundance area were heated with wood; coal was used wherever it was available. Pupils brought their lunches in lard pails or tobacco cans.

Teachers were a hardy lot in early Wyoming. Clara Works, Mandell's first teacher, toured Yellowstone Park by horseback in 1880. Winona Condit, who taught the Kearney school, arrived in response to a brother's letter that Wyoming paid twice as much as Iowa. One former Ranchester principal, Jennie Williams, attended school in the Big Horn stone house when it practiced segregation of the sexes, girls entering by one door and the boys by another; Jennie later was told she had "disgraced womanhood" when she began wearing pants to cut hay, after her brother left for World War I and no one else could handle his high-spirited team.

War Comes to Classroom

Schools were caught up in the World War II emergency, as the state war board of the U.S. Dept. of Agriculture asked them to go on a six-day week so students could be released a month early for field work. Not all schools did, and Supt. Esther Anderson was kept busy protecting fundamentals in the curriculum. High schools in 32 cities adopted courses in preflight aeronautics, and nearly all expanded curriculum in physical education, science, math, history and geography.

Equalizing financial support for education in a state where vast mineral wealth was extracted from some counties and none from others required development of a formula, which was devised in 1935. Twenty years later, the legislature refined this, giving every district general operating money equal to $5,500 multiplied by the number of classroom units, later increased to $20,300 per unit. A 12-mill levy for schools was mandatory in each county by 1966; previously, state support was given in the form of a permissive six-mill property levy. Fifty percent of Wyoming's 37.5 percent share of federal oil and gas royalties was funneled into the schools.

Junior Colleges Time Arrives

After the war, an upsurge in enrollment occurred, with ten times the pre-war level of 2,000 registering at the university. The junior college system, approved in 1945, began in Casper that year. Five others opened soon, Northwest Community College in Powell in 1946, North-

First schoolhouse at Arvada, 1897, in log cabin

ern Wyoming College in Sheridan in 1949, Eastern Wyoming College in Torrington in 1948, Western Wyoming College at Rock Springs in 1959, Central Wyoming College at Riverton in 1966, and Laramie County Community College in Cheyenne in 1968. A commission to oversee this system was created by the legislature in 1971, and $20,527,263 was appropriated.

Financial affairs at the University of Wyoming improved with fortunes of the state—up from what was once only $5,000, to $62,077,229 in 1976. Enrollment leveled off to about 10,000. Physical facilities improved, as the legislature supplied matching funds. The able president of the UM board of trustees, former governor Milward Simpson applied his considerable persuasive powers to obtain a donation of several million dollars from William R. Coe of Cody and Oyster Bay, Long Island; this helped build Coe Library and endowed the School of American Studies.

The 1940s and 1950s were golden years in which Wyoming's "Four Horsemen" built an athletic program. The "Four" were Simpson, an alumni Tracy McCracken, UW president Duke Humphrey hired in 1945 after he built Mississippi State's football program, and Glen "Red" Jacoby, the new athletic director.

JEHOVAH JIREH—THE LORD HAD TOO MUCH GROUND TO COVER

Culture was no stranger to the frontier, as the call of the west lured people of all walks of life—but Jehovah Jireh was unique. This dryland town between Manville and Keeline was built by idealists, Christians and educators, who believed "the Lord provideth."

They were warned by an irreverent cattleman: "Out here, the Lord has so much ground to cover, sometimes us mortals has to take his place."

The colony of Jireh, endowed by the Congregational Church of Dayton, Ohio, was intent on building a cultural center on the prairie. A college opened in 1910, attracting faculty from many eastern colleges. By then, 200 families were building a community of "no liquor, no cards, no smoking, no dancing."

The college received an appropriation for an experimental farm from the 1911 Wyoming legislature; Jireh people were farming the barren land—until the drought came. Jireh died in 1920, its building and experimental farm moved to the university at Laramie.

DEDICATION TO: LUCILLE KENDRICK WHITE

Who first opened my eyes to the lure of Wyoming history—to dream of the humanity on cattle roundups, in rock cairns piled by long-ago people, or in abandoned cellars. Lucille lived much of it—and collected even more.

With her, I hunted deer, antiques and precious morsels of western history. Together we shot Pike Mefford's muzzle-loader, visited in lonely cabins, and broke trail off the Big Horns into the Hole-in-Wall.

Her acquaintances were prodigious, the full range of the social scale—she was at home in the fireglow of peyote tepee, on poor or wealthy ranches, and in drawing rooms—anywhere interesting people were to be found.

Her father, Tom Kendrick, and uncle, Sen. John B. Kendrick, rode up the Texas cattle trails. Her husband, Ed White, her son Tom and her grandsons, Kenny and Eddy are today's version of the long-trail drivers—in 18 wheelers.

Lucille was one of northern Wyoming's best known "private persons." She was born 1911 in Briggs, Texas, and died in 1982 "with her boots on" in Reno, Nevada, of a heart attack after winning at the casinos. —BB

ACKNOWLEDGEMENTS

In sifting through Wyoming's past, many people extended help, and I was repeatedly impressed by the universal concern for historic preservation which has created important archival collections many places in the state. I made liberal use of public library facilities such as the Wyoming State Historical Archives in Cheyenne, the State Historical Library in Laramie, the University of Wyoming Library, Sheridan Fulmer and several other county public libraries, as well as those in community colleges. Museums throughout the state also contain much useful material. In each facility, I found officials and staff who willingly helped me in locating often obscure fragments of history. Specialized libraries at state offices, such as the Minerals Division and Game & Fish, contained invaluable insights with which to flesh out the bones of facts. Newspaper archives were also utilized.

As Wyoming people cherish history, so many shared private research of a lifetime. Foremost among these is Dr. George C. Frison, head of the Department of Anthropology at the University of Wyoming, from whose lectures, books and personal observations was derived much data for the section on prehistoric human lifestyles. The past comes alive as he uses foot-long tooth and mastodon jawbone to illustrate an ancient dental replacement system, or taps a bison skull with grapefruit-size hole through which brains were scooped.

Neal Blair, now retired from the Wyoming Game and Fish Department, generously made available his writings from a life-long fascination with history and wildlife. Ulla Pedesen at the University of Copenhagen in Denmark was so interested in this project that she supplied results of wolf behavioral studies, as well as contributing little-known works on Indian culture. Historian Dr. Peter K. Simpson, director of the UW Foundation who is also a former state legislator and enthusiastic Wyoming booster, supplied encouragement and information when it was needed.

One who is not only an expert wildlife photographer but also a meticulous researcher, Ron Mamot at St. Stephens Mission opened to me years of work on early military and Indian movements. Also on the Wind River Indian reservation, historian Pius Moss was generous in sharing personal insights as well as materials developed for his lectures on Indian history and culture. Northern Cheyenne activities in Wyoming were enriched by Ted Rising Sun, Jack Badhorse, and Josephine Stands-in-Timber Glenmore.

As a state's history is the sum of all its parts, so research for this book has delved into remote localities, striving to draw the state "personality" as a composite of its inhabitants throughout the ages. In the northeast corner of the state, Ann Thomas generously made available research and photographs from private collections in the northern Powder River country. Similarly, many in other areas contributed their early ranching, homestead and depression memories.

I am particularly indebted to the efforts of those in state offices like Paula West Chavoya of the historical archives; Dorothe Cable, communications officer of the Wyoming Recreation Commission; Sherry Hughes of the Wyoming Travel Commission, several specialists in the Minerals Division of the Department of Economic Planning and Development. Dr. John Ravage at the UW Department of Journalism and Telecommunications not only opened his private photo collection, but also obtained access to a documentary tape library. For information on contemporary economics and social concerns, staffers of the Powder River Resource Council located archival material, photo files, and devoted their time.

PICTURE CREDITS

Hecla Silver Crown refinery

Brink, Beverley Elaine: 7a, 20a, 28, 30a, 32, 40, 41, 46b, 50b,d,g,i,j, 55b,d,e, 60, 66, 70a,b, 73b, 86a,b, 127b, 146a, 148, 149, 156a,b, 163

Casper Tribune: 20b

Custer Battlefield Museum: 94c,d, 95a,c, 96d, 104a,b,c

Engraf, Eileen: 138b

Frison, George: 81b, 82b, 85, 87

Harpers Weekly: 89

Ken's Photo, Casper: 55a, 71b, 146b, 147

Jackson, W. H.: 93

Lozier, Irv: 36a, 37a,b

Lytton, Jack: 159

Mamot, Ron: 1, 4, 9c, 13, 18a,b, 19, 23b, 26a, 27b, 30b, 31b, 83a,b, 120b, back cover a,b

Morales, Dan: 17c, 25a, 31a, 50f, 64, 123a, 166a

N.D. Game & Fish: 6a, 38a, 42

N.D. Travel: 72b,c, 102

Peoples, Evalyn: 35b

Powder River Basin Resource Council: 5a, 52a, 55c, 69

Ravage, Jack: 142a,b

Riverton Ranger, 58c

Schott, Robert: 71a

Simpson, Alan: 53b

S.D. Game, Fish & Parks: 23c, 39, 44a

S.D. Historical Society: 97a, 115, 122a,b, 124c, 126a, 134, 137b, 138a, 154b

S.D. Travel: 6b, 50c, 90, 91, 98a, 124a, 137a

Smith, Tony: 18c

Smithsonian: 94b, 97c

Thermopolis Chamber of Commerce: 17a

Thomas, Ann: 2b, 34, 35a, 50h, 51, 53a, 118a,b, 123b,c, d,e, 127a,c, 131b, 135b, 136, 137c, 140a,b, 141a,b, 155, 170

Thompson, Scott: 68, 105a

U.S. Bureau of American Ethnology: 97b

U.S.D.A.: 139

U.S. Geological Survey: 105b, 106a,b

U.S. Library of Congress: 154a

U.S.D. Archaeology: 81a

University of Wyoming: 46a, 47a,b, 75a,b,c, 169

Wallop, Malcolm: 54

White, Lucille: 117, 124b, 125, 128, 129b, 130b, 131a, 160, 161b

Wind River Rendezvous: 12, 33a,b, 36b, 48, 56, 57, 58a,b, 59, 73a, 84, 96a, 98b,c, 99, 101, 103b, 119a,b, 150a, 152a,b,c,d, 153a,b, 165a,c

Wyoming Game & Fish: 8a, 24, 27a, 38b, 40b, 43, 76a,b, back cover c

Wyoming Recreation Commission: 21a, 25b, 49a,b, 50e, 96b

Wyoming State Archives: 94a, 103a, 107a,b, 108a,b, 109, 110a,b, 111a,b, 112b,c, 113a,b, 114, 120a, 126b, 130b, 133a,b, 135a, 150b, 161a, 162, 164a,b, 165b,d, 166b,c, d, 168

Wyoming Travel: 2a, 3, 5b,e,f, 6c,d, 7b, 8b,c,d, 9a,b, 10a,b, 11a,b, 14, 15, 16, 17b, 21b, 22, 23a, 26b, 45, 49a,b, 50a, 72a, 77, 78a, 79, 80a,b, 82a, 92, 112a, 129a, 143, 144, 145, 167, end pages, front cover

Color separations courtesy of the Wyoming Travel Commission and the Wyoming Game & Fish Department.

Cover photo: in the Tetons, Wyoming Travel Commission.

ABOUT THE AUTHOR

Beverly Brink Badhorse grew up on a southeastern Montana ranch and has lived in Sheridan, Laramie and Story. She could be called a native of that no-man's land once named Absaroka—northern Wyoming, southeastern Montana and western South Dakota, whose residents wanted statehood in 1935. She earned her Master's degree from the University of Wyoming, her Bachelor's from the University of Montana.

A long-time reporter and editor, she has held these positions on such newspapers as The Miami Herald, Dayton (O.) Daily News, and Mexico (D.F.) News. She has covered Wyoming affairs for The Billings Gazette, Country Journal, and KROE Radio in Sheridan. Her many awards in Florida, Ohio, Wyoming, and nationally include two Herbert Bayard Stokes national awards for Wyoming historical writing.

BIBLIOGRAPHY

Agricultural Credit Summit. Report on Wyoming 1984, Wyoming Department of Agriculture

Arvada Historical Group, *Wheel of Time, 1800s-1984*, State Publishing Co., Pierre, S.D., 1984.

Athearn, Robert G., *High Country Empire*, University of Nebraska Press, Lincoln, 1960. Also, *William Tecumseh Sherman and the Settlement of the West*, University of Oklahoma Press, Norman, 1959.

Atherton, Lewis, *The Cattle Kings*, Indiana University Press, Bloomington, 1961.

Badhorse, B., "Petroglyphs—Possible Religious Significance," *The Wyoming Archaeologist*, Dec. 1979, Vol XXIII, No. 4.

Billings Gazette, "Ancient Fire Pits," Nov. 4, 1984.

Bolton, H.E. and Marshall, T.M., *The Colonization of North America 1492-1783*, New York: The MacMillan Company, 1922.

Borne, Lawrence R., *Dude Ranching, A Complete History*, University of New Mexico Press, Albuquerque, 1983.

Buffalo's Centennial Book Committee, *Buffalo's First Century*, Buffalo Bulletin, Inc., WY, 1984.

Burt, Nathaniel, *Jackson Hole Journal*, University of Oklahoma Press, 1983.

Cahn, H.A., "The Petroglyphs of Dinwoody, Wyoming," *American Antiquity*, XV, No. 3, 1950.

Carbone, Gerald, "Surface Report of the Tongue River Drainage Area," *The Wyoming Archeologist*, Vol. XV, No. 4, Dec. 1972.

Census of Agriculture, Wyoming, 1978 and 1982.

Chittenden, *The History of the American Fur Trade of the Far West*, Academic Reprints, California, 1954.

Coolidge, Grace, *Teepee Neighbors*, University of Oklahoma Press, Norman, 1984 reprint of 1917 printing by The Four Seasons Co.

Davenport, Joseph and Judith, ed., *The Boom Town: Problems and Promises in the Energy Vortex*, The University of Wyoming, 1980.

Ewers, John C., "The Medicine Rock of the Marias," *Montana, Magazine of Western History*, II, 54, 1952.

Frison, George C., *Prehistoric Hunters of the High Plains*, Academic Press, Inc., New York, N.Y., 1978. *Linear Arrangements of Cairns in Wyoming and Montana*, University of Wyoming, Laramie, 1984.

Galloway, E., and Agogino, G.A.; "Pictographs at Wall Rock Cave, Albany County, Wyoming," *The Wyoming Archaeologist*, Sept. 1962.

Gebhard, David, "Petroglyphs of Wyoming: A Preliminary Paper," *El Palacio*, LVIII, No. 3, 1951.

Gilbert, H., "Indian Picture Writing," *The Wyoming Archaeologist*, Vol. V, No. 3, Sept. 1961.

Gould, Lewis L., *Wyoming, a Political History 1868-1896*, Yale University Press, 1968.

Grant, Campbell, *Rock Art of the American Indian*, New York, 1967.

Irving, Washington, *The Adventures of Captain Bonneville*, Binford, 1954.

King, Bucky, *The Dude Connection*, Jelm Mountain Press, Laramie, 1983.

Kehoe, Thomas F. and Alice B., "Boulder Effigy Monuments in the Northern Plains," *Journal of American Folklore*, 1960. "Stone Medicine Wheels . . .", *Journal of the Washington Academy of Sciences*, Vol. 44, No. 5, May 1954.

Homsher, Lola M., ed., *James Chisholm's Journal of the Wyoming Gold Rush*, University of Nebraska Press, 1960.

Larsson, T.A., *History of Wyoming*, University of Nebraska Press, 1978.

Laubin, Reginald and Gladys, *Indian Dances of North America*, University of Oklahoma Press, 1977.

LeFors, Joe, *Wyoming Peace Officer*, Laramie Printers, Inc., 1953.

Lopez, Barry Holstun, *Of Wolves and Men*, Charles Scribner's Sonx, N.Y., 1978.

McLean, Mick, tape, "Twentieth Century Mining," University of Wyoming, 1983.

McCoy, Tim, *Tim McCoy Remembers the West*, Doubleday, Garden City, N.Y., 1977.

McCracken, Harold, *The American Cowboy*, Doubleday, 1973.

Mokler, Alfred James, *History of Natrona County, Wyoming*, Argonaut Press LTD, N.Y., 1966.

Murray, Robert A., *Miner's Delight, Investors Despair*, Piney Creek Press, Sheridan, 1972.

Neihardt, John G., *The Song of Jed Smith and the Song of the Indian Wars*, MacMillan Co., 1949.

Noggle, Burt, *Teapot dome: Oil and Politics in the 1920s*, Louisiana State University Press, 1962.

Pence, Mary Lou and Homahwe, Lola M. *The Ghost Towns of Wyoming*, Hastings House, N.Y., 1956.

Powder River Heritage Committ, Kaycee, *Our Powder River Heritage*, Frontier Printing, Inc., Cheyenne, 1982.

Powder River Resource Council, *Powder River Breaks*, issues 1980 through 1984.

Powell, John Wesley, *Report of the lands of the Arid Region*, U.S. Geological Survey, Washington, D.C., 1978.

Riegel, Robert Edgar, *The Story of the Western Railroads*, University of Nebraska Press, Lincoln, 1967.

Rocky Mountain News, Denver, 1860, etc.

Rollinson, John K., *Wyoming Cattle Trails*, Caxton, Caldwell, Idaho, 1948.

Rise and Fall of the Public Domain Exclusive of Alaska and Other Outlying Possessions, Conservation Branch of the United States Geological Survey, Dept. of the Interior.

Scott, Mary Hurlburt, *The Oregon Trail Through Wyoming*, Powder River Publishers, Aurora, CO, 1958.

St. Stephens Foundation, *The Rendezvous*, issues 1975 through 1984, St. Stephens, WY.

Stegner, Wallace, *Beyond the Hundredth Meridian*, Houghton-Mifflin, Boston, 1962.

University of Wyoming, "Archaeological Investigations in the Shoshone Basin of Wyoming," and "Petroglyphs in the Boysen Reservoir Area," 1954.

Vestal, Stanley, *Joe Meek, the Merry Mountain Man*, University of Nebraska Press, 1963.

Wall, J.T., *Life in the Shannon and Salt Creek Oil Fields*, Dorrance & Co., Philadelphia, 1973.

Wasden, David J., *From Beaver to Oil*, Pioneer Printing Co., Cheyenne, 1973.

Webb, Walter Prescott, *The Great Plains*, Grosset and Dunlap, New York, 1931.

Werner, M.R., and Starr, John, *Teapot Dome*, Viking Press, N.Y., 1959.

Wind River Indian Tribes, Directory of Human Resources, Ft. Washakie, 1982-1983.

Wyoming, State of, *Wyoming Agricultural Statistics, 1983, 1984; Wyoming Game and Fish Department Annual Report, 1983; Annual Report of the State Inspector of Mines of Wyoming, 1984; 1984 Wyoming Mineral Yearbook*, Mineral Division of State Department of Economic Planning & Development; *Wyoming Wildlife*, issues 1974-1984, Wyoming Game and Fish Department.

Canada geese fly in to rest

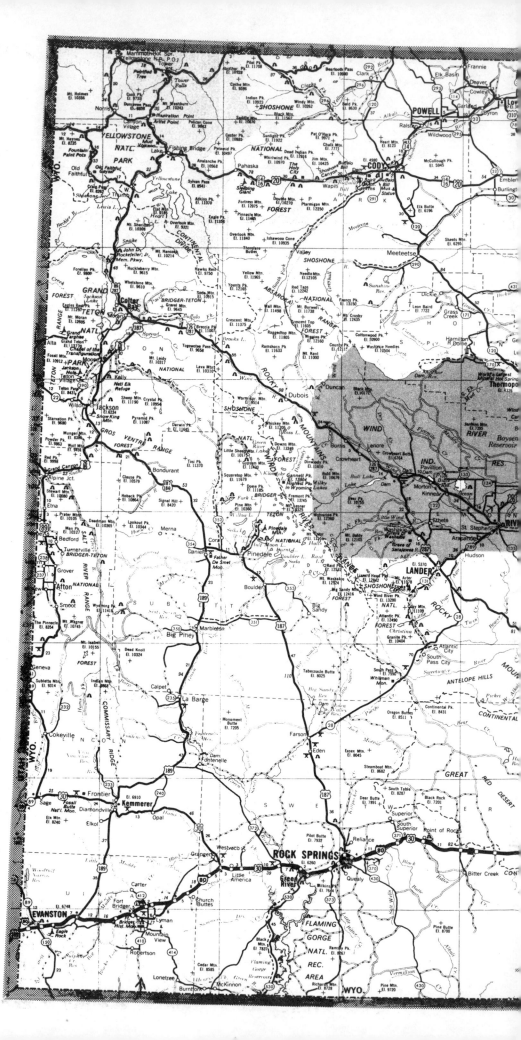